BELFAST
TOWARD A CITY
WITHOUT WALLS

VICKY COSSTICK

Photographs by Frankie Quinn   Foreword by John Paul Lederach

COLOURPOINT BOOKS

Glenbryn

This book is dedicated to the memory of Monsignor Tom Toner
and to all those working to build a lasting peace in Northern Ireland

Published 2015 by Colourpoint Books
an imprint of Colourpoint Creative Ltd
Colourpoint House, Jubilee Business Park
21 Jubilee Road, Newtownards, BT23 4YH
Tel: 028 9182 6339
Fax: 028 9182 1900
E-mail: info@colourpoint.co.uk
Web: www.colourpoint.co.uk

First Edition
First Impression

A catalogue record for this book is available from the British Library.

Designed by April Sky Design, Newtownards
Tel: 028 9182 7195
Web: www.aprilsky.co.uk

Printed by W&G Baird Ltd, Antrim

ISBN 978-1-78073-072-1

Front cover: Bryson Street, Short Strand

CONTENTS

VICKY COSSTICK has worked as a writer and journalist, academic, and organisational change consultant. She lives in London and Ireland, which she first visited in the late 70s, when she wrote her first article on the conflict for *The New York Daily News*. She realised about the extent of the peacewalls and interfaces when researching articles on the 15th anniversary of the 1998 Belfast Agreement.

JOHN PAUL LEDERACH, Professor of International Peacebuilding with the University of Notre Dame and Senior Advisor for Humanity United, has been involved in conflict transformation work since the early 1980s, working in settings of protracted conflict in over 25 countries. He accompanied the early growth of Mediation Network Northern Ireland and advised the Community Relations Council during the 90s, often visiting his parents, John and Naomi, who lived close to the peacewalls in Belfast for four years. He is author of more than than 20 books including *The Moral Imagination: the Art and Soul of Building Peace* and the recent publication with his daughter Angela of *When Blood and Bones Cry Out: Journeys through the soundscape of healing and reconciliation*.

FRANKIE QUINN is from Short Strand and since 1993 has been photographing the 'Peacelines' in Belfast. He has published two books on the subject, *Interface Images* 1994 and *Streets Apart* 2008. With support from the Arts Council NI (Support for the Individual Artist Programme) Frankie has embarked on another project, partly in response to the OFMdFM's desire to dismantle the walls by 2023. He is using a Fuji 617 camera and Ilford HP5 film. Big thanks to Stevie Raelynn for the post production work on the negatives. His work can be seen at: www.frankiequinn.com

ACKNOWLEDGEMENTS

Researching and writing this book has been an extraordinary adventure and privilege. I interviewed over a hundred people, sometimes more than once, and I am grateful to them for their warmth, their generosity with their time, openness and honesty. I hope I have not let them down. Belfast's greatest resource is its people and I was invariably humbled and moved by their utter dedication to the city they love and to continuing to work for peace in their diverse and myriad ways.

Early on, I noticed and noted that the progress of the book seemed to be accompanied by 'opportunities, coincidences and invitations'; it appeared to gain a momentum of its own – partly because both John Paul Lederach and Frankie Quinn agreed without hesitation to work with me, compelling me to try to deliver a text that would deserve their contributions.

There are three people without whom I think this book could not have happened, and who have given me unflagging practical and moral support, particularly in the tough moments. I reconnected with Sr Consilia Dennehy at Mgr Tom Toner's funeral in November 2012. She introduced me to key contacts in Belfast for articles I was writing, and from the very first moment that my idea of a book on the walls and interfaces emerged has been a bottomless source of wisdom and encouragement. My good and long term friend Diane Toner, and her equally hospitable husband Henry, welcomed me repeatedly into the Toner household and she and I shared a good few late night chats and glasses of wine. Máirtín Ó Muilleoir invited me several times to shadow him as Lord Mayor and the contacts I made during those visits and those he shared with me from his vast network were invaluable. These three people helped me to feel I belonged in Belfast.

I also received particular help, support and connections from journalist Martin O'Brien, Paddy McIntyre, Fr Martin Magill and Frank Liddy. Chris O'Halloran, then at Belfast Interface Project, was very helpful giving me initial lists of community contacts. Many thanks for reading and commenting on drafts of the book or particular chapters are due to journalist Martin O'Brien, Consilia Dennehy, Kirstein Arbuckle, Jimmy Burns, Martin Farber, Rita Duffy, Revd Lesley Carroll, Anthony Weldon, Tom Lee and Gordie Walker. They gave invaluable advice and set me straight on a number of things, but for any flaws and *faux pas* that remain responsibility is entirely my own. For their love, help and support during the research and writing many thanks to my wonderful friends Trisha Edwards, Rosemary Cunniffe, Kate Winter, Sinead McIntyre, Bishop Declan Lang and Paddy Rylands, Fanny, Noel and Pamela Russell, and to my cousins Caroline Bull and Theresa Murray Magee, and Theresa's great friend Kathleen Roberts of Ballymacarret/ Short Strand. My thanks are also due to Bob McKenzie and the AMED writers' group, and, for years of personal support and friendship, to Judith O'Grady. I am so sorry that Emily O'Rourke of Inniskeen, a warm host and friend during and since my first visit to Ireland in 1977, did not live to see this book published.

One inspiration for the book was my son, John Walton. In 2010, he spent five months cycling from Cairo to Capetown, raising £5,000 for charity. The four young people who travelled together had not met before, nor had they been to Africa. John said afterwards that he promised himself at the start of the trip that there was never a chance that he would not finish it. That is how it has been with this book – from December 2013 when I made the commitment to doing it, there has never been a chance that I would not finish it. It did, I have to say, get easier from the time – somewhat and rather agonisingly later – that Malcolm Johnston decided that it was a book worth publishing and I am grateful to him also for his interest and encouragement.

Finally, of course, eternal thanks to my wonderful husband of almost 45 years, Kelvin Walton, for his unwavering support for all of my schemes and dreams. None has been more important to me than this one.

Vicky Cosstick
April 2015

FOREWORD

Vicky Cosstick has woven a web of a good book. I read these pages once and then a second time, slowly. The reading merits the spider's approach – forth and back, criss-crossing the same space differently each time, sort of the way Vicky wrote the book I imagine, following wall-strand stories.

Belfast has stitched itself a fine history of walls.

Robert McLiam Wilson suggested that in Belfast "it's always present tense" and "all the streets are poetry streets." True, and presently tense. The stories in this book unfold the on-the-street experience of interface communities living alongside the labyrinth of 'peacewalls' throughout the city. Captured on page in the extraordinary photography of Frankie Quinn, the walls sit static in time. Immovable. But they are anything but static. The heart of this book suggests the opposite. Walls live. Like poetry lives. Words on pages, yet when spoken with breath and bone, a poem comes alive again with old and new meaning. That's because a poem can never be contained in the universe of black on white. Poems like Belfast walls live in the imagination – alive, begging for interpretation and effusing significance.

The stories flowing from Vicky's pen leave us a poetic challenge. A good poem transports you into *noticing* something about life, yourself, what surrounds you, and the world *we* inhabit. If you listen to Belfast walls with the ear of the heart you may catch the pulse of their good questions. Who am I? Who are you? Who are we? Where are we going?

I have walked many of the streets mentioned in this book. I have sat with a good number of those quoted. My parents lived for a period of their life within a 'stones-throw' from the brick and mortar of one sectarian divide.

I have touched the walls.

They touched me back.

After reading through these pages I felt uncertain how to adequately write a foreword. Some of the stories in this book reminded me of other conversations, in places where people faced larger than life challenges. I remember sitting for days in Yangon with informal ethnic mediators shuttling between the powers of the military junta and the jungles of armed oppositions. Their task seemed doomed from the start. One would be peacemaker had to travel through a dozen military blockades, at times arrested and held for weeks, to arrive from near the border of Bangladesh to Burma's capital city of Yangon in order to receive messages and a passport. He then flew to Bangladesh and again travelled by land to the other side of the border he had just left. And back again. He turned in his one-trip passport and eventually arrived home – months for one message of potential peace. They called themselves the Mediators Fellowship. Their voice kept haunting my thoughts when I heard the tales of the growing Belfast walls.

Advice from the Mediators Fellowship

Don't ask the mountain
to move, just take a pebble
each time you visit

I decided to let my first thoughts just bounce out, and what bounced came in little windows and vignettes. And a series of '*maybes*' I found arriving with each story and chapter. Let me start with the big one.

Maybe the long and high vocation of Belfast walls provides a street level poetics of peace, a place long divided but held together by the wars they fight. The walls were not built overnight. They will not come down quickly. Some walls last a century, a few for millennia.

The journey *toward a city without walls* will require fissures and cracks, windows and gateways, pebbles and a few weedy vignettes that crumble the long arc of stone-laid history.

I visited people inside the Maze prison several times during the early 1990s. Past those turn gates that marked the out from in, we would usually walk H-block by H-block until we had completed the warren tour of carefully marked habitats. Inevitably the long corridors would lead to a single small room. Crowded, we'd talk inside four walls.

Inside the Maze

"My fear of peace?"
the Commander responds.

We sit hunched under bunks.
Men with tattoos bring us tea.
Roll cigarettes.
And watch even our breathing.

"That at the end of the day,"
he says to us twice,
"I'll be back in this prison visitn'
me children's children."

Wandering around Belfast in 2014 I saw what Vicky and Frankie capture so well in this book. Since 'peace' came to Belfast the walls have spread. At times I wondered if maybe the prison had closed but the maze had crept into Belfast. Alongside creeping labyrinths, people still seek safety inside four walls.

Walls always hold a paradox. The stories and voices Vicky shares describe this without pause.

On one side, a wall keeps *them* out.

On the other, a wall keeps *us* in.

Us and them.

Dead clear.

Some say walls have frozen the conflict with no horizon in sight. I once heard a lament around a lunch table in Belfast. I jotted it down later as a near perfect haiku memory of everyday conversation.

Rainbow's End?

Maybe, he says, *this*
is as good as it will get
peaceful bigotry

In Belfast, for all its pain and trouble conflict always provided a certain relief for the mind. At least it eliminated ambiguity.

We humans don't much like living for long in ambiguity. It's confusing because we don't know who we are. That's the problem with peace on the Island. The gift of conflict delivered absolute clarity about identity. I know who I am by knowing who I am not. Few questions asked. Answers known.

Peace on the other hand comes shrouded in mystery. It messes with truth.

Maybe walls provide comfort because they are so concrete. Some of the stories in this book point this way. Entering Peacelandia without maps, a good wall gives you the 'you are here' arrow.

Yeat's long ago suggested that "peace comes dropping slow", something he touched only when he could find himself somewhere near the "deep heart's core".

At times in the midst of this book it felt as if the Belfast walls strung along neighbourhoods had replicated themselves round the hearts of those living in the shadow of the walls. Many stories in this book speak from embodied trans-generational pain and loss. Living with and in the aftermath of violence, we humans don't just build walls. We dig murky moats that keep the world from getting close to even the outer edge ring of stone that protects our damaged heart's core.

But that's not the whole story.

Over the decades I found myself talking with people across Belfast who had suffered a great deal through the Troubles. Interface folk. Prior to meeting someone for the first time, colleagues would prepare me with a phrase like "your man's hardened" or "he'll suffer no fools." At times we did indeed meet the cold steel, but more than not Belfast life and people held surprises. Mine was this. Even the most hardened soul of the Troubles inevitably had a golden vein of warm hospitality. Maybe this hospitality comes from the salt, peat and air of the Island for it did not know a sectarian origin.

I always experienced this vein of hospitality through a single ritual: I would be called by my first names and my names would never be forgotten. "John Paul" sometimes got interspersed a couple of times per paragraph of craic.

It was as if a deep desire to know and be recognised bubbled inside. Thich Nhat Hanh once wrote a poem titled *Call Me By My True Names*. This captures what I felt: Heart reached toward heart. Beyond the wall and moat, the desire and offer to be known by true names shines through.

While at times Belfast seems hell bent on concealing its hidden gems of compassion, a city without walls will not start when the dozers smash the cement and the shears cut the wires. A city without walls will come when people reach through to touch and share the true names of the heart.

Where in our bodies do we humans carry history?

Memories as thoughts seem to reside in the mind, the location from where we story ourselves into place.

Several wisdom traditions suggest something about the origin of stories. Let me put this in the form of two old sages walking and talking.

One says, "I think God created humans because She liked to hear stories."
After a bit of silence, the other responds, "I think God created humans because She liked to tell stories."
"You may be right," the first answers, "We certainly *become* the stories we tell."

This book brims with stories. We tell stories to find our way. We tell stories to remember. We tell stories to dream. And no matter the story, we live into what we *story* about others and ourselves.

I have found one rule of thumb about stories in the midst of deep conflict: We need to fit in our own story. We don't want to be bothered with stories where we don't fit, where we don't have a place, you know, to call home.

Maybe this is the Belfast wall dilemma: How to raise kids in a story and place where they fit.

In Australia the aboriginals travelled vast landscapes without maps on paper. They sang as they walked. Stones and mountains, grasses and ponds marked with a note, a melody that became the Songlines, the musical maps of the landscape they carried in their body, not just their head. Some report that they could taste the music. Some said the songs related to the feel of the place, like the earth on their feet. To know their location and not feel 'lost' required a whole body experience. With a songline the travellers felt at home wherever they ventured.

Maybe walls hold the Belfast Songlines. They mark the known maps. They have a taste. They resonate with the body. Hear a wall sing and you sense your location.

Some will sing the walls to stay home, afraid to venture past the edge of the known map to those places where there be dragons. They will live into a story locked in time. These songs will carry melodies of fear. They will know their landscape well and the tune will never change.

Some will sing the taste at the ambiguous edge of the known maps. The walls, whether they crumble or stay, will matter very little for these emergent songlines will hold memoirs and dreams.

The great son of Belfast, Van Morrison, sang it well in the seamless way he stitches memories and horizons. "Got to go back", he says, "for the healing and go on with the dreaming."

View of Belfast from Blackmountain, showing
Million Brick Wall, Springmartin

Here is one of the many gifts of *Belfast: Toward a City without Walls*. The very title suggests a journey in search of the rooted reminders yet capable of soaring with the courage of the heart's core to places not yet fully known.

The poetry emergent in the stories and images sings a city in search of healing that will both remember and change.

Take time to read and listen with the ear of the heart.

John Paul Lederach
April 2015

ABBREVIATIONS

ACE	Action for Community Employment
BCC	Belfast City Council
BGFA	Belfast (Good Friday) Agreement
BIP	Belfast Interface Project
CBI	Confederation of British Industry
CCRF	Cliftonville Community Regeneration Forum
CNR	Catholic/Nationalist/Republican
CRC	Community Relations Council
CRI	Cromac Regeneration Initiative
CVS	Commission for Victims and Survivors
DDTW	Draw Down the Walls
DoJ	Department of Justice
DRD	Department for Regional Development
DSD	Department for Social Development
DUP	Democratic Unionist Party
EU	European Union
HIPA	Hate Incident Practical Action
IFI	International Fund for Ireland
IRA	Irish Republican Army
IWG	Interface Working Group
LSCA	Lower Shankill Community Association
MIW	Make it Work campaign
MLA	Member of Legislative Assembly
NBIN	North Belfast Interface Network
NEET	Not in Education, Employment and Training
NIHE	Northern Ireland Housing Executive
NILT	Northern Ireland Life and Times Survey
NIO	Northern Ireland Office
OFMdFM	Office of the First Minister and deputy First Minister

OTR	On The Runs
PCSP	Police Community Safety Partnership
PMR	Peace Monitoring Report
PSNI	Police Service of Northern Ireland
PTSD	Post Traumatic Stress Disorder
PUL	Protestant/Unionist/Loyalist
PUP	Progressive Unionist Party
RHC	Red Hand Commando
RUC	Royal Ulster Constabulary
SDLP	Social Democratic Labour Party
SF	Sinn Féin
SHA	Stormont House Agreement
SLIG	Suffolk Lenadoon Interface Group
SRRP	Stewartstown Road Regeneration Project
TASCIT	Twaddell, Ardoyne, Shankill Communities in Transition
TBUC	Together Building a United Community
UDA	Ulster Defence Association
UU	University of Ulster
UUP	Ulster Unionist Party
UVF	Ulster Volunteer Force
VSS	Victims and Survivors Service

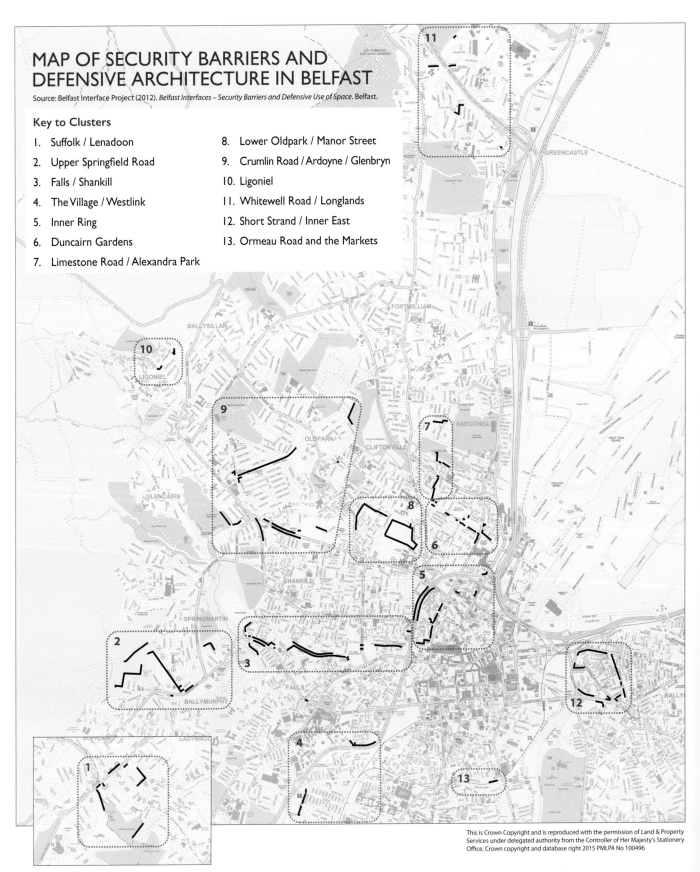

MAP OF SECURITY BARRIERS AND DEFENSIVE ARCHITECTURE IN BELFAST

Source: Belfast Interface Project (2012). *Belfast Interfaces – Security Barriers and Defensive Use of Space*. Belfast.

Key to Clusters

1. Suffolk / Lenadoon
2. Upper Springfield Road
3. Falls / Shankill
4. The Village / Westlink
5. Inner Ring
6. Duncairn Gardens
7. Limestone Road / Alexandra Park
8. Lower Oldpark / Manor Street
9. Crumlin Road / Ardoyne / Glenbryn
10. Ligoniel
11. Whitewell Road / Longlands
12. Short Strand / Inner East
13. Ormeau Road and the Markets

INTRODUCTION

Iₙ ᴀʟᴍᴏꜱᴛ ᴇᴠᴇʀʏ ᴄᴜʟᴛᴜʀᴇ, walls are a feature of daily life. They mark the boundaries of our homes; they protect our privacy. In suburban estates, gates and walls are a sign of status; around gardens they create micro-climates; on country estates they may be policed by guard dogs and 'no trespassing' signs. In many places they define distinctions of class and wealth. Walls have often been used for political and military purposes: Hadrian's Wall was built by the Romans to outline the empire's furthest limit and keep marauding Picts at bay; the Great Wall of China protected the first Chinese empire from Mongolian invasion; the Great Hedge of India was built in the mid-19th century by the British, ran for over 1500 miles and was used to collect an oppressive salt tax and control the opium trade. The original Berlin wall was made of barbed wire and concrete posts and was erected in dead of night on 12–13 August 1961 to suddenly separate communist East Berlin from democratic West Berlin.

My curiosity about the peacewalls and interfaces in Belfast dates from early 2013, when I was researching articles on the 15th anniversary of the Belfast Agreement (BGFA) for *The Tablet*. Soon afterwards, in May 2013, First Minister Peter Robinson and deputy First Minister Martin McGuinness made their striking promise to bring down the walls in Belfast by 2023 in Together Building a United Community (TBUC) (OFMdFM 2013).

Like many visitors to Northern Ireland, I had walked along the art and graffiti-encrusted Cupar Way wall, first built in 1969, which divides the Protestant Shankill from the Catholic Falls Road in Belfast. I since learned that there are some 100 sectarian walls, barriers and interfaces across working class North, West and East Belfast. The last was erected in 2007, in face of great official reluctance, in the grounds of Hazelwood Integrated Primary School in North Belfast – the last, that is, until November 2013 when a missile-proof, retractable, steel mesh 'curtain' went up in the grounds of St Matthew's Roman Catholic Church in Short Strand, East Belfast. This book tells the story of the walls, now the last in Europe and still standing over 15 years after the Belfast Agreement of 1998 and 25 years after the fall of the Berlin Wall in November 1989, and asks for how much longer these physical signs and symbols of sectarianism and the Troubles will disfigure the cityscape.

The real work for this book began with an email to Department of Justice Minister and Alliance Party leader David Ford. He responded immediately and followed up with a phone call and an invitation to meet him at Stormont. It turned out to be a good place to start: Minister Ford has a personal passion to bring down the walls, even if not necessarily according to the 2023 deadline. He was the first of many I met who see the removal of the peacewalls and interfaces as essential to the peace process. The bulk of the work for the book ended when the Stormont House Agreement was reached on 22 December 2014. With implications for the work around the peacewalls, it provides a convenient second 'bookend', neatly matching the May 2013 TBUC commitment.

For almost 30 years, from 1969 to 1998, the year of the Belfast Agreement, a brutal conflict raged among a profusion of Protestant and Catholic paramilitary groups, the British army, and the Northern Irish police force. Over 3,600 people died, mostly in Northern Ireland, as a result of the conflict, more than 100,000 were injured and half a million (or 30% of the population of the province) are defined as victims: directly affected by bereavement, injury or trauma (CVS 2012). The main battlefields were the streets of working class Belfast. During that time, physical walls, fences and gates were flung up, sometimes apparently overnight, in attempt to keep warring factions apart.

The walls were erected mostly by the British army and government; according to some, the only possible tactic in the face of vicious and uncontrollable savagery; to others it was a strategy of desperation. Now, it is common to hear that "the real walls are in people's minds" – that is, the walls of fear, hatred and mutual suspicion – and that these mental walls will need to be removed before the physical walls can come down. The actual walls, meanwhile, have reinforced and exacerbated sectarianism, segregation of Protestant from Catholic, and cycles of deprivation. They literally block regeneration. The walls, as one senior housing official says, "get in the way of everything". The walls are relics of and memorials to the conflict and a reminder of the unfinished nature of the peace process. They are, says one Republican community worker, like the tips of icebergs: below them are "anger, sectarianism, violence, strife, poor education, alcoholism and drug abuse". Decades, even centuries of sectarian attitudes and behaviour are also spilling into alarming incidence of verbal and physical race-hate attacks on recent Asian, Eastern European and African immigrants to Belfast (*Andersonstown News*, 24 Mar 15). Because of the walls and interfaces, says one writer, "people are not getting comfortable with the multi-cultural city" (di Cintio 2013).

The walls were easy to put up, but they are devilishly difficult and hellishly expensive to take down. *Belfast: Toward a City Without Walls* explores whether, when and how the walls and interfaces will be removed. It uses a narrative approach to tell a quieter but compelling story of the current peace process, through the stories and from the points of view of the complex network of people and the different communities and agencies that are involved in maintaining peace at the interfaces and working toward a 'city without walls'.

Fifteen years after the Belfast Agreement, it sometimes seems as though beyond the province it is only the big, bad stories about Northern Ireland that make headlines: anything to do with Gerry Adams, the 'On The Runs' (OTR) scandal, the stalled Haass process, the flag protests. As Bill Rolston points out, by the mid-70s, the pattern for the portrayal of Northern Ireland in the British, US and European media was established, and persists to this day: "Ireland could be out of the headlines for long periods of time, but when it did appear, the news was undoubtedly bad" (Rolston 1995). In 2013, journalist Roy Greenslade wrote in his blog that "unless violence breaks out, the 'national press' turns a blind eye to events in the six northern Irish counties. Anything outside of the pre-peace process narrative of conflict and division is ignored. The old editorial mantra 'Ulster doesn't sell' is still in place. Worse, the lack of coverage implies 'Ulster doesn't matter'" (Greenslade 2013). But beneath the flare-ups in the headlines, as the 2014 Peace Monitoring Report (PMR) notes, are the "long slow processes of reconciliation at community level" (Nolan 2014). As with the ocean, there may be turbulence and quite fierce storms at surface level, while deeper below there is more stability and calm. From my research, an intricate picture has emerged, a thus far untold story of how the fragile peace process is being worked out in the current life of the city.

In the past 18 months, I have met community workers, including former combatants from both sides, and visited all eight International Fund for Ireland (IFI) funded peacewalls programmes in Belfast and Derry/Londonderry. I spoke to politicians and civil servants, church ministers and leaders, bureaucrats and 'securocrats', artists and architects, city council and Housing Executive employees, black taxi drivers and the Lord Mayor. I visited community groups, attended conferences and sat in on cross community dialogues. I interviewed academics and read PhD theses and many reports, articles and other materials held in the Linen Hall Library political collection. Everywhere, people honoured me by speaking frankly and often confidentially. Many people in Belfast are working tirelessly for peace and for the regeneration of devastated neighbourhoods. They told me often impressive, moving and unpredictable stories of their own lives, and what they think and feel about the walls.

Belfast can be viewed through a conflict lens or a peace lens. A conflict lens is more dramatic, makes for better headlines and can reinforce negative beliefs about Belfast. This book is written from a 'peace' perspective and from a generally positive point of view. It assumes that, by whatever uncertain and circuitous route, the peace process is advancing – an assumption further supported by the reaching of the Stormont House Agreement in December 2014. The book aims to accompany and echo the doggedly persistent work of the many people and groups whose lives and work are defined by the walls and interfaces, to give a real time picture of the complex process by which constructive change is being worked out in the life of the city. To write with a peace lens needs patience and attentiveness, like the peace process itself. It requires acute awareness of the impact of both my presence as a writer and the written word on the situation I am describing.

John Berger once famously called for a 'new way of seeing' which involved the recognition that all seeing is relative, limited, partial and subjective: "What we must work towards is the greatest possible aggregate of constructive viewpoints and perspectives" (Berger 2008). I have tried to tell the story of the walls in an as accessible and readable way as possible. I have brought to the work my experience as a journalist and published writer, but it is not intended to be purely journalism. I have brought the experience and skills of an academic, but it is not intended to be an academic study. I have brought my experience and some of the methodologies of a consultant, but it is not intended to be a consultancy report. My approach is underpinned sometimes invisibly by decades of theoretical and practical work and influences. These have included, from my first degree in sociology, a commitment to ethnomethodology and phenomenology, and the idea that reality and meaning are socially constructed. From all three degrees, in sociology, theology and change agency, an unwavering commitment to systems thinking. As for practice, the single skill that has linked years as a journalist, adult educator, group facilitator and coach/mentor has been listening.

I have long been fascinated by putting theory and practice together. One without the other risks being either arrogant or futile. In the theoretical literature of understanding how change actually happens, I have never found a more extraordinary and insightful book than Lederach's *The Moral Imagination: the Art and Soul of Building Peace*. This book has been my professional bible for a decade. For Lederach, peacebuilding and facilitating "constructive change" are one and the same. I thought all my Christmases had

Springfield Road

come at once when I found myself face-to-face with John Paul Lederach himself in the Bobbin Café at City Hall in Belfast, in January 2014, in a meeting set up for me by then Lord Mayor Máirtín Ó Muilleoir and his Buddhist chaplain Frank Liddy. That encounter was fundamental to the progress of this book – as indeed has the book *The Moral Imagination* itself also been, although I did not reread it until a year later, at the end of my writing process. John Paul Lederach has been a frequent visitor to Northern Ireland and contributor to its peace process, and I am immensely proud that he has contributed the Foreword to this book. Like him, I am strongly influenced by complex systems theory[1] – and this is a further prism through which the 'conundrum' or complex problem of the

---

1 A complex systems approach recognises that social phenomena are uncertain, dynamic and made up of multiple interconnected actors and factors. They do not change in a linear fashion and cannot simply be managed or controlled. They are subject to 'emergence': patterns emerge "beyond, outside of and oblivious to any notion of shared intentionality" (Patton 2011).

walls is viewed in this book. In complexity thinking, my presence itself, the listening, the questions I ask have an amplifying effect on the situation, for good or ill. This means there is an additional responsibility to tell and reinforce the good news of what is happening in Belfast, to identify where, in John Paul Lederach's phrase, constructive change – or peacemaking – is happening.

Since I have not seen my role as that of an investigative reporter or an academic researcher, the challenge for me is not to be 'objective' but to be balanced and aware. It is a cliché but I accept that everything is connected – body, mind, emotion and spirit – we are always 'involved', influencing and influenced by what we experience and engage with. Lederach understands that the more complex the system we are trying to explore and understand, the simpler the questions we need to ask. *The Moral Imagination* addresses the questions: "How exactly do we transcend cycles of violence? How do we create genuine constructive change in and with the human community?"

Those questions are equally relevant when it comes to understanding the dynamic around the peacewalls and interfaces in Belfast, as are some aspects of Lederach's own response to those questions. Lederach believes that "social change is the art of seeing and building webs". In researching this book I attempted to 'see' and explore as much as possible of the complex social system or web around the walls. The moral imagination involves, he says, "the capacity to imagine that it is possible to hold multiple realities and world views simultaneously as part of a greater whole"; it "pursues complexity as a friend rather than as an enemy", and it "refuses to frame life's challenges, problems, issues as dualistic polarities" (Lederach 2005). That implies following a "both/and" rather than an "either/or" approach.

The research and writing of this book has been a personal as well as a professional journey. It began with a battle with myself about self-confidence and courage. In outline terms the destination was quite clear and defined by the core question raised by the 2023 commitment – but the route and path were not, and remained foggily unclear beyond the immediate foreground. All along, the way ahead was pointed out by the people I met, and over and over again by synchronicities and serendipities which always presented themselves to me as gift, as food for the journey. While I was initially led to be anxious that people at the interfaces might be tired of researchers and surveys, I found little resistance to my desire to simply listen to people's experience and the stories they tell; and I tried as far as possible to stay in touch and keep people informed of the book's progress. I can count on the fingers of one hand those who either refused my request for an interview or asked afterwards not to be included. In addition, I did, was encouraged to, twice request an interview with First Minister Peter Robinson and deputy First Minister Martin McGuinness, but never received any acknowledgement or reply. I also feel bound to underline that I have no political allegiance in Northern Ireland.

Few people in Belfast know the walls and interfaces better than photographer Frankie Quinn, who was born and still lives in the Short Strand, and who has produced two collections of photographs of the walls: *Interface Images* (1994) and *Streets Apart* (2008). I am enormously pleased that Frankie agreed to work on this book with me and his pictures – taken specially in the first months of 2015 – complement the book perfectly.

Frankie's perspective is that of the insider; mine of course is that of the outsider. It is often said that the closer you get to the walls, the less you see them: a privilege of my position has been that I have been able to gain a 'helicopter view' of the world around the walls – and I continue to be shocked by them. The greatest difference between myself and the people that populate that world is that I have not suffered through or survived the Troubles. Many of those I interviewed said they would welcome a fresh eye on the subject. This book aims to offer another angle on the unfolding and incomplete peace process in Northern Ireland – to the extent that it succeeds, the primary credit goes to those I interviewed who unfailingly shared their thoughts, hopes, stories and insights with great trust and frankness.

Chapter One

SETTING THE SCENE

"Your neighbour is your other self, dwelling behind a wall.
In understanding, all walls shall fall down."

Kahlil Gibran, The Prophet

THE PHOTOGRAPH, A CALENDAR picture for March 2008, shows a simple but surreal, Photoshopped image – a bulldog suspended in mid-air above a non-descript roundabout. A tall CCTV camera scrutinises the scene. The text states: MARK YOUR TERRITORY.

This is the roundabout at Twaddell Avenue, at the top of Ardoyne in North Belfast. It is one of many 'invisible' interfaces: there is no wall but Catholics walk on one side of the street and Protestants on the other, and young people speak of 'our side' and 'their side' of the circle. This became the site of the Twaddell Loyalist protest camp, founded in summer 2013 when a Loyalist march past Ardoyne was banned, still consuming extra policing at a cost of £30,000 a day.

Dogs mark their territory. Community workers Brendan Clarke and Rab McCallum from North Belfast Interface Network (NBIN) pointed out to Sean and Mikey, who were waiting with their cameras for the dog to cock its leg, that this was in fact a bitch and a puppy – "you could be there a while", they joked.

This was the start of Draw Down the Walls (DDTW), which began with £600 leftover project money in summer 2007. Cameras were given to 15 'hard core' boys from the Catholic neighbourhood of Ardoyne, who were asked to capture images that showed how they experienced territory and identity within one square mile. Launched with an exhibition at the newly restored Crumlin Road Gaol, the pictures show the teenagers' awareness of being under constant surveillance, of needing to choose carefully where they walk. They illustrate Ardoyne's claustrophobic feel, one way in and one way out, the Black Mountain hills on the near horizon but beyond reach. Consciously or unconsciously the bulldog image echoes the story that, even before there were physical walls, the 'dogs in the street' knew the boundaries of sectarian territory.

Disaffected youth, the claustrophobia of interface neighbourhoods: these are emblematic of the story of the walls. The calendar also suggests young people's intrinsic capacity for joy, hope and humour. The project was not presented to them as art, but the result is art, a series of compelling images that encapsulate their experience.

The years of the calendar's production, 2007–2008 were, as we shall see, a *kairos* moment when politicians, statutory agencies and communities began to 'see' the walls as a problem to be solved. DDTW brought together the NBIN, the Loyalist Lower Shankill Community Association (LSCA) and the Golden Thread Gallery to use art to raise issues and open discussions. Rab McCallum's and Brendan Clarke's work was inspired by imagining 'a city without barriers'. "I can live with that," responded their Loyalist partner from the LSCA, Ian McLaughlin. "We are", says Rab McCallum, "always looking for ways to start conversations around conflict". It led next, as we shall see later, to Colombian artist Oscar Munoz's remarkable 2012 *Ambulatorio,* installed between the closed steel gates at Flax Street, off the Crumlin Road, which in turn has led to hopes that this interface can be permanently opened. DDTW has shown how art can kick off transformative conversations, the value of creative approaches to conflict, the unpredictability of outcomes, and the need for long term funding.

In May 2013, First Minister Peter Robinson and deputy First Minister Martin McGuinness made the commitment to remove the peacewalls and interfaces by 2023 in response to direct pressure from Westminster. It was greeted with derision and widespread cynicism in the media. Commentators argued that it will not be possible to bring the walls down within this time frame or perhaps ever; that the political impasse amongst the five power-sharing parties in the Northern Ireland Assembly will inevitably frustrate any real progress; that the promise was itself cynically made in advance of the June 2013 G8 summit, held in Fermanagh, and to secure funding. It also met with fear and disbelief from local communities, certain that the target cannot be achieved in practice. "It set us back three years", says one community worker, "that target and the flags protest."

By early 2015, however, the Flax Street gates are among a number due to be transformed across the city within the next few months. The work faces continual setbacks as it gets snagged by bureaucratic delays and macro- and micro-political agendas. Nonetheless, protective window grilles have been removed from houses in Moyard estate at Black Mountain and on Duncairn Gardens; a steel extension has been taken down from the wall in Duncairn Business Complex. One of two sets of gates have been removed from Springmartin Road and the traffic barrier on Newington Street has also been removed. Most importantly, the forbidding security gates at Workman Avenue were replaced in April 2015 by decorative see-through gates. These may seem to be insignificant actions – a gate open for a few hours a day here, a fence lowered there; toughened glass replacing steel grilles on windows that have not been cleaned for decades. But these small changes are testimony to the turning of the tide and to the reality that in many places in Belfast, there has been no significant violence in six or seven years.

This might surprise those who follow the news from Northern Ireland. But as many recognise, there is a distinction between the political process and the peace process, which trudges relentlessly if wearily forward. Richard Haass warned the US Congress in April 2014 that a return to violence was possible if the process he began with Dr Meghan O'Sullivan during 2013, and which took a further step forward with the Stormont House Agreement, was not completed. However, no-one I spoke to in the course of interviewing for this book said, and in no public forum was it expressed, that a return to havoc is remotely likely. There is disagreement about whether Northern Ireland is in a post-conflict phase or whether the conflict has simply shape-shifted – Rab McCallum says, "We are not post-conflict, we are just carrying on the conflict in a different way" – but no-one believes a return to large-scale violence is on the cards. And this, John Paul Lederach said, is due to the "safety net of the myriad of community activity" in Belfast for which, some would say, not enough credit has been given. "Northern Ireland is changing", says academic John Brewer "and changing for the better. It just doesn't feel like it. We have yet to make peace with peace…" (Brewer 2014).

Belfast is a small city. Its population has stabilised – or increased slightly due to multinational immigration – at around 300,000 having dropped by 200,000 or 35% during the three decades of conflict. It is contained by attractive low hills on three sides while the iconic giant yellow Harland and Wolff gantry cranes still tower over the Titanic shipyards. From the city centre, the famous arterial roads stretch to the North and West: the Antrim, Crumlin, Shankill, Springfield and Falls Roads. Across bridges over the Lagan, the Newtownards Road leads east to Stormont. The Stormont Estate, gifted to the

St Matthew's Roman Catholic Church, Short Strand

province in 1921 at partition by Westminster and home of Northern Ireland's Assembly, known colloquially as The Hill, dramatically overlooks the city. The neo-classical symmetry of the Parliament Building itself – patterns of sixes in the number of windows and columns to reflect the six counties, and an exactly mirrored design on both sides – belies the chaos which has afflicted the province for much of its history.

It rarely takes longer than 20 minutes by car to get from any place in Belfast to any other place. It is hardly six miles as the crow flies from Greater Whitewell, hugged by the dual carriageway to the north, where the fence was erected in Hazelwood Integrated Primary School in 2007, to Suffolk, a walled and threatened Protestant enclave in far south-west Belfast. And barely three miles from the outer northwestern sectarian divides of Ligoniel to the still deeply conflicted East Belfast. Here, the most recent peace fence was erected in November 2013 in the grounds of St Matthew's Roman Catholic Church in Short Strand, there was persistent rioting during the late summer and autumn of 2014, and the Protestant area is becoming notorious for vicious race hate attacks and 'locals only' protests against incoming migrant residents.

Downtown Belfast, dominated by its own gracious and iconic building, City Hall, and the newly developed docks and Laganside areas, gives the impression of a normal, bustling, thriving city – but things are not normal: there are two Belfasts, two parallel worlds that are so close in places that you can slip from one to another simply by crossing a bridge or traffic lights. Alongside the glittering new Belfast of the Titanic Belfast centre and Waterfront Hall lies a deeply divided society, within which segregation between Protestant and Catholic has steadily hardened since the 1994 ceasefire and the 1998 Belfast Agreement. While violence has abated in much of the city, fear and tension between Unionist and Nationalist communities remain – and the most tangible sign of the conflict are the walls and interfaces, a third of which were built in the decade since the Belfast Agreement.

No-one knows exactly how many walls and interfaces there actually are. In 2012, the Belfast Interface Project (BIP), the long-established communities network, published a numbered and photographed catalogue listing 99 with, if known, their year of construction and owner, and grouped them into 13 clusters (BIP 2012). But there may well be more, since each local community has its own list, and in any event the interfaces are continually changing. There are also the many invisible interfaces, including, for example, a stretch of Ligoniel Road, or the stretch of Clifton Street below Carlisle Circus. Here there is an Orange Hall on one side of the road; next to it the listed and abandoned Methodist Church, which has been cut in half and the other half, pinned incongruously between the church and the Orange Hall is the Indian Community Centre with its sparkling Hindu temple. The almost unnoticeable presence of the Indian community here on the interface is a powerful symbol of how a number of immigrant communities, including Indians, Chinese and Polish, have been long established in Northern Ireland. This building was bought by them for £3,500 and opened in 1981. One hundred and twenty families from the Punjab during the 50s and 60s, possibly landing "by mistake", according to Dr Satyavir Singhal. The early migrants were door-to-door salesmen and the "first creditors in Northern Ireland". The Indian community were "not troubled much" during the Troubles, he says, and have done very well – most are now professionals. More recent waves of immigrants have included IT specialists, and Christians, Muslims, Sikhs and Jains as well as Hindus.

Interfaces may be ritualised to an extraordinary degree – in White City there are said to be segregated bus stops, while near Bryson Street in East Belfast there is a designated 'shared bus stop'. The interfaces and walls represent a single complex systemic problem while each cluster presents a quite specific local context. And each cluster requires its own unique strategy for transforming or bringing down the walls.

The wall usually said to have been the first built is Cupar Way, the best known and most often visited by tourists: a four and a half metre edifice, embellished by art and graffiti, which divides the Catholic lower Falls from the Protestant lower Shankill and runs for half a mile out of the city centre. Begun by the British army as a barbed wire barricade in September 1969 it is now topped by three metres of steel fencing and a further six metres of open mesh. The most dominant and effective interface is the dual carriageway, Westlink, which slices the city like a crooked smile from north-east to south-west Belfast. It formed a convenient 'natural' division between the troublesome areas of North and West Belfast and the city centre and prosperous and leafy areas of Queen's University Belfast and South Belfast (Processions 1971). Frank Higgins, a community historian in Brown Square, a tiny Protestant enclave cut off to the east of Westlink and close to city centre, is confident that the corrugated iron interface in their children's playpark is in fact the earliest – a photograph from August 1969, the month before Cupar Way, shows two soldiers leaning on the original waist-high fence, reinforced by barbed wire, with a Union Jack hanging from the old gas lamp.

An interface can be defined as "the contested space where intercommunity tensions have the potential to lead to a confrontation between segregated Unionist and Nationalist communities" (Persic 2004). An interface may or may not be marked by a physical wall, gate or barrier. Some are high concrete walls such as that on Cupar Way. Others are tall green fences running between the backs of gardens down side streets. Some are locked or lockable steel gates or traffic barriers. Many, like the reinforced steel security gates on Lanark Way, are ugly and militaristic. Some are vacant plots of land or carparks. Some may be decorative steel fencing. A section of wall on the Springfield Road is a 'boast wall' – it appears to be solid brick but is hollow cladding held together with steel rivets and designed, ironically, to be easily deconstructed. Many of the gates and walls have smaller pedestrian gates open during the day. Houses on interfaces may have metal grilles over

Bryson Street,
Short Strand

their windows, or perhaps almost no windows at all, or wire cages over back gardens, creating a sense of incarceration. Interface areas often have further signs of blight: derelict houses, shops and factories; abandoned wasteland. Some interface areas have become dumping grounds for rubbish, and, some would say, for vulnerable people. Parts of North Belfast recall bomb-damaged postwar London and are presided over by the monstrous burnt-out roofless hulk of Crumlin Road Courthouse – an ironic neo-Greek echo of its grander cousin on The Hill.

At many levels, practical, psychological, metaphorical, the walls are a real problem for post-conflict Belfast. They are a concrete sign of the "normality of the abnormality" of Belfast (Byrne 2012). They have replaced the guns and bombs as a physical manifestation of the conflict and hatred; they are the debris of the unfinished peace process; they are, Gabbi Murphy writes in the introduction to Frankie Quinn's photographs, *Streets Apart* (2008), "the faultlines that define the tectonics of sectarian division". The walls scar the cityscape, and are described by Maurice di Cintio in his travelogue as "self-harm" and "mutilation" (di Cintio 2013). To all intents and purposes, this remains a fortified city, shaped by the architecture of conflict: bomb-proofed new buildings, ubiquitous CCTV, fortress police stations.

The walls also inhibit the progress of the peace process. According to Scott Bollens, effective peacebuilding in divided societies requires the sharing of space, everyday interactions across the divide, and the potential for new cross-ethnic political factions to form: "rights are created as much through everyday urban social practices built on unrestricted flows and involving places of encounter as they are created through formal means". Speaking of urban divisions as "ethnic hinges", he says that when these hinges are hardened, the city is "handicapped as a place of interaction and cross group pluralism". For the hinges to be "lubricated" there need to be multi-cultural encounters at the everyday level, porosity in urban activity patterns, inclusivity and fair political representation, and economies dependent on multi-ethnic contacts (Bollens 2013). In other words, healthy societies are dynamic, fluid and promote diversity.

The barriers "freeze the geography and demography of single-identity communities and prevent all sorts of normal freedom of movement" (CRC 2008). Residents may avoid moving beyond their immediate vicinity and thus have restricted access to shops, health centres and other amenities. Particularly at night, when gates may be closed, people must walk or drive long distances to get where they need to go. What architect Mark Hackett calls "tubes" have been created – long stretches of street with no exit to left or right, which make the city "impermeable" and people feel unsafe. The walls are "just there," says a senior serving Police Service of Northern Ireland (PSNI) officer. "Everything is organised around the fact that they are there. I wonder what life would be like without them."

Literally and metaphorically, the walls restrict vision, says Revd Lesley Carroll, Presbyterian minister and peaceworker. They are an "obstacle to the future"; they "repress in advance the novelty of experience" (Phillips 2013). They prevent people from imagining new possibilities. They make people "look inward rather than outward", said 2013–2014 Lord Mayor Máirtín Ó Muilleoir. Interface communities are isolated and insular. Segregated neighbourhoods such as Short Strand and Ardoyne have a curiously calm, sheltered and stifled feel to them, not unpleasant, rather as I imagine a fortified mediaeval encampment might have felt. Now, says Ian McLaughlin, from the lower Shankill, "people need to be meerkats, to look up and over the walls."

The walls are a "site of contradiction" (Ravenscroft 2006). Their intention is to protect from violence, and many residents say that the walls make them feel safer, but they are also a target for violence and teenage anti-social behaviour. "The interfaces aren't a place where people don't get on," says veteran community worker Roisin McGlone, "they attract those who want to come and throw stones." 'Recreational rioting' is the term invented in the early 2000s to describe the low level but persistent trouble caused by children and young people in interface areas. Although motivated by boredom and bravado rather than politics, it can feed into sectarian violence. In 1969, young people might have seen themselves as defenders of their own communities, says Rab McCallum, but "at some point things changed and we realised they were coming into areas from outside". Young people are being recruited, mobilised and exploited by criminal gang leaders – sometimes more romantically presented as former political combatants. In interface areas, the "marginal location and relative lack of adult presence turns them into spaces they can define for themselves and claim as their own" (Jarman 2001). Now, the rioting can be organised in a flash through mobile phones, Facebook and Twitter, frustrating and outwitting the police and terrifying local residents. What might be relatively normal ritualised gang behaviour and hanging out takes on a more sinister timbre in the volatile sectarian context of Belfast. Some of the visitors to Crumlin Road Gaol, closed in 1996 but now restored and open as a tourist attraction, are former prisoners who bring their sons to try and put them off risking a prison sentence. Even so, some 700 youths passed through criminal courts and faced possible prison sentences and crippled lives for their participation in the Loyalist flag protests.

War is a young man's occupation, on the whole, and in Northern Ireland during the years of conflict the paramilitaries – and the soldiers and police – were often very young. Sam 'Chalky' White, a former Loyalist combatant from East Belfast, recruited at 15, says: "We were child soldiers". This reality, and its long term impact on both the survivors and the perpetrators, is powerfully conveyed in the 2008 film *Five Minutes of Heaven* with Liam Neeson and James Nesbitt. Now with other former prisoners in the Prisons to Peace Programme, Chalky visits schools to persuade children to stay out of trouble. Chalky White learned as an Ulster Defence Association (UDA) prisoner in mixed wings, with Red Hand Commando (RHC), Ulster Volunteer Force (UVF) and Irish Republican Army (IRA) all mixed together, the benefits of dialogue and the harm caused by conflict. They learned from one another about human rights and equality: "Our conversations were based on total respect." He has learned that "we live in a society divided by walls and united in poverty."

Some would say it is not the walls that are the problem, but fear and mistrust: a fear that is very real for those who live near the walls. Ask a resident for the reason they are afraid, and they will often quote an incident from decades ago, recounting it as if it were yesterday. "When I look at that gate," says Maureen, a member of Grace Women's Development Group in Ardoyne, of a rusted and bolted gate on Alliance Avenue, "I still see the Loyalist gunmen coming through it." From 1969 to 2004, a third of the victims of political violence were murdered within 250 metres of an interface, and 70% within 500 metres (Shirlow 2006). The walls have become sites of memory and commemoration. Roisin McGlone, employed on the interfaces for over 20 years and now director of InterAction on the Springfield Road, says: "This is where people were killed. The walls are our wounds. Sometimes it seems the politicians want to wash away evidence of the Troubles, but there is still a subconscious, unintentional need for memorialisation."

Sectarian fear is transmitted through the generations, says Chris O'Halloran of BIP. Since serious violence has largely abated in the last seven years in many areas, it is 'fear itself' to a significant degree that is now the problem. "The reality of the threat becomes irrelevant, the perception is all" (di Cintio 2013). "The legacy of the conflict", says Sally Smyth, the coordinator of Grace, "is just as raw as when the conflict was happening". During the months of February and March 2014 she referred close to 100 people to the new Victims and Survivors Service. As another community worker said, "Yesterday isn't history and it impacts on everything." Belfast remains a captive of its past, a past enshrined in the walls themselves.

Some would say it is not the walls themselves that are the problem, but the wider economic situation in Northern Ireland. Oft-quoted is New York Mayor Bloomberg's speech of 2008 to the Northern Ireland Investment Conference. It was in the interests of peace, prosperity and investment to remove the walls, he said. As the annual Peace Monitoring Report bluntly states, in the first paragraph of the first chapter, the Northern Ireland deficit is over £10 billion, an eye-watering gap between the revenues of £23.2 billion and the income of £12.7 billion (Nolan 2014). The economy is also unbalanced, being two thirds public to just one third private sector. The priority for Westminster was the economic sustainability of the region, and as Prime Minister David Cameron has made clear in a number of public pronouncements, the walls were seen as essential to achieving it.

Some would say it is not the walls themselves that are the problem, but social deprivation. According to the Multiple Deprivation Index of 2010, the 25 most deprived wards in Belfast are all in interface areas. In February 2013, the End Child Poverty Campaign named West Belfast the parliamentary constituency with the second highest rate of child poverty (46%) in the UK – after only Manchester Central. Life expectancy in West and North Belfast is around 73 years old for males and 79 for females, over 7% for men and 4.5% for women lower than in the most privileged areas of Northern Ireland. West and North Belfast register higher levels of unemployment. Mental health is also poor: there is a direct link between numbers of suicides and the Multiple Deprivation Index. In November 2014, the Department of Health announced that there have been 7,000 suicides in Northern Ireland since 1970, with numbers increasing since the 1998 Belfast Agreement, and plateauing since 2007 at around 280 annually (*Irish News,* 11 Nov 14). Studies have linked suicide and attempted suicide specifically to the "unexpurgated traumas suffered by children during the worst years of violence in the 70s" (Nolan 2014). Furthermore, the levels of poverty have not fallen despite the estimated over £2 billion of funding poured into Northern Ireland by the EU, IFI, Irish government and Atlantic Philanthropies by 2008 (Deloitte 2007).

Some would say it is not the walls that are the problem, but segregation and sectarianism. Sectarianism is still not criminalised in Northern Ireland; there is no accepted definition and no law against it. Northern Ireland has been "arguably one of the largest social laboratories in history as investment has flowed in, in an attempt to create liveable social and political integration" (Herbert 2013). The proportion of social housing in working class areas of Belfast ranges from 50% to over 80%, of which 96% is segregated. Yet, while to varying degrees people want and can imagine a reduction in the walls and interfaces, few envisage an end to segregation between Protestant and Catholic communities. The 2012 research report notes that over 78% of people believe that segregation would remain without the peacewalls. For the general public, addressing the problem of segregation is a larger and different problem to that of the peacewalls (Byrne et al 2012).

Comparisons are odious and it can be argued that in human terms, the Catholic/ Nationalist/Republican (CNR) working class communities and the Protestant/Unionist/ Loyalist (PUL) communities share far more than divides them, including levels of deprivation, although Catholic communities score consistently higher on all indices of poverty. Nonetheless, there are also significant differences, although as we shall see the use of terms Protestant, Unionist, Loyalist and Catholic, Nationalist, Republican are increasingly euphemistic.

Catholics have been less likely to move out of interface areas; the Catholic population has increased proportionately, leading to pressure on housing stock. In very broad brush strokes, and at the risk of generalisation, what may be described as Catholic/Nationalist/

Glenbryn

Republican (CNR) working class communities are relatively coherent and united as they have just one Christian denomination, the Roman Catholic Church, and Sinn Féin (SF) predominates politically although is widely perceived to be closely allied to its former military wing, the IRA. Dissident Republican influences remain; and there is a significant gap between the Catholic Church and Republicanism. Mass attendance varies from around 10% to 35% in Belfast (*Irish News,* 13 Jan 15).

Meanwhile, the Protestant/Unionist/Loyalist (PUL) community is fragmented, and this fragmentation contributes to its declining confidence: on the lower Shankill, for example, there are over 40 separate Christian denominations, and very low levels of church attendance. Some congregations survive only because of the number of middle class commuters who return on Sundays to worship in the church in which they were baptised or married. There is rivalry and violent feuding within and between some former members of the Ulster Defence Association (UDA) and Ulster Volunteer Force

(UVF). There are several Unionist parties, including the dominant Democratic Unionist Party (DUP), Ulster Unionist Party (UUP), and Progressive Unionist Party (PUP). There is a perceived gap between working class PUL and their political representatives.

Protestants have been in general geographically and economically more mobile, and Protestant interface areas often have extensive open or waste ground, while Catholic housing is often backed right up against the walls: "working class nationalist areas are bursting at the seams, while houses in nearby Protestant areas lie empty" (Heatley 2004). Social housing – its appalling quality and discrimination in its allocation – was one of the primary triggers for Catholic unrest during the 1960s. Although Northern Ireland now has some of the best social housing in the UK, it continues to be a source of dissatisfaction, friction and envy between communities. In 2011, less than 1% of social housing was unfit and some 4% failed to meet the Decent Homes Standard; much of the housing stock requires some improvement. There were about 40,000 on the waiting list in September 2012, more than half of whom were in 'housing stress' (Northern Ireland Housing Market Review 2014).

Dr Orna Young, a conflict researcher on the panel at the launch of the Anti-Sectarian Charter (Appendix 2) at Belfast Metropolitan College campus E3 on the Springfield Road in April 2014 pointed out that "sectarianism thrives amongst people who are most alike". Sectarian attitudes in Northern Ireland have hardened: a research update to the Northern Ireland Life and Times Survey (NILT) of 2012 found that the proportion of respondents who believe that relations between Protestants and Catholics are better now than five years ago has fallen by 7% since 2012 to 45%, its lowest level since 2003. Sectarian attitudes have worsened particularly among young people, who have less memory of the violence and therefore less fear, and unlike their parents no memory of the more integrated society that existed prior to 1969. While many might have assumed or hoped that young people would be more open and tolerant than their parents, the walls – and continued segregated education – have actively ensured that they are less likely than their parents to be mixing with peers from the other tradition, at least until they go into third level education.

Meanwhile, there is deep concern about the decline of the Protestant working class neighbourhoods. Flight to the suburbs has led to estates emptying and schools closing. Four out of five Protestant boys receiving free school meals are leaving school without minimum qualifications of 5 GCSEs including English and Maths (Nolan 2014). Only Irish travellers and Gypsy Roma do worse. After the decline of shipping and other traditional industries and during the conflict, many Protestants went into the police, the Ulster Defence Regiment and support roles for security forces that Catholics felt unable to take. The UDR was merged into the regular army in 1992, the PSNI halved in number (from about 14,000 to about 7,000) and began to attract a higher proportion of Catholics, and most army barracks closed – leading to a second wave of job loss for Protestants in the 1990s.

There is a need to listen to and understand the Loyalist position. Young mothers, residents of Lower Oldpark, where the 'yellow wall' has cut across Manor Street and divides the Protestant community from the Catholic Cliftonville on the other side, tell me that they may never have voted or attend church; for them Protestant culture is defined primarily by the celebrations of the 11th and 12th of July. Helping to unite a very fragmented 'community' and boost its morale, the parades have doubled in number since 2008, and although the vast majority of them are non-contentious, their proliferation may not be a sign of the strengthening of Protestant culture but a greater defensiveness.

Nationalist areas are characterised by optimism, Protestant areas by despondency according to academic Peter Shirlow (quoted in Heatley 2004). As Paul Nolan, author of the 2014 Peace Monitoring Report said in his presentation to the Community Relations Council (CRC) Annual Policy Conference in June 2014, the changing demographic pattern is clear. Belfast no longer has a Protestant majority; "the axis of politics has shifted." It used to be between Republicans and Loyalists; soon it will be between Unionists and everyone else; "Unionists are pulling their wagons into a circle", said Denis Bradley, the influential former priest and co-chair of the Consultative Group on the Past, at the same conference. By 2021, the centenary of partition, which precedes the 2023 deadline for the removal of the walls, the very reason for the founding of the province, the Protestant majority, will no longer be germane.

Protestant and Catholic identities are formed in opposition to one another, they exist in "an entrenched dialectical relationship to one another", writes Emily Ravenscroft – in other words each tradition requires the quarrel with the other in order to survive. The need is generated "to maintain the other as a threat in order to keep a stable sense of identity". In Ardoyne, an older member of a women's group defines herself as Republican "just to spite the other side" – a phrase I hear more than once. And the peacelines "create, reinforce and exacerbate these dialectical identities". As a former senior PSNI officer says: "the problem is each community's concept of the other, their images of who the others are. The peacelines contribute to the distrust." For Catholics, the peacewalls are an echo of the prison walls of Long Kesh and the martyrdom of the hunger strikers; while for Protestants they represent the walls and siege mentality of Londonderry's walls, keeping out the invading Catholic hordes. Furthermore, the state "does not fully understand the rhetorical work that these peacelines do" (Ravenscroft 2006).

The divisiveness is reproduced at higher levels of the political system. The leadership of Northern Ireland is perceived as failing to model the 'united community' promoted by its rhetoric. Minister of Justice David Ford, head of the moderate Alliance Party, notes that the two main political parties, Sinn Féin and the DUP, have something to lose by what is commonly called 'Good Relations' because their support has traditionally come from the more extreme ends of the spectrum. As a consequence, Ian McLaughlin says: "an argument on The Hill is magnified toxically at grassroots level". The ubiquitous complaint is of a provincial government unable to put the desire of a silent majority for peace and prosperity above the parochial pettiness of party politics. Stormont, says journalist Barney Rowan at the CRC Policy Conference, is a "cold, shrill, screaming and scowling place". Brewer notes that the negative characteristics of the political arena are themselves reflected in the media, which in turn becomes "curmudgeonly, cantankerous and crabby" (Brewer 2014).

"If truth is the first fatality of war, perspective is the casualty of peace. Perspectives are distorted in peace processes by focussing on the difficulties ahead and ignoring what we have actually achieved", says Brewer (2014). I repeat that in all my interviews I met no-one who said they believed Northern Ireland could return to the mayhem of the decades of conflict. "Belfast won't go up again", says Chris O'Halloran of BIP. "We are resolute that there will be no more suffering", says Glenn Bradley, a former interface resident and British paratrooper, at the launch of the Anti-Sectarian Charter in April 2014. Sporadic violence, dysfunctional politics, lack of leadership, a failure to deal with the 'toxic' residue of the past, flags and parades – these overtones cause a certain stuckness in the conversation – but, as two Loyalist leaders, one from East and one from West Belfast independently assure me, "we are now in the endgame".

The walls are a problem, and so are fear, sectarianism, segregation, deprivation and the need for economic growth in Northern Ireland. Unfortunately, to a significant degree, the barriers have been "deemed only of concern in the areas within which they are present, with little attention given to the social ramifications posed to the province as a whole" (Hatch 2013). This is a complex problem with many interdependent facets and no obvious solution. The great challenge of peacemaking, says John Paul Lederach, is how to build creative responses to patterns of self-perpetuating violence in a complex system made up of multiple actors and many simultaneous activities (1997). There are thousands of individuals and groups intensely involved with the walls: individual residents and community forums; former paramilitaries and community development workers; police and civil servants; families and older people; politicians working at local and regional levels; tourists and taxi drivers; artists, photographers and architects; academics, church leaders and funders. There are many stories, those of individuals and groups, within the wider narrative of the peace process.

When we listen, when we hear, when we converse, post on Facebook or Twitter, consciously or unconsciously we are always making choices. We are magnifying, amplifying and mirroring what we perceive. In other words, people choose whether to reinforce elements of conflict or peace in this complex situation. Viewed as a static problem, the goal of removing the interfaces can appear unattainable. But when viewed as a dynamic situation, in terms of what is changing, a different picture emerges. Lederach says that the lived reality in post-conflict societies is of "a dynamic context in which people simultaneously live and face elements of both conflict and peace – a context in which reconciliation and healing are embedded."

Peace processes are iterative and can't be forced. As we have seen with the flag disputes, Twaddell, the On The Runs and Haass, progress is made and then stalls or even appears to go backwards. As if to prove Lederach's conviction that change processes are non-linear, the trajectory from the May 2013 Office of the First Minister and deputy First Minister (OFMdFM) promise demonstrates the fragile and sometimes contradictory path of the peace process. Initial cynicism was tempered by hope as good work by community groups and more effective collaboration with and between statutory agencies gained momentum. By June 2014, there were specific projected late summer dates for transformations and opening of gates and barriers at Townsend Street, Flax Street, Crumlin Road and Workman Avenue. Belfast had its most trouble free 12th of July and marching season in years. But as the long hot summer wore on, plans were repeatedly delayed. Communities dug their heels in and it seemed that the discussions over the interfaces were getting snagged in the larger negotiations to kickstart the stalled peace talks over parades, flags and the legacy of the past, and Unionist demands for a separate inquiry into the Ardoyne parades. The peacewalls were perhaps being used as poker chips in the 'graduated response', the unspecified strategy threatened by Unionists to accomplish their demands. "It is not a crisis," said Sinn Féin Member of Legislative Assembly (MLA) Pat Sheehan during a panel discussion for American students at Farset on the Springfield Road in June, "and however bad it gets, it's not going back to the way it was." Now, some believe the wheels are oiled again and the reaching of the Stormont House Agreement (SHA) will translate into further progress on the peacewalls and interfaces.

During what was widely seen as a remarkable year in office, from which he emerged as a "political celebrity", according to journalist Alex Kane (*Belfast Newsletter*, 12 Jan 15), Lord Mayor Máirtín Ó Muilleoir's guiding principle was to "edit out the negative". In this he was influenced by his Buddhist chaplain Paul Haller, and also by the organisational change methodology of appreciative enquiry, an approach which aims to stimulate constructive change by looking for what works, accentuating the positive (Hammond 2013). This approach does not mean being in denial or turning a blind eye to dysfunction, and it does not fight shy of challenge or critique, but it recognises that we learn as much or more from what is being done right or well as from what is failing.

By early 2015, since OFMdFM's apparently impetuous pledge to bring down the peacewalls and interfaces by 2023, progress is indeed being made. The IFI funded peacewalls programmes have developed an effective model, building on previous successful cross community work, which will be promoted beyond the eight current programmes in Belfast and Derry. These programmes have carefully targeted interfaces and areas of blight, and used cross community dialogue and consultation to negotiate local support for positive change. They have also used holistic approaches to regeneration of their local contexts so that the peacewalls are not seen in isolation from wider socio economic issues. The Housing Executive and Belfast City Council have been among those using artists and architects to help transform interface areas.

When Northern Ireland's most senior politicians spearheaded the initiative to bring down the walls, there was widespread concern that interface residents themselves should be involved in the local decision-making process. Now that communities are coming on board, one threat has been from lack of finance. Although in early 2015 the Irish government offered £5 million to allow Phase II of the IFI peacewalls programme to go ahead, the UK government and Northern Ireland Executive are offering minimal financial support to implement the Together Building a United Community (TBUC) strategy. Budgets have been slashed. There will be a gap between the end of EU Peace III funding in December 2014 and the start of Peace IV in late 2015. No-one is quite sure how the actual cost of demolition is to be paid for. Some say: the British government paid to put them up, and now should pay to take them down.

Meanwhile, at one of the invisible interfaces, where Glendore Avenue meets Skegoneill Avenue in North Belfast, William Haire bought a vacant site on the sharp corner of the junction and five years ago opened a tiny shop and café in an open-sided shipping container which is used by both Protestants and Catholics. The Catholics might have seen it to begin with as a "wee Protestant shop", he says, "but if anyone had ever put a flag on it I would have closed it down."

"I don't care how much it costs to bring them down," says former Lord Mayor and Alliance Party city councillor Alderman Tom Ekin, "the walls are stupid. The cost of a segregated Northern Ireland is a billion or more a year, and if the barriers coming down saved us one tenth of that, it would be worth it."

Springhill Avenue

Chapter Two

HISTORY: THE NORMAL ABNORMAL

The Great Wall of China "is one of the wonders of the world, and also proof of a kind of human weakness, of an aberration, of a horrifying mistake; it is evidence of a historical inability of people to communicate."

Ryszard Kapuscinski, Travels with Herodotus

BEFORE THE TROUBLES, SAYS Tony Macaulay in *Breaking the Barriers*, a film made in 2014 by young people from the Falls and Shankill Roads, you could go anywhere. A similar tale is told by others including community worker Sam 'Chalky' White. Chalky grew up on a mixed estate in Castlereagh in East Belfast, then a suburb on high ground overlooking the city. Religion, he says, was never an issue. He had Catholic friends and bonfire night, 11th July, was huge for everyone. But in 1969, as the conflict began to get out of control, clouds of smoke could be seen below, billowing over the city. Before long their community too was being divided. "You would get a tap on the shoulder," he says, "and be told, don't be mixing with Paddy or Mick, now." The army and Royal Ulster Constabulary (RUC) put a fence down the middle of the estate, and families moved from one side to the other, their belongings piled onto flatbed lorries with a tricolour or Union Jack stuck on the top.

That was 1969, the same year that the Cupar Way wall began to be built. For the next 30 years, the walls proliferated, spreading like triffids down arterial roads and back streets, almost unnoticed.

The resort to division between Protestant and Catholic in Northern Ireland has a long history. It can even be dated to the consequences of the 1609/10 Plantation of Ulster. "Segregated living patterns which continue to exist today were laid down during the 17th Century and frequently refreshed with bouts of rioting, intimidations and expulsions." By 1704, just 5% of land in Ulster was owned by native Irish, and by the time of partition in 1921 "a type of economic, social, cultural and political apartheid had evolved in the North, and while many working class and rural Protestants also suffered poverty and deprivation, Catholics tended to occupy a much more disadvantaged position" (Ó hAdhmaill 2012).

The first physical barrier is said to date from 1866, separating Protestant from Catholic graves and buried nine foot deep in the city cemetery (Nolan 2014). Temporary walls were erected in Short Strand in 1920 and in Sailortown in 1935 (Byrne 2011).

In July 1920, sectarian strife began after the Belfast Protestant Association had marched to expel Catholic workers from factories. By the end of July, about 5,000 had lost their jobs and violence spread to East and North Belfast. These Troubles lasted over two years, and 489 people lost their lives. One hotspot was East Belfast where 76 people were killed in the communities of Short Strand and Ballymacarret.

Fr Patrick J Gannon, a Jesuit visiting St Matthew's in the Short Strand, wrote:

"I may say that if there was any serious desire on the part of authorities to protect the Catholic quarters, a judicious erection of these barricades would make the task very simple. The few in existence were only put up after 18 months of massacre and incendiarism and are not nearly numerous enough" (Kernaghan 2000).

On 10 September 1969, referring to the Cupar Way wall between lower Falls and Shankill, army chief Lt General Sir Ian Freeland famously said that "the peaceline will be a very very temporary affair. We will not have a Berlin Wall in this city." By April 1971, however, a government working party report records the existence of 17, mostly catwire fences but including seven corrugated iron walls. The working party had been convened in October 1970 "to consider existing areas of confrontation and peacelines and advise as to future policy." Its chair, John Taylor, writes to Northern Ireland Prime Minister Brian Faulkner: "We saw fit to consider our remit primarily from the relatively short term security aspect and our recommendations on this are intended to suggest means of easing the burdens falling on the security forces and of restoring and preserving public order." He went on: "We do however believe that it would be completely wrong to suggest that security considerations can be divorced from the longer term issues."

The 'peaceline' is a "spectacular and controversial" means of security control, the report says, but it recommends that they stay, at least in the short term. "It is an ugly thing to see a barrier of this kind in a city in the United Kingdom… Its continued existence one moment longer than necessary creates an atmosphere of abnormality which is psychologically damaging." In addition, the planned Belfast Urban Motorway could provide "some sort of *cordon sanitaire*", creating a wide cleared belt to the west of the city centre, said the report, which recommended that other opportunities to create 'natural' divisions between difficult areas should be explored.

Prophetically, a minority report by A Hewins Esq attached to the main report warned: "when a city is redeveloped a pattern of life is laid down for at least a century." The recommendations of the report are a "counsel of despair" which could lead to "ghettoisation": "these proposals would give the name substance and would attract criticism from all over the world" (Working Party 1971).

The report recommended that the peacelines should be reviewed in four months and removed as soon as possible, but its intentions were overtaken by events as Northern Ireland was plunged into even deeper chaos. 1972 was the bloodiest year by far of the conflict and 497 lost their lives (Fay 1999). In March 1972, the Stormont government was dissolved and Westminster reestablished direct rule. In the early 70s, there was

Mayo Park,
Shankhill

the largest population shift in Europe as 60,000 people moved home: "Loyalist and Republican communities began to solidify into two homogenous ethnic groups" (Murray 2006). The Northern Ireland Housing Executive (NIHE), created in 1971 to take over responsibility for public housing from local councils, was under huge pressure, as Jennifer Hawthorne, head of the Social Regeneration Unit at the NIHE, recalls – both from the conflict and the appalling housing conditions. In the lower Falls and Shankill areas, for example, over 90% of housing stock was without inside toilet, bath, hand basin or hot water (Working Party 1971). In March 1973, there were 17,183 residents on rent strike, and 5,184 properties affected by intimidation, vandalism and squatting. In Belfast, in 1972–1973, 14,000 properties were affected by 284 explosions (Weiner 1975). "As the landlord," says Hawthorne, "we were facing the worst housing conditions, rent strikes and divided communities – and in the midst of it, the walls were being built."

Segregation between Protestants and Catholics was also subject to what has been called the "ratchet effect" (Boal 1995). Over past decades, every period of intercommunal conflict has led to newer and higher levels of segregation.

Between 1969 and 1994, the army, the Northern Ireland Office (NIO) and the police had the mandate to erect barriers and walls became a common crisis management mechanism. In the late 70s, the walls were fortified with brick or concrete, with metal bollards and steel gates across roads. During the 80s, described euphemistically as "boundary treatments", the Housing Executive used walls where there were security issues around new housing estates. The walls, says Hawthorne, emerged as a policy response by government and Housing Executive to civil disturbance. They were a "necessary evil" to deal with the "most savage terrorist conflict in Western Europe." With reference to a broader international context, according to Bollens, partition in divided cities has typically been promoted by external parties, usually colonial, "for the purposes of ethnic group conflict management". This strategy was also associated with cities at the periphery of empires "during the end-game of their empire building" which "left certain cities with antagonistic indigenous populations extremely hard to be self-governed" (Bollens 2013).

During the 1980s, the Housing Executive began to transform walls to make them more aesthetically pleasing and less obvious. They were embellished with brickwork, ornate railings or plantings of shrubbery and flowers. Despite these attempts, many of the walls were and remain deeply oppressive militaristic structures, the "architecture of fear". The city evolved into a "brutal fortress landscape"; the walls "pockmarked a city ravaged by conflict". Inner city neighbourhoods became "fortified residential camps" (Neill 2006). Businesses, factories and shops in their vicinity closed because customers could not get to them. Janice Beggs, of Lower Oldpark Community Association, who moved into the Protestant area as a child with her family in 1969, recalls that she used to be able to walk to Cliftonville Primary School along Manor Street, and there was a row of shops including a butcher. Now Manor Street is truncated on the Nationalist side and has vanished on the Protestant side, cut through by the 'Yellow Wall', corrugated and at least 20 foot high. Houses on the Protestant side of the wall were 'vested' and therefore eventually demolished. When new houses were built back-to-back with the Catholic houses, there was conflict and so the wall was built, and the new houses were also demolished to make a 'no man's land'. A further steel fence was put up inside the wall to protect the houses from missiles.

The planned Belfast Urban Motorway never came to fruition for a range of reasons, including delays, lack of funding and public objections. However, Westlink, the dual carriageway that links the motorways north and south of Belfast, was finally opened in 1983 (Johnston 2014). It is often mentioned as the most significant interface, albeit primarily one of class, for it cuts off troublesome West and North working class Belfast from the city centre and the middle class areas of South Belfast and Queens Quarter. Since Westlink reduces access to the city centre to five easily manageable access points, it is presumed to have been built with security in mind. Johnston writes: "While it is certainly true that Westlink must have assisted the security forces in monitoring traffic entering and leaving the central area of the city, it is wrong to conclude that this was the strategy behind the road's design – decided almost 20 years previously." There is no doubt, meanwhile, that it has had a negative economic impact on West and North Belfast, contributing to the "ghettoisation" that was foretold in the 1971 report. It "significantly reduced connectivity between the city and West and North Belfast – a fact that is very evident 30 years on" (Johnston 2014). "Westlink acted as a moat, cutting off the city centre from the Catholic and Protestant housing areas of the Falls and Shankill, with access to the centre from the many small backstreets of the once more permeable residential area" (Neill 2006).

In late 1993, Secretary of State Patrick Mayhew established a working group to consider peacelines issues. It concluded that each one is different and there could be no single blueprint for action; any proposals should depend on security considerations; long term development could lead to the removal of the walls; and "in light of the political situation, segregation had to be accepted as a reality by urban planners" (Byrne 2011). In 1994, the year the Irish Republican Army (IRA) and Loyalists declared ceasefires, Lord Mayor Hugh Smyth called for the removal of peacewalls in his installation speech. From then until 2010, the consultation process for the building of new walls expanded to include political representatives and residents as well as the security forces and the Northern Ireland Office. In the wake of the ceasefire and as violence spilled over from the Drumcree protests in Portadown of 1995–1997, there was a flurry of wallbuilding. Street violence increased: "paradoxically the end of the 'shooting war' opened up the space for large scale street violence." Barriers replaced guns and bombs in Belfast as the physical manifestation of conflict. "The walls became the face of the other community," says Niall Ó Dochartaigh (2007).

One of the last areas to experience segregation and violence was Greater Whitewell, the area embraced by the flyovers and under Cavehill, to the far north of the city. Things kicked off here later than elsewhere, remembers community worker Brian Dunn. "They were beating the ten bells out of each other up on the Falls and Shankill, but there was very little happening here. There were hanging out spaces, like at the bottom of Whitewell Road, where people mixed." But then, as whole neighbourhoods were burned out and needed rebuilding, people were shifted into outlying areas. White City became predominantly Protestant; Lower Whitewell became predominantly Catholic. "It got so you were afraid to speak to someone in case something happened to them."

After Drumcree, Dunn recalls, all hell broke loose between Serpentine Gardens and Gunnell Hill. There was a plan to tear down the houses on Serpentine Gardens to make a no man's land. Instead, on 9 April 1998, the day the Belfast Agreement was signed, a decision was made to put the wall up, a green steel fence, with wire fencing above, running up the road between the back gardens.

In the late 90s, mobile phone networks and the widespread use of CCTV emerged as a means to control and reduce street violence. Roisin McGlone started the first phone network in West Belfast in 1996. A retired senior police officer from North Belfast recalls working with Loyalists and Republicans – "responsible prominent people from both communities" – and the peace organisation Corrymeela, around the same time, on the Limestone Road, a key interface where there is no wall but which is now monitored by CCTV. "We would be standing under the tree with our mobile phones. The former paramilitaries had the authority to break up gangs of kids," he says. "Some of them would be as young as 7 or 8, throwing stones at each other. Normal childhood behaviour but on Limestone Road in Belfast it's a different phenomenon with more serious consequences." "In the late 90s and early 2000s," says Roisin McGlone, "the phone would've gone all the time. You would always think the call you missed would be the one that would make the difference." Brian Dunn of White City recalls: "We used to go to bed with our clothes on."

Ciaran Shannon of Duncairn Community Partnership, the first of the IFI funded peacewalls programmes, recalls that traders at Yorkgate shopping centre at the bottom of Duncairn Gardens had threatened to leave. The Loyalist former prisoners' association got together with local residents' associations, "literally standing on street corners during the summer time". By 2007 they were down to six minor incidents, giving the traders confidence to remain. The shopping centre was rebranded as 'Cityside', and now thrives, employing up to 500 people, many of them locals.

From 2007, something in the system began to change; it was as if the walls had become visible as a problem to be solved. By 2007, there was a palpable reduction in street violence. For example, according to PSNI statistics, the number of shooting incidents dropped from 1,000 for the five years 2002–2006 to 305 for the years 2007–2011. This was for a number of reasons: the IRA had decommissioned in 2005; the mobile phone networks had been effective. No longer on continual alert, community workers began to look around themselves and they saw the walls. Asked when and why they began to pay serious attention to the walls, many of those I interviewed date the change back to events of 2007–2008. Although not always remembered in the same way or the same order, it is possible to piece together a series of events and developments.

Rab McCallum also remembers an earlier event, the 'Moving On' conference, held in June 2004 by the Belfast Interface Project, which had been founded in 1995. The conference aimed to identify problems in interface areas and to explore the challenges posed by the web of relationships among the many public agencies responsible for disadvantaged interface communities, and between them and the communities themselves. The effect of communal violence was pinpointed, along with the inadequate level of provision for young people and the need for "communities to articulate their own responsibility for development of interface communities."

A participant commented: "We see a haphazard approach compartmentalised into the spaces of violence. *We have failed to push for an acknowledgement that coming out of violence is a massive endeavour* [my emphasis]. We need to invest in creating spaces for dialogue." Even 10 years later, a persistent question that emerges from my research for this book is the extent to which the communal post traumatic stress in working class Belfast remains unhealed – and whether this helps to explain why residents cling to their walls.

In January 2007, Sinn Féin announced its decision to support the PSNI and the recommendations of the Patten report on policing in Northern Ireland. Roisin McGlone tells the story of how prior to this, between 2004–2006, police protocols were developed in West Belfast.

The 1999 Patten report on Policing in Northern Ireland had recommended that police should work "in partnership with the community" to "mobilise resources to solve problems affecting public safety over the longer term, rather than the police, alone, reacting short term to incidents as they occur." However, because Sinn Féin had not yet agreed to the Patten recommendations and would not cooperate with PSNI, community safety was a major concern and a priority for InterAction. "The legacy of a generation of non-cooperation with the police by the nationalist community remained," explains McGlone.

She recalls her experience of intensive facilitated workshops between volunteer attendees from West Belfast PSNI of various ranks and Republican activists – with the minutes passed between them. The PSNI's subsequent action plans to improve policing in the community had a knock-on impact on PSNI strategy and practice across Northern Ireland. The West Belfast protocols have continued to be adapted and are in use today, to ensure that local incidents are dealt with by the local community and not unnecessarily escalated.

The retired police officer says:

"There was a recognition that policing is too important to be left to the police alone. We wanted to encourage the community to take responsibility for low level anti-social and youth behaviour. Partly it was also about mathematics. After Patten, numbers of police dropped from 14,000 to under 7,000."

In North Belfast, he says, "we didn't have formalised protocols as such, the situation and the relationships were more informal. A lot of relationship building went on prior to the 2007 Sinn Féin announcement." He recalls slipping covertly into the Parochial House at Ardoyne to negotiate policing arrangements with a senior Sinn Féin figure for the 12th July parade.

The need to install a fence in the grounds of Hazelwood Integrated Primary School in North Belfast in May 2007, just prior to devolution, concentrated minds. The private, mainly Catholic estate of Throne is on one side of the school, and the Loyalist estate White City on the other. There had been an attack the previous summer on Throne via the school grounds: an oil tank was set on fire, a house was destroyed and a woman and baby almost injured.

Jim Brown, who performs a successful Elvis tribute act in Belfast and internationally, remembers the night well. He had moved to Old Throne Park from Newington when he made his first record deal, unaware that he was moving onto an active interface. Jim and his wife came home from a gig after midnight, later than usual that night. It was, he says, a matter of God putting a person in the right place at the right time. They noticed a flickering of light at the end of the road, and thought it was someone's barbecue, except that the flames got bigger. Jim Brown made his way down, realised that an oil tank was on fire and called the fire brigade. Within minutes it had turned into an inferno, and several houses had caught fire. Fourteen people needed to be rescued, including an old couple, whom Jim Brown and neighbours helped to safety over the railings. "The way it was done, it wasn't kids that had done it," he says, "There was too much know-how and planning." Jim Brown and others set up a residents' committee and fought to have the fence erected. Before it was put up, his family would have stuff chucked into their garden while they were sitting out; since then there has been no trouble. The incident "made me all the more determined to live in a non-sectarian way", he says.

Newington Street/Limestone Road

If Scott Bollens is correct and physical separation has usually been the 'kneejerk reaction' of external powers to fragment space as a means to control it, it is neither coincidental nor surprising that with devolution came a determination to avoid erecting walls in the future. The Alliance MLA David Ford vehemently opposed the Hazelwood fence and took his passion to do something about the walls into his role when he was appointed Justice Minister in April 2010. Following Hazelwood, Duncan Morrow and Dympna McGlade of CRC got together with then Secretary of State Paul Goggins to ask if there was anything else that could be done. The Interface Working Group was founded in November 2007. A review of the walls led to the publication of the first attempt at a comprehensive list (CRC 2008). There was agreement that no more walls would be built.

Rab McCallum, Director of the North Belfast Interface Network (NBIN), also recalls that leading up to that moment, there had been a decrease in the violence and a palpable desire to live differently. The need for a fence at Hazelwood Primary caused a "real moment of reflection". In North Belfast, a cross community interface monitoring group was set up which has met fortnightly since then.

Two other events of 2007 were also widely remembered: the Deloitte report and a maverick intervention by Trina Vargo, then president of the US Ireland Alliance.

The Deloitte report was commissioned and completed just prior to the restoration in May 2007 of the Northern Ireland Assembly by Prime Minister Tony Blair. It was released after devolution, in August 2007, only after a demand under the Freedom of Information Act by David Ford and the Alliance Party. Speaking in an Assembly debate in December 2014 on the 'costs of division', OFMdFM Junior Minister Jennifer McCann recalled that while the Deloitte report had been commissioned and finalised under Direct Rule, it was "independent research" and did not represent the views of the Executive, nor was it accepted as an agreed basis for policy development.

The report assessed the price of a divided society in Northern Ireland, including the direct costs, for example of building the walls; the less obvious costs, for example from the need to duplicate services such as parks, leisure and medical centres; and finally the other costs, for example of community relations work, the promotion of Northern Ireland to tourism and investment markets, and the opportunity cost of lost tourism or investment. The Deloitte report estimated and summarised the cost of division at £1.5 billion a year. It also noted that in 2005–2006 public spending in Northern Ireland as a percentage of GDP was 71.5%, compared with 43% for the UK as a whole (Deloitte 2007).

And several interviewees, ever conscious of external perceptions of the country, particularly by the US, vividly recall two American interventions. The US Ireland Alliance published results of a survey of 1037 people in 6 interface communities which said that 60% of people wanted the walls to come down when it was safe to do so, but only 21% wanted them to come down immediately. Sixty two percent believed the walls were still necessary, while 43% agreed that the walls maintained levels of tension and antagonism between communities (CRC 2008). Trina Vargo, President of the US Ireland Alliance, announced in *The Irish Times* that the following year, on the 10th anniversary of the Belfast Agreement, she would bring Senator George Mitchell, the facilitator of the Agreement talks, former Taoiseach Bertie Ahern, former Prime Minister Tony Blair and former US President Bill Clinton back to Belfast. She challenged "the people of Belfast to take down at least a part of the peacewall" (*The Irish Times*, 5 Feb 2008). This was, says one community worker scathingly, Vargo's proposed "CNN moment" and she was told in no uncertain terms by the people of Belfast "where to go." DUP MLA Sammy Douglas, then an advisor to Peter Robinson, met Trina Vargo – he told her he loved the idea, but not yet. The former PSNI officer remembers that he received a call about the stunt. "I said to them, who am I to interfere? Go ahead, and bring in a bricklayer, and as soon as you have taken the wall down and had your photos taken, I shall be putting it back up again."

2008 was a key year for community workers, civil servants and officials, and politicians in which removal of the walls began to seem both necessary and possible. The CRC report identified and listed 88 barriers – a figure often still quoted – it counted the number of CCTV cameras and identified 'intrusive security at police stations'. The report began to identify barriers that could be removed, and quotes a number of studies commissioned by Belfast City Council (BCC) in a series on Conflict Transformation. The report notes that walls that were built to offer a short term solution had become part of a long term problem and, while they offered some respite for anxiety, did not offer sustainable security. It notes the number of ethnic minorities moving into interface areas including Chinese, Indian, Jewish and Sikh, and says: "This growing diversity provides an opportunity to reimagine the future of interface areas beyond the simple orange-green divide." The report concludes that the policy agenda needed to assume that the walls and barriers "must be removed if the aspiration to develop a more shared and integrated city is to come to fruition" (CRC 2008).

In March 2008, following a motion by Councillor Alban Maginness, Belfast City Council resolved "that it is now time to begin to work towards the reduction and ultimate removal of the so-called 'peacewalls' and barriers that presently divide our city." Belfast City Council was given £10 million under Peace III over five years for a two phase peace strategy covering four themes, the first of which was transforming contested space – the other three are securing shared city space, developing shared culture, and building shared spaces.

Mayor Bloomberg of New York City visited Belfast in May 2008 to address the Northern Ireland investment conference and said "removing the barriers is in the interests of peace and prosperity and the sooner the physical barriers come down, the sooner the floodgates of private investment will open." "The best and brightest don't want to live in a city defined by division. They don't want to live behind walls."

Deputy First Minister Martin McGuinness mentioned the walls to the Assembly, acknowledging the responsibility of the Northern Ireland Office. On 23 June 2008, he said:

"We can and should seek the removal of peacewalls when local communities feel safe and comfortable. It is essential that plans to remove peacewalls must be community driven. Policy responsibility for the erection and removal of peacewalls remains with the NIO" (Byrne 2011).

Meanwhile, in his thesis on the development of public policy on the walls, Jonny Byrne notes that the Jarman report of 2008 for the Institute of Conflict Research concluded that "over 1/3 of barriers could be removed or transformed with minimal difficulty within a process of regeneration or normalisation, provided there was local support, political direction and economic investment." However, getting the three ducks of local support, political direction and economic investment in a row has not proved easy, for each of these comprises a complex system in itself. Jarman recommended that any approach should be conducted in a "joined up, coordinated manner with strong cross-government departmental support" (Byrne 2011).

The 20th anniversary of the fall of the Berlin Wall in November 2009 came and went without much visible change around the walls. A conversation began about the removal of a simple traffic barrier in Newington Street, which in a foretaste of things to come stuttered on the question of who was to take responsibility for its removal and how it would be paid for. Residents, now used to being able to see their children play safely in a cul-de-sac, demanded speed bumps. The Department for Regional Development (DRD), said that there was no documented need for traffic calming and therefore it was not a priority to pay for it. In the end, Department of Justice (DoJ) found £10,000 to pay for the speed bumps. The traffic barrier was finally removed in November 2014.

In May 2010, responsibility for the 59 walls that had been erected by the army and Northern Ireland Office was devolved to the new Department of Justice under the leadership of Minister David Ford, and on 27 July 2010, the Cohesion, Sharing and Integration document announced that "OFMdFM will lead in the development of a cross-cutting programme with departments, agencies and the community on how best to work actively toward the removal of peacewalls." This created an irony identified by Byrne in August 2011 in his thesis: "What makes Northern Ireland unique is that the devolved administration has to respond to a security policy issue that was not conceived or implemented by local politicians." And, one could add, the local administration is also expected to find funding for it.

In mid-2011, Jonny Byrne was able to conclude in his thesis: "The issue of peacewalls, according to this research, will not feature on the decision-making agenda at this moment in time." The aim of his thesis however was to "place the issue of peacewalls back into the narrative of the NI conflict and the subsequent peace and political processes". It is likely that Jonny Byrne did in fact contribute to a higher profile for

Glenbryn

peacewalls issues, and that he was also, in a way, jumping onto a moving train. Having made a commitment in the 2011–2015 Programme for Government to "actively seek local agreement to reduce the number of peacewalls," the Department of Justice formed the Interagency Group, which brought together all the key statutory agencies around the problem of the walls, including OFMdFM, Belfast City Council, PSNI, Northern Ireland Housing Executive, Department for Regional Development (DRD) and Department For Social Development (DSD). During 2011, the walls moved higher up the priority list for Belfast City Council. To fanfares, the gate in Alexandra Park was opened in September 2011. Alderman and former Lord Mayor Alliance Party councillor Tom Ekin took on the walls as a personal cause. On 1 September 2011, echoing the earlier Council motion of 2008, Alderman Ekin proposed: "This council can demonstrate true civic leadership by agreeing to tackle one of the biggest problems which affects all the citizens of this city, that is, the continued existence of the so-called 'Peacewalls.'" The Ekin proposal, says one council official, "created a lot of fear, but very positive conversations resulted and it became less scary."

Since the Council does not own any barriers – other than the fence in Alexandra Park – it has no direct responsibility for putting them up or taking them down. It did agree a detailed framework for action under five strategic themes and a cross cutting interfaces strategy. Its role was identified as: firstly, civic leadership – setting the vision of a city without physical barriers; secondly, influencing – to ensure that urban development contributes to a city without barriers; and, thirdly, practical – using its resources to complement wider initiatives. On 18 November 2011, a detailed action plan was proposed and agreed, and in 2012 the Council received £421,313.00 of Peace III money to "soften, adjust, transform, or remove" 14 barriers in North and West Belfast identified by the Department of Justice on the basis of police reports as "quick wins" or "low hanging fruit."

In December 2011, there was a joint conference of the Interface Working Group (IWG) and the Interface Community Partners – which had been formed in 2009 to give community groups a forum parallel to the IWG for discussion of the interfaces. It noted that following a wide consultation on the Community Safety Strategy, four priority areas relevant to the interface areas had been identified: anti-social behaviour, early intervention, concerns about drug and alcohol abuse, and promotion of a shared society – but nothing, we now notice, about levels of post-conflict trauma. At that conference, Rab McCallum observed in a speech (CRC 2011) that:

> "the failure of government departments, statutory agencies and the voluntary and community sector, 17 years after the 1994 ceasefire, to make any real impact on the removal of interface walls and barriers is not indicative of a failed process. Rather, it reflects the lack of any cohesive process at all."

Duncan Morrow, then Chief Executive of the CRC, said in his concluding comments at the conference:

"After 17 years of ceasefire we need to ask is this fear [of removing the walls] grounded in real threats to people's safety or only in historic memory? If it is memory, then the solution is confidence building and therapeutic investment. But if the threat is real, here and now, and not just imagined as I suppose most of us would concede, then how come we can't tackle it after 17 years? Just who is threatening who, in a world where 14 years ago we all signed up to purely political means, and where is the action plan to tackle this completely unacceptable threat?" (CRC 2011)

In 2012, Justice Minister David Ford said in a press release: "I believe this is a particularly important year for those living at interfaces", referring to the Northern Ireland Executive Programme for Government 2011–2015, in which Target 68 to "actively seek local agreement to reduce the number of 'peacewalls'" was assigned to the Department of Justice. Over in the Housing Executive, Jennifer Hawthorne discovered from a mapping exercise that the Housing Executive owns 20 of the walls. The interfaces were included as one of five Community Cohesion priority themes in the Corporate Plan for 2012–2015. In an imaginative intervention, she worked with architects Tony Stevens and Agnes Brown from Urban Innovations to see how interfaces could be transformed. Stevens and Brown also facilitated some conversations with communities about their options for redesign of the barriers.

Belfast Interface Project (BIP) published its own study and identified 99 walls, barriers and other kinds of interface (BIP 2012). Each one is numbered and photographed. According to this study, 58 are owned by the Department of Justice, 19 by the Housing Executive; seven are privately owned, and 15 are owned by others; some are fences with unidentified private owners, vacant plots of land and car parks. A June 2012 report to OFMdFM recorded that the proportion of people wanting to see the walls come down had dropped from the 67% recorded in the US Ireland Alliance survey of 2007 to 44%, while over a fifth (22%) were saying they wanted things to remain the same (Byrne et al 2012).

Meanwhile, the IFI decided to support eight peacewalls programmes with specific targets around the walls, six in Belfast and two in Derry/Londonderry. These programmes were designed to be the final flourish in IFI's investment in the peace process in Northern Ireland, an involvement that had begun in 1986. Gordie Walker, who had worked for the CRC with the IFI funded projects until Christmas 2013, says:

"from the IFI point of view, the last bastion of any divided society post-conflict is the structures that divide people, and here they are manifested as the peacewalls. Demilitarisation of Northern Ireland needs to take place through the removal of the barriers."

At Christmas 2012, after the Council's controversial decision to fly the Union Jack at City Hall on only certain days of the year, Belfast was brought to a standstill by Loyalist flag protests during the critical commercial period of Christmas and New Year. At Twaddell protest camp, established in July 2013 when an Orange march was banned from passing through Ardoyne, the cost of policing alone is estimated to be £40,000 a night, reaching a total by December 2014 of £12 million (*Belfast Telegraph* 6 Jan 15). In a submission to the Haass process in autumn 2013, the Belfast Chamber of Commerce estimated a £234 million loss of income the previous year due to Loyalist parades and marches, the flag protests – but also the Olympic torch ceremony and St Patrick's Day parade.

In April 2013, Conservative Secretary of State Theresa Villiers 'bluntly' threatened to withhold financial aid unless there was more progress towards a shared society (*Belfast Telegraph,* 10 April 2013). Hot on foot of Villiers' threat, on 23 May, and not coincidentally, OFMdFM released Together Building a United Community, usually affectionately referred to as 'T-Buc'. It was also widely and somewhat cynically believed that TBUC was released in anticipation of President Obama's visit and the G8 summit in Fermanagh. It contained in an early paragraph the commitment to remove the walls by 2023. In its own response to TBUC, in a statement signed jointly by Prime Minister David Cameron, Secretary of State Theresa Villiers, as well as First Minister Peter Robinson and deputy First Minister Martin McGuinness, the British government headlined the 2023 walls commitment and promised £100 million of additional loans for shared housing and education schemes "conditional on the Executive demonstrating progress on the implementation of this strategy" (NIO 2013).

TBUC headlined four priorities: children and young people, shared community, safe community and cultural expression. Removing the interface barriers was the first objective under the third of these priorities, 'Our Safe Community', and the sixth of seven targets set out by TBUC – the others refer to shared education, housing, sporting events and volunteering programmes. Perhaps not surprisingly, it is removing the walls which is listed first in *Building a Prosperous and United Community*, the Westminster government's response to TBUC.

In April 2014, Alliance MP Naomi Long raised in Prime Minister's Questions the findings of a *Belfast Telegraph* poll of 16–24 year olds, 67% of whom said that they believed their future lies outside of Northern Ireland, and 70% of whom said they did not believe Northern Ireland politicians were capable of agreeing a shared vision for the future. Mr Cameron replied: "What we need is politicians in Northern Ireland to build a shared future, to take down the peacewalls, and make sure the economy can grow and opportunities are there for everyone in Northern Ireland."

This signals the central significance in Westminster's mind of the need to remove peacewalls and barriers. Nevertheless, the Office of First Minister and deputy First Ministers and the Northern Ireland Office can determine and influence policy but are able to do frustratingly little to actually remove the barriers, especially as there is no central fund for this purpose. The Department of Justice is responsible for the physical maintenance, including construction, adjustment or removal, of the walls it owns. All statutory agencies have signed up to the principle that the walls will not be touched without residents' consent. That consent is negotiated, painstakingly, and often with excruciating slowness, to some degree by the Department of Justice and/or Belfast City Council, and/or the Housing Executive, working with the peacewalls programmes and other community and residents' groups and their 'gatekeepers'. Community peacewalls programmes are funded, and likely to continue to be funded in the absence of an alternative, by the IFI; meanwhile the Department of Justice, Department for Social Development, and Department for Regional Development, responsible for roads, must bid for budget to transform or remove the walls independently and within their own departmental priorities. Belfast City Council, the Housing Executive and the PSNI must also work within their own budgets and strategic plans. In other words, although agencies, funders and communities operate within an interrelated, complex and dynamic web or network, action to transform or remove any given structure requires decision-making and, most significantly, expenditure from agencies and budgets which are siloed.

When I talk to Alderman Ekin in January 2014, he is seething with exasperation. Little progress has been made with the 14 quick wins; he says the blocks are the local residents, the police, paramilitaries and the people who own the land.

"The walls are stupid. I don't care if they are costing us £100 million or £1 billion, if we save 10% of it, it is worth it to bring them down. My passion is as a taxpayer, I am one of the people that pays for these things. And the big issue we need to address is the underachievement of working class kids, the future terrorists."

A year later, Alderman Ekin acknowledges the slow progress that has taken place. He continues to be annoyed that OFMdFM proposed the 2023 deadline, but then "passed the buck to Department of Justice without giving them any money." Alderman Ekin has also realised that progress on the walls and interfaces sometimes means "softening", rather than removal – replacing solid gates with see-through ones, or opening them for longer. Removal of the interfaces will be a "long and difficult task", but there is a lot that can be done to make the interface areas more attractive in the meantime. However, there has been a lot of work done by a lot of people, he says. He will leave the Council at the end of March 2015; before he goes he will host "tea and buns" at City Hall for all those involved in trying to make a difference to the interfaces. Councillor John Kyle will propose a motion to Council that he will second requesting of OFMdFM that it "provide a progress report on the development of this strategy and that it provide resources to enable the Council to take the lead with other statutory agencies in order to work with local communities to create a process leading to removal of these barriers."

This is the fluid and evolving web that is delivering peace and change, what one civil

Oranmore Drive/
Malinmore Park
Suffolk

servant calls the "busy busy busyness of all that is going on around the interfaces." A network of agents of change, including on the one hand the anonymous civil servants, bureaucrats, 'securocrats' and officials of the OFMdFM and the Department of Justice, of the Northern Ireland office and Belfast City Council, and the PSNI; on the other are a more amorphous multitude of community workers and groups, including former paramilitaries, who communicate with and on behalf of the residents of the interface areas. Also in the mix are concerned politicians, church ministers, and activist academics, architects and artists. There are formal and informal groupings under a dizzying array of acronyms. All across the web are people utterly passionate about maintaining and furthering the peace, desperate to ensure that no further lives are lost, universally motivated by wanting a better future for the children and young people of Belfast and Northern Ireland. As in a real spider's web, the filaments of the web are elastic, almost invisible, the relationships, conversations, interactions amongst all these people and groups – it is these conversations and relationships that make up the peace process in Belfast.

The web operates across space and time. Perhaps the greatest distance is between the Westminster government and the devolved Stormont Executive and the disadvantaged communities and blighted land at the interfaces; at each end of this particular spectrum the actors perceive those at the other end as having the power. Deprived communities want decisions made – about planning and regeneration, about strategies to reduce poverty – meanwhile politicians and civil servants hand communities the say in whether and when the interfaces should be removed. "That's an awful lot of responsibility on the shoulders of the communities," comments one former Republican combatant turned community worker. The communities meanwhile see themselves as victimised, and may lack the vision to see a bigger picture beyond their own fears. A civil servant – formerly a community worker – echoes the sentiment: "I believe the notion that we won't bring down the walls until the communities say so needs to be challenged."

This is how change happens: through small steps forward and sometimes back, through synergistic relationships, serendipity, through 'emergence': patterns of apparently unrelated but coincident events bubbling up across a complex system. Through fleeting moments in private and group conversations virtually impossible to track or record. Through people noticing, listening, echoing.

People noticed what Trina Vargo, Mayor Bloomberg and Alderman Tom Ekin said. They might have been irritated, but their interest and conversation were stimulated and directly or indirectly the ecosystem around the walls, both at government and community levels, began to shift and change over a period of years, creating the basis for policy change which in turn led to further cycles of action and intervention.

The story of the interfaces would not be complete without mention of the history of community development in Northern Ireland, which has been and remains critical in the narrative of the peacewalls. From very early on, as we saw in deputy First Minister Martin McGuinness's 2008 intervention in the assembly, the government and statutory agencies have recognised the central role to be played by local residents in decision-making about the walls. There have however historically been tensions between government and communities; how the different elements of the system have managed these tensions and begun to work together is important.

The roots of the community development sector in Northern Ireland lie in the Catholic civil rights movement and Republican-backed social protests of the late 1960s, which fed into sectarian strife. During the 1970s, reconciliation and peacemaking were predominantly community-led activities. Community groups sprang up in self-help initiatives during the conflict in Catholic/Nationalist no-go areas such as the lower Falls and Ardoyne. "Working class Catholics, confident that Stormont cared little for their plight, had no hesitation in organising self-help groups" and this led to a "heightened self-awareness and confidence among many Catholics/nationalists" (Ó hAdhmaill 2012). To some degree this was mirrored in Protestant areas – William 'Plum' Smith tells the story of how Gusty Spence founded a people's taxi service to support the local community as well as the prisoner population (Smith 2014). According to Ó hAdhmaill, community action and self-help did not take place in Protestant/Unionist areas to the same degree partly because while community organisation for Nationalists was motivated by revolutionary ideals and the desire to boycott state services, in PUL areas people were supportive of the state, and tended to remain cooperative. They were less likely to campaign or protest, partly because that was what Catholics were doing – and in some cases this lack of protest almost amounted to a fatalistic acceptance of situations and problems. During the 1980s and 90s, when funding flowed freely into Northern Ireland,

Catholic/Nationalist groups appeared to be more effective at accessing funding, partly because the community infrastructure was better developed (Ó hAdhmaill 2012).

Several interviewees vividly recall the Hurd Principles of 1985. Under the leadership of Conservative Prime Minister Margaret Thatcher, and in the wake of the Hunger Strikes, then Secretary of State Douglas Hurd became concerned at the growing influence and popularity of Sinn Féin and withdrew funding from local organisations where a member had alleged links to a paramilitary organisation. Funding was redirected to churches, considered safer, which bent over backwards to distance themselves from any paramilitary links. The Hurd Principles remained in force until 1995, when after the 1994 ceasefire, the government became more amenable to working with paramilitaries to promote the new peace (Ó hAdhmaill 2012).

With the advent of the New Labour government in 1997, under Prime Minister Tony Blair, and after the Belfast Agreement of 1998, funding began to flow into Northern Ireland, and the political tide turned towards support for community relations work and indeed towards engaging more directly with Sinn Féin and Loyalist groupings. One billion in EU peace funding came in between 1995 and 2013; the IFI, one of the earliest major funders, spent £465 million between 1986 and 2004; The Atlantic Philanthropies spent £230 million between 1982 and 2004.

Community groups exist, and have always existed, to varying degrees and at different times, in a state of tension with local and national government departments and bureaucracies such as the Department of Justice, Belfast City Council, the Housing Executive and the PSNI. Government and bureaucracies have seen community groups as both 'friend' and 'enemy' (Ó hAdhmaill 2012); this is partly because of their sometimes commitment to social change and protest as well as the involvement of former paramilitaries in many groups. However, the value of their role was recognised in the Belfast Agreement (BGFA, para 13). By 2008, there were 29,000 employees in the community and voluntary sector in Northern Ireland (Edwards 2010). The sector had received over £2 billion in funding since 1997.

Ó hAdhmaill posits a distinction between a 'good relations' approach – as promoted by national and local government – which stresses the need for cross community education and relationship building to reduce ignorance and prejudice, and the more radical political agenda based on addressing endemic structural inequalities and power relations. The research for this book suggests, however, that these are mostly theoretical distinctions. From a peacewalls perspective, there is a need and community groups' activity is directed both to improving cross community relationships and to addressing structural inequalities. In *The State of Play*, InterAction Belfast is clear about its agenda:

"We have a long history of working in the community… in this regard the relationship between conflict transformation and socio economic development is interconnected. Community development cannot be dealt with in isolation and must include work towards securing social and economic rights and ensuring these communities benefit from the peace process."

Community groups, therefore, often "adopt both approaches in their work" and are more often at micro level more focussed on a specific goal – for example, the removal or transformation of specific barriers. According to Edwards & McGratton, community relations workers have not been given enough credit for the vital role they have played in the consolidation of the peace (2010).

People in Belfast frequently say that the walls themselves are not important, it is the people and communities that are important. From a complex systems perspective, the interesting thing is how a diverse group of actors has come together over the last few years to deliver effective decision-making and implementation around the walls. Targeting the structures has forced community groups and the statutory agencies to focus on the people, community issues and need for regeneration around the walls. Each situation and interface forms a complex system in its own right, with the same dynamics and factors playing out in different ways. Each plan to transform or remove a barrier requires coordination of several agencies and separate project management. For example, in order for any change to happen, the owner or owners of the wall or walls and land need to be identified. Residents' approval needs to be negotiated. A community safety/PSNI report needs to be prepared. Budget needs to be found for removal. Art works or design of new gates or fences needs to take place. Actions, therefore, need to be coordinated between some or all of the local cross community groups, Department of Justice, Belfast City Council, Housing Executive, PSNI, the Department for Regional Development (Roads).

The Department of Justice Interagency Group, the Interface Working Group and the Interface Community Partners have been effective at bringing these 'stats' together and building relationships with the community groups. The membership of the groups has been remarkably stable, and there has been a determination to work together effectively. Stats and communities have been coy about seeking media attention, fearing a negative backlash at grassroots, but this is changing. In August 2014 there was a double page spread by Rebecca Black in the *Belfast Telegraph*, with the headline "Flashpoint talks bring down the peacewalls". On 20 November 2014 The IFI launched a Twitter feed giving updates on the peacewalls programmes (@FundforIreland).

By January 2015, the 14 "low hanging fruit" or "quick wins" have been reduced to 10. The walls in North City Business Centre carpark have been lowered; North Howard Street is considered to be too large to tackle at this time; the fence in Torrens has already been removed; the Newington Street barrier has been taken away. Tenders for environmental improvements at 10 sites were decided by end August 2014, along with selections of artists and artworks for six artists and eight of the sites. Nevertheless, making visible progress proves painfully slow and complicated. The Belfast City Council employee responsible for interfaces, asked what she has learned so far from working with the "14 quick wins" replies, quick as a flash, "they weren't quick wins".

At the annual Interface Community Partners and Interagency Group held on 16 December 2014, CRC Chair Peter Osborne and Justice Minister David Ford both commended the "inspirational work on the ground" and the "quality of engagement" at community level. When and if the walls come down, people say, it will be to the credit of the communities – they are the ones that have borne the brunt of the conflict and have done the hard work since to build the peace. Minister Ford told the conference

Distillery Street

that the University of Ulster (UU) would be working with the Department of Justice as a critical friend, supporting policy development and assessing the evidence base. The Department was also increasing its level of interdepartmental engagement – they have come to see that interface work involves almost all government departments – apart from Agriculture. Speaking for OFMdFM, Linsey Farrell, Director of Good Relations and Financial Governance, explained that a revised delivery architecture for TBUC would include a panel involving all executive ministers to determine strategic direction and delivery. There would be a number of thematic subgroups reporting directly to the panel, including a subgroup for the interfaces, which would include representatives from the youth, faith and business sectors, as well as the statutory agencies, aiming, it appears, to be a more effective and representative mechanism to support delivery of the 2023 commitment. Minister Ford underlined yet again the importance of the walls: he told the conference that the credibility of Northern Ireland and the Stormont Executive is at stake over their removal.

Chapter Three

DIALOGUE AND REGENERATION:
THE COMMUNITIES

*"A ten year conversation has to start somewhere… we know it's not one conversation.
In the end it becomes a series of different conversations, in different places, appropriate to
different experiences, different needs and different circumstances".*

Duncan Morrow, Challenge of Change conference 2009

WORDS ARE SYMBOLS, AND in Northern Ireland many words and symbols are problematic, including the use of the word 'community'. The word community is a meme – a word or phrase that contains within it multiple layers of meaning and cultural assumptions but which is rarely challenged or questioned. It is, suggests Raymond Williams in *Keywords,* a "warmly persuasive word" and, unlike any other word used to describe social organisation, "it seems never to be used unfavourably" (Williams 2014). In Northern Ireland, however, the use of the word 'community' is more complex and may not always have such cosy connotations.

People speak of the 'Protestant community' and the 'Catholic community', or of the PUL (Protestant/Unionist/Loyalist) and CNR (Catholic/Nationalist/Republican) communities. People speak of 'our community' or 'my community', referring to this wider ethnic identity. These phrases are now in themselves euphemistic, since a member of the PUL community may – or may not – be a practising church goer, and/or identify themselves as a political Unionist and/or a Loyalist; similarly a member of the CNR community will variously identify themselves as a practising Catholic and/or a Nationalist and/or a Republican. Within these communities there remain – sometimes violently warring – factions and cliques. At the same time, as we have already seen, on either side of the walls and barriers are 'communities' that share more history and culture with one another than they do with those on the other side, and yet the identity of each is maintained in opposition to the other. The word 'community' therefore inherently implies the 'divided community' that is Belfast – it speaks more of division than of unity.

As an aside, a novel set in Canada in the first half of the 19th century against the backdrop of segregation and sectarianism between French speaking Catholics and English speaking Protestants is called *Two Solitudes* – a phrase that speaks perhaps more accurately of the isolation and aloneness caused when two peoples living side by side choose to turn their backs to one another (MacLennan 1945). A similar sentiment is echoed by Seán Mistéil in *From Ashes to Aisling*:

"The two communities can only partially and imperfectly function while remaining in splendid isolation from each other, and the city of Belfast which both roads feed cannot in turn fully flourish with the limited interaction which it has with the Shankill and the Falls" (MacGoil et al 2010).

TBUC speaks hopefully of a "united community"; the aspiration to a single community in Belfast or Northern Ireland. This concept officially includes the notions of improved attitudes among young people, a limited number of shared educational campuses and housing schemes, equality of opportunity, safety and good relations, and respect for diversity and cultural expression. It includes the removal of all interface barriers – but it does not go as far as to speak of integration, of schooling or of housing and neighbourhoods (OFMdFM 2013).

People also speak of 'communities' – the patchwork of multiple tiny distinctive neighbourhoods or urban villages that make up Belfast, their names now as familiar as the shipping forecast to anyone who has followed the news within or from Northern Ireland over the last 45 years: Falls, Shankill, Turf Lodge, Ballymurphy, Ardoyne, Short Strand … Meet anyone in Belfast and they will quickly identify which village they are from; which village their partner is from; which villages their parents came from.

If Williams suggests the word community is never used unfavourably, in Northern Ireland it is sometimes referred to cynically – perhaps because of its association with the reality of division and conflict. "Community is a construct put on us", says artist Rita Duffy. Speaking at the Ulster Museum conference on Art and the Troubles, academic Colin Graham noted that 'community' has replaced 'traditions' to describe the two identities in the Northern Ireland context. The notion of "traditions" referred to the "archaeology of past harmony and the promise of future harmony"; "community" meanwhile is "reliant on the idea of shared identity and homogeneity" - it "resists any alternative", it is "tradition in a time of self-consciousness, rhetorically directed inwards". The idea of communities, he said, is built into the Belfast Agreement, which accepts the concept without irony or cynicism – there are six references to "both communities" and "two communities". The Belfast Agreement also refers to "the community" 21 times, most frequently in the context of policing and justice; and 14 times to "cross community", a phrase which itself implies a divided community or the two communities.

From early in the story of initiatives to bring down the walls, we are repeatedly reminded that this will not happen until 'communities are ready to do so'. This phrase is so frequent and so rarely challenged that it too has become a meme. In this usage, the communities are the villages, the areas adjacent to and separated from one another by the walls and interfaces. Community in this context implies a physical territory, sharply defined. It means a jumble of residents, their political and other representatives, their community workers, the local paramilitaries, the people called 'gatekeepers'; it implies a shared narrative, of poverty and the legacy of the Troubles, and also of extended families and celebrations and moments of humour. These communities are made up of the lives of women, younger and older people, families, workers, students and unemployed, former combatants. There are issues of drug and alcohol abuse, physical and mental health, safety, the challenge of regeneration, the impact of recession. The villages have community and health centres, pubs, shops and churches – although religion itself is a fading influence in many places.

These communities, sometimes also referred to as the 'grassroots', were the killing fields during the conflict and are now where the peace process is happening, where it plays out. As Peter Osborne, chair of the CRC, said at E3 in April 2014 during the launch of the Anti-Sectarianism Charter: "The peace process is about managing change in a highly complex environment" and: "Politicians don't own the peace process, people own the peace process." John Paul Lederach credits the engagement of community groups for the fact that Belfast has not collapsed back into violence, and he expresses concern that at the highest political levels there might be a retreat from understanding the importance of the community sector.

Ultimately the idea and reality of community depends on funding – indeed community and funding are two sides of one coin. It is no coincidence that the concept of and infrastructure for community relations in Northern Ireland emerged in the late 80s just as vast amounts of funding began to be injected into the province to underpin the peace process. Many social services – children, pre- and after-school, youth, health, women's groups, reconciliation initiatives, support for elderly, citizens' advice, victims' and survivors' support, unemployment and training – in addition to the peacewalls programmes – are delivered by community groups in community centres funded from national and local government and other sources. Because much of this funding is short term and major pots are drying up – both because of austerity policies and because of the perception beyond the borders of Northern Ireland that the peace process is complete – 'community' is increasingly fragile.

The CRC Policy Conference held in June 2014 was called 'Finish the Job', echoing Bill Clinton's phrase at the Guildhall in Derry/Londonderry in February 2014, when he urged Northern Ireland to complete the unfinished task of the peace process. The subtext of the conference, however, was the uncertainty of the community relations sector, an uncertainty of leadership, purpose and funding. The highly respected Presbyterian minister and community leader, Revd Lesley Carroll, noted in her final comments that the community sector needed to be clear about its strategy, and that its own lack of leadership mirrored, in some way, the lack of leadership perceived at the highest levels; she warned that a lack of connectedness or sense of shared task could pull the movement down.

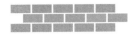

In the forefront of the emerging ten year strategy to bring down the walls by 2023 are the eight IFI funded peacewalls programmes: two in Derry/Londonderry – Triax and St Columb's Park House – and six in Belfast – Black Mountain Shared Space, TASCIT (Twaddell, Ardoyne, Shankill Communities in Transition), Cliftonville and Lower Oldpark, Greater Whitewell, and Duncairn Community Partnership.

The parallel development of the IFI peacewalls programme and the TBUC strategy appears to have been somewhat serendipitous. It was coincidental, although not unlikely, that IFI made a strategic decision to invest in programmes to bring down the peacewalls, as the final flourish in its long term support of the peace process in Northern Ireland, at the same time that OFMdFM were making the interface barriers a priority within the overall TBUC strategy. As we have seen, OFMdFM had the aspiration, but no mechanism or power, to carry out the required action. While the Department of Justice and the Housing Executive are responsible for the physical maintenance and ultimately the removal of the walls that they own, they have not necessarily had the relationship with nor the reach into the communities that IFI had established over many years, particularly through its 67 Community Bridges programmes. Meanwhile, while IFI are prepared to fund programmes which carry out the hard graft of building cross community relationships and negotiating community support for changes to the walls, that funding did not at least initially include the cost of the transformations or removals themselves – which reverts to the owners of the walls. In fact, in practice, IFI has proved willing to stump up some of the necessary cash in some circumstances.

IFI has invested £4 million over 2–3 years in the initial phase of these peacewalls programmes, due to end by August 2015. By then the work will be far from complete – although IFI recognised that to begin with the work was all about starting to create the conditions for the removal of the peacewalls. Even part-way through it is clear that the

Malinmore Park

eight programmes have been effective and are likely to merit continued funding. It is also likely that the 'IFI model' will be replicated in other interface areas.

The eight peacewalls programmes were selected according to common criteria: they needed to involve cross community collaboration; they needed to aim at the actual removal of the structures; each one needed a management or reference group including local residents and the statutory agencies. IFI originally asked CRC to manage the peacewalls programme, although they took back responsibility for the management in December 2013. It was, said Gordie Walker of CRC, a very difficult task to identify the target walls and groups able to do work with them. There were 35 or 36 initial expressions of interest in the programme, and he and Joe Hines of CRC whittled these down to 12 or 13 and then to the current eight which met the criteria and directly addressed the structures. Each peacewalls programme has a specific list of sites and targets, with a phased community engagement and planning process.

There were a total of 91 barriers and 139 objectives, across the two cities, included in the eight projects and by late 2014, 39 objectives had already been achieved. The programme was set up, sources note, before the flag protests of December 2012 – that and the ongoing protests at Twaddell over the Ardoyne Orange march route, which have escalated into the Unionist 'graduated response', have slowed progress, but IFI are generally pleased with the overall level of progress.

The peacewalls teams have quickly seen they needed to be able to work ingeniously and organically on issues. By focussing on very specific interface sites they have had to acknowledge and address the complexity of issues within each neighbourhood. They have needed to develop strategies that are both generic – addressing removal or transformation of the peacewalls and engaging in cross community dialogue – and context-specific.

At the top of Springfield Road, IFI funded Black Mountain Space Project has ten sites, including fencing, gates and ultimately the 'Million Brick Wall' along the Springmartin Road and around the PSNI station (Cluster 2). Seamus Corr, the project coordinator, grew up in a staunchly Republican family in Turf Lodge and became involved with Republican politics at 16 or 17 years old. He sees that as seamlessly connected to his current commitment to building the peace and community work: "Everything we done was for the community. There was a natural transition from street battles to community involvement at a formal level, people trying to organise for the community better."

The Black Mountain Shared Space team includes Stephen Maginnis, who is working with the Nationalist community in Sliabh Dubh, Moyard and Springfield Park, and Joanna Felo, from the US, who originally came as a volunteer and lived with the Curragh community on Workman Avenue. She spent four years researching her PhD and is now working in the Loyalist communities of Highfield and Springmartin.

Stephen Maginnis says that much as he is himself from West Belfast, he was surprised at the levels of neglect and low self-esteem he found in these communities. Black Mountain Shared Space was originally set up to lobby the developers of the abandoned Finlay's site, a massive 8.2 acres of wasteground, surrounded by a curious graffiti splattered green interface fence and opposite the slopes of Black Mountain, where cattle graze and a lane leads up to Quaker Cottage. They wanted the development to include both jobs and houses, but Samuel Hughes, the developer, went bust in the recession and IFI offered Black Mountain funding to tackle the interfaces.

Maginnis thought he would be "straight into interface issues"; "the thing with this game is," he says, "you can get too far ahead of yourself. You can't go in and deal with the walls in isolation." There was a serious lack of community infrastructure. Programme efforts have focussed on building confidence and capacity. They have established residents' groups and youth projects, combating anti-social behaviour by reaching out not only to young people but their families. They have painted murals at the entrance to Moyard and a 'superheroes' mural at Sliabh Dubh which now attracts people wanting their photos taken; levels of trouble at the interface have fallen. Black Mountain have had their support to residents' groups well received; they have brought in football coaches and run anti-sectarian workshops, set up over-50s cross community groups, and hosted an annual Christmas dinner where both communities celebrate together.

Highfield and Springmartin have well run community centres, says Joanna Felo, and she has focussed on facilitating centre development and supporting single parent families, young people and ex-combatants. She asked the Springmartin Community Association what they would like to happen to improve the look of the area. They asked for hanging baskets and an entrance feature artwork – a steel tree with the local children's names engraved on the leaves. Fortuitously, installing the sculpture required removing one of the sets of traffic barriers across Springmartin Road.

Autumn 2014 and Black Mountain is making good progress. One patch of land beside an interface fence on the upper Springfield Road has already been cleared and the fence itself is repainted. Grilles have been removed from windows in Moyard estate. Corr has accessed £500,000 funding from Belfast Education & Library board to move the playpark in Moyard next to the Matt Talbot youth centre. Black Mountain stress they have a structured approach to developing the area and a clear plan for the next nine months, when the IFI funding is projected to end. They have been granted £30,000 IFI Peace Impact funding to train and employ four local young people as peer leaders in Highfield and Springmartin. They are heading to Derry/Londonderry to visit the 4rS Recycling Resource Centre to see whether the model might work for Black Mountain. Most ambitiously, Belfast City Council is putting in a bid to the receivers to purchase the Finlay's site – if that is successful, they hope to start by building a shared community facility.

It is February 2014 and at Balmoral Hotel in outer West Belfast, there is a meeting of some 50 people to discuss a community safety strategy for Suffolk Lenadoon (Cluster 1). There are representatives, including former Republican and UDA paramilitaries, of three community groups: the Safer Neighbourhoods Project, Suffolk Community Interface Project, and Suffolk Lenadoon Interface Group, sitting at separate tables. There are representatives from PSNI, Belfast City Council and the Housing Executive. There is a facilitator with a flip chart.

This is the latest in a series of meetings, and after a hesitant start and a repetitive conversation that goes on for a while, someone in the group asks: "What are the real

Manor Street,
Lower Oldpark

problems?" "What has brought each of us here today?" The atmosphere in the room shifts. The real issue, it seems, is the decline of the Protestant Suffolk community, and intra community tensions within the Protestant enclave. The population is now around 350 families, while there are over 10–12,000 residents in Catholic Lenadoon. Suffolk has lost its primary school, and so even more families are leaving; the houses need new roofs; now there are empty houses. The Protestants have no political representation as the area is too small so they are outvoted by Sinn Féin. There are private landlords on the estate; a diverse population is moving in. "Suffolk survived the war and is losing the peace." "How can Suffolk move from erosion to inclusion?" There are few serious safety issues – there is trouble sometimes from young people coming in from outside the area, and groups of volunteers have a mobile phone network and monitor the interface; the Suffolk Loyalist march is non-contentious and is facilitated by the Catholic community of Lenadoon and Blacks Road. But there are splits among Loyalists and Suffolk is unable to speak with one voice at the meeting. The group agrees that smaller conversations need to take place, and that Suffolk needs to sort out its own issues first: "We're in that kind of twilight zone." The group agrees a timescale for the next series of meetings and then breaks up for lunch.

Suzanne Lavery is the coordinator for the IFI funded Suffolk Lenadoon Interface Group (SLIG) peacewalls programme. She has worked her way up since becoming a SLIG volunteer in 2000 when she was 16 and had to leave school when she had her first child. She began to get qualifications and do university modules and now has a degree in community youth work from the University of Ulster. For a couple of years she was a youth worker on the Donegall Road, and came back to SLIG as a peace worker in March 2013.

Suzanne was born and brought up in Suffolk. She attends the local Church of Ireland, the only Protestant Church remaining in Suffolk with a congregation of just 35–40 worshippers, and describes herself as Protestant but not Loyalist or Unionist. When she started, there was hostility: "When I started due to the media attention to the TBUC announcement, they assumed we were here to take the walls down." SLIG has an IFI grant of £250,000 for a two year peacewalls programme, involving 10 sites. The first task has been to get the fencing at the Suffolk entrance to the Stewartstown Road Regeneration Project (SRRP) shared space building replaced so that the Suffolk community can have equal access to the site from their estate.

"We've held various community groups and I tell all participants that this is about changing things so you can live with not as many fears. I'm not asking residents to move into each other's areas or stand at the interface and shake hands. Our aim is to move forward and not back to the past. We had a petrol bomb in July, the first in 13 years and it has caused major challenges. To move on, we have to convince the community it's not the end of the world. If the gate wasn't there, and they could have seen on the other side, would the kids have thrown a petrol bomb? The peacewalls programme is here to create dialogue to give different options to the community and then the community get the opportunity to lead on it and decide what they feel is appropriate for each site."

Suzanne Lavery has also achieved her second target to improve the riverpath interface and replace fencing. She trained six volunteers to consult with the local community, and then matters progressed more quickly than she had hoped because Belfast City Council and the Housing Executive found extra money in their budgets to pay for the work. Suzanne is also hoping to put some public art, focussing on history, peace and reconciliation, around three of the sites – the Arts Council is currently giving grants for such installations.

Jean Brown has lived in Suffolk since the estate was built in 1952 and is a founder and director of the Stewartstown Road Regeneration Project. Now close to retirement, she has been active in community work since the 80s. She met her Catholic husband when she was 17; Tommy, also 17, picked her up on the dodgems on a day's holiday. It was 1967 and the Troubles were starting – a terrible time, she says – and he asked her to marry him two weeks later. His parents wouldn't give permission so they had to wait until they were 21, and his father didn't speak to them until their daughter was born three years later. Her family always accepted him: "an uncle got drunk and said to me: 'You're marrying a Fenian'. My dad took him by the scruff of the neck and threw him out. 'Don't you ever speak about Tommy Brown that way, for we love him.'"

In the 80s, when the government started an unemployment scheme, Jean and a few others typed up a proposal on an electric typewriter and got funding to start a programme, which ran until 1999 and found jobs for hundreds of people. The Stewartstown Road Regeneration Project was founded the following year. The regeneration project transformed a row of derelict houses into shops, a post office, a café, counselling and family support services; they also built a day care centre, Sparkles, providing integrated preschool childcare for 48 children. Jean says she always felt called by God to her work for the community.

Jean says she has in the past been isolated and branded a traitor for promoting cross community work against the expressed wishes of Loyalist paramilitaries. She is planning to retire shortly and realises that things might develop very differently afterwards, and that those who once openly opposed the work could end up running it. She genuinely believes it is time for her to go and says: "I've done the best I can and have no desire to control what happens afterwards."

Two powerful symbols of the new and old Belfast are the refurbished Crumlin Road Gaol and, directly opposite it, the scandalously crumbling Crumlin Road Courthouse. They are umbilically connected a few feet below ground by the tunnel which brought convicted prisoners straight from court to jail, a passage now blocked by its own wall.

The gaol, which closed in 1996, is now beautifully restored and was visited by the Queen during her July 2014 Belfast tour. The gaol is open to tourists and for conferences and weddings. The guides are former prison officers, and the star feature is its fully functional gallows. Some visitors are former staff and prisoners, some of whom apparently bring their sons, to warn them of the consequences of their choices. The former chapel is used for concerts, including Jailhouse Rock, with local performer Jim 'The King' Brown. It is an excellent example – as was the use of Ebrington Barracks for the Tate Turner Prize in 2013 – of how a space formerly associated with the conflict can be 'reframed' in the imagination by being put to a different use, especially when that reframing involves art and music. Meanwhile the Courthouse, designed by Charles Lanyon and completed in 1850, was closed in 1998. It was privately purchased in 2003, before being badly damaged in a fire. Its future is uncertain. One creative proposal I heard – one apparently submitted to the Haass process – was that it should become a hub for all community groups in Belfast, a sort of grassroots iteration of Stormont.

Behind the gaol, the former Girdwood Barracks has been razed to the ground and after years of squabbles the cranes and hardhats have finally moved in; the site is being transformed for shared housing, a shared community hub and enterprise centre, and a football pitch – funded to the tune of £10 million by Belfast City Council from Peace III. There will be 60 houses and the hub will include a gym, sauna and youth space; it is due to be opened on 1 July 2015.

When the construction is finished, the green security fence around Girdwood's perimeter will be removed. With other smaller peacewalls sites, says Manus Maguire of Cliftonville Community Regeneration Forum (CCRF), work is proceeding, despite the dysfunctional wider political context (Cluster 8). Some old fences need to be repainted and they would like the yellow wall to be repainted blue. In order to make any changes it is necessary to "stack up all the ducks": community support, progress in the Stormont peace talks, and movement by various government departments. Budgets are being slashed and departments are running out of money. Meanwhile, he remains hopeful: "There are good people in government and good people in the communities."

The huge 'yellow wall' runs shockingly from Rossapenna Street to Clifton Park Avenue, on the edge of the Girdwood site, and cuts across Manor Street. Here the Cliftonville Community Regeneration Forum, on the Nationalist side and the, Lower Oldpark Community Association (LOCA), on the Protestant side, are working together in one of the IFI funded peacewalls programmes. They have been involved from the start in the plans for Girdwood and continue to pay close attention to how it will be managed and the opportunities for local businesses and employment.

Janice Beggs is centre manager of the Lower Oldpark Community Association. Beggs has lived in this Protestant area since 1969 when she came as a six year old child with her family. She trained and worked as a secretary for many years, and has always been active in community work. She has no memory of the wall being built in the 80s. Her passion, like other community workers, is the regeneration of the community which, she says, was "all empty houses, blight, dereliction and deprivation." People might work in the city, but are so ashamed of the squalor and desolation they feel unable to bring friends home or tell them where they live, she says. "I love the people and want to help rebuild the community."

While Catholic houses are backed up against the wall except for a small section where Manor Street used to go, there is a large grassed open area on the Protestant side and the wall has a second mesh fence inside it to prevent anyone from climbing up or throwing objects over the wall.

A children's playpark lies near the wall, with its own hazards: on one side a brick wall, perpendicular to the yellow wall, left over from a row of demolished houses, means mothers cannot watch over their children playing in the park, and, according to them, a local man nicknamed 'hammerhead' comes into the park and chases the children with a hammer. They have been involved in making an animated film with plasticine figures called *Walled In*, designed to lobby the council to remove the park wall.

In this, as in other Protestant areas, there is a fear of 'encroachment', even of the yellow wall being moved further in to allow Catholics to build more houses on the other side. There is a live memory of Torrens, up the road, where an entire Protestant community was forced out almost overnight in 2004. Fear is ingrained into people, says Janice. On Oldpark Road, houses are still regularly attacked. Lower Oldpark is now one of six pilot areas under the 'building sustainable communities' strategy of the Department of Social Development. As part of the area's regeneration, 26 houses have been refurbished having been empty for 20 years, and then 45 new ones will be built. Janice says it has brought "new people and new life" into the area.

In PUL communities, former paramilitaries are active, feuding violently among themselves and intimidating young people, community workers and residents. "They hover", say the young mothers, laughing, although it is hard to laugh with them when you hear what these bullies are capable of. As in other parts of Belfast, on both sides, people in Oldpark speak of being themselves, or of others being or having been 'put out' of their houses. Being 'put out' means being intimidated, verbally abused, petrol bombed, or otherwise harassed and forced out of your own home by paramilitary thugs from your own or the other side, in criminal, sectarian, or, increasingly, racist attacks. People use the phrase often in a matter of fact way, a way that gives no hint to the naïve listener of the reality of what it means, that ordinary people do not have the right to feel safe in their own homes. Being 'put out' is an experience common to many.

Janice Beggs works on the peacewalls programme with Sarah Lorimer, a fulltime peacewalls worker appointed in January 2014, and Manus Maguire and Malachy Mulgrew from the Cliftonville Community Regeneration Forum. The forum has three priorities: peacebuilding, youth and regeneration. There is intense engagement with young people through teams of detached youth workers, offering activities and mentoring and coaching. There are cross community days and shared history trips, aiming to build mutual understanding and respect. "The smoke on the Crumlin Road used to be from petrol bombs and bonfires," says Manus, "now it's from barbecues."

Further North and under Cavehill, lies Hazelwood Integrated Primary School, where the fence was erected in 2007, and the Protestant area of White City and the Catholic area of Whitewell (Cluster 11). Geraldine O'Kane of Greater Whitewell Community Surgery and Brian Dunn of White City Community Development Association have

Navarra Place
playpark, White City

been working individually in community development for 30 years and together for the last 10. Their IFI funded peacewalls programme concerns six sites, including the Hazelwood school fence. In Graymount Crescent there is a gate across a laneway which can be closed automatically by the PSNI if there are disturbances in the area. A massive fence runs between Serpentine Gardens and Gunnell Hill, installed in the late 90s, and on Longlands Avenue a fence divides the estate and derelict factory sites from playing fields.

Initial programme priorities have been to redevelop the Navarra Place playpark, which is separated from Serpentine Road by an ugly high military fence. On the park side of the fence is a memorial mural to Thomas McDonald, a teenager killed locally in a sectarian attack, and family members have agreed to the mural being moved so that the fence, which has an open pedestrian gate, can be replaced by see-though fencing. Belfast City Council have also agreed to new park equipment. The project has also engaged a researcher from the University of Ulster to carry out an 'emotional mapping' of residents' feelings about the interface. While it seems to Geraldine that things are moving slowly, she says that there are many connections developing between people on both sides of the interface: "the talking, the conversations, that's what's happening." Meanwhile, she says, of her work with Brian Dunn, "ourselves, our whole thinking is together".

Also in North Belfast, Rab McCallum of TASCIT (Twaddell, Ardoyne and Shankill Communities in Transition), whose IFI funded peacewalls programme covers 11 sites, is confident that, despite delays, the proposed changes to the Flax Street gates – between the abandoned Hillview Retail site and the empty flax mill on the Crumlin Road – will take place (Cluster 9). Originally planned for September 2014, the aim is to replace the gates with ornamental see-through gates which will be open 9–5, and an artwork is to be installed. There have, as at other sites, been issues and concerns expressed by the Shankill PUL community, but McCallum describes the patient and dogged process by which each specific issue is being identified and addressed, and a timeline laid out.

For example, one woman was objecting to the changes because her neighbour had been shot dead during the conflict. TASCIT has arranged for a steel panel to be inserted into the new fence near her house and now she is 'happy enough'. They have also agreed an aftercare package for residents to cover the cost of any damage if there are opportunistic attacks after the alterations are made. In general, says McCallum, they are in a 'see how it goes phase' – understandably, residents need to be able to see some improvement or reward for the changes. There has been significant frustration at the lack of a plan to reinvest in Hillview Retail Park, which would provide a major incentive to open the Flax Street gates. He understands, as do many community workers, that changes to the interface barriers need to be seen as part of larger regeneration schemes. Furthermore, he notes, each specific interface presents a different set of problems.

One of TASCIT's partners is Ian McLaughlin of the Lower Shankill Community Association (LSCA). Described as the 'go-to' man on the Shankill, he has continued to work for the peace process despite the setbacks in recent years and months. He is a representative on some 15 groups and networks, including the board of Belfast Interface Project. His priority is the economic regeneration of the lower Shankill, which reaches from Carlisle Circus near the city centre up through Lanark Way and the Springfield Road – and a redressing of what some Protestants believe to be an unfair emphasis of funders and investors in Catholic areas. McLaughlin "takes offence at being called a gatekeeper." "I'm an agitator," he says, "I would agitate my community to try and change people's minds. I'm a conduit between areas of multiple deprivation". He is working on a range of multi-million pound projects with the Department for Social Development and Belfast City Council, as well as the building of 33 new homes in lower Shankill.

Ian left school at 16 and was looking forward to joining the Merchant Navy – he had a place booked on the Ulster Star out of Rio de Janeiro – when his father suddenly died; while his brother left for university, he stayed home with his mother. He joined Mackie's in 1978, worked his way up to be maintenance manager for the entire plant, and was the last employee on the books when the factory closed in 1999. He worked in Derry/ Londonderry for a year.

In 1982 a good friend of his, Mark – they were both in the UDR – was shot dead right in front of him at the gate of the factory "one bright summer's day", and for many years that "shaped my mind". Eventually, a church minister approached him and asked: "How do you feel about talking to your neighbour on the other side of the fence?" "Once you get married and have kids, you start asking, do you want your children to go through the same thing? I entered into the conversation. So many of the things my neighbour talked about were the same things I was thinking about. Deprivation didn't know the barrier."

The LSCA was formed to foster relations with Nationalist neighbours and to mediate in internal Loyalist feuding. Although not himself a former paramilitary, McLaughlin sees himself as having influence with them. McLaughlin notes that the Protestant population of Greater Shankill fell over 40 years from 71,000 in 1971 to 23,000 in 2011. Under the guise of redevelopment, he says, the whole lower Shankill was 'bulldozed' and many Protestants moved out to Bangor, Newtownards and Carrickfergus. At the same time, there was the oft-mentioned collapse in traditional sources of employment for Protestants in heavy engineering, ship and aircraft construction. In the worsening conflict situation, many Protestants went into the security industry in the UDR and part time RUC, or into maintenance and support roles in police and army barracks, roles that couldn't be taken by Catholics who saw working in security as 'collaboration'.

Following the Belfast Agreement and the Patten report, army bases closed and the PSNI reduced from 12,000 to 6,000, of whom a third are now Catholics; and the recession hit. "There's almost a siege mentality," says McLaughlin, "the world – Brits, Americans, Dublin – is against us." Meanwhile every disturbance in the wider political system – Haass, the On The Runs, the flags protest, Twaddell camp, and unresolved toxic issues of the past – all cause great anxiety in the Loyalist community: "Republicans have achieved more and Loyalists want the same." Meanwhile, McLaughlin remains "steadfastly committed to the peace process" – and to the support of PSNI. "If I detect crime I report it." He was involved in the Connect Programme, which trained 240 local people and 120 police officers in 2007; in 2012 the LSCA joined the local Police Community Safety Partnership (PCSP).

The Duncairn Community Partnership in North Belfast has six partners: Intercomm, the North Belfast Interface Network, North Belfast Community in Transition, North Belfast Prisoners' Aid, and two residents' associations, Tigers Bay and Newington (Clusters 6 & 7). Their IFI funded peacewalls programme includes responsibility for Alexandra Park, where a gate was opened, to much media fanfare in September 2011, in the fence which cuts the park in two.

Duncairn is one of the longest established peacewalls programmes, and has made good progress. The interface wall in Northside Business Park has been lowered, and grilles and toughened glass are being installed in the windows of houses there and on Duncairn Gardens. Even such an apparently small job can turn out to be tricky – in the case of Housing Executive houses, the Housing Executive will pay for grilles to be removed and replaced out of Hate Incident Practical Action (HIPA) funds; in the case of private housing, IFI has stepped in. Duncairn have facilitated the reimaging of some Loyalist murals. At the end of November 2014, the traffic barrier on Newington Street was finally removed – after years of objections from residents and delays in having street alterations implemented by the Department for Regional Development.

The partnership has needed to face a range of difficulties – ongoing tensions between Loyalist factions in Tigers Bay, with families only recently being 'put out' of their homes. There were accusations that there had not been enough consultation over the Alexandra Park fence; a council-funded review was generally positive about the process, although it recognised the challenges in maintaining the involvement of the local community in decision-making. Now a further 30 metres of fencing in the park will be removed, opening up space for an outdoor classroom that can be used by local schools. Ciaran Shannon of the Partnership says that apart from the difficulties in Tigers Bay, which have had a negative effect on local confidence and ongoing attempts to undermine the work, finance is the biggest issue, both to support voluntary sector employment and the physical changes required.

The Fountain is an extraordinary and tiny Protestant enclave underneath and looked down upon from the South side of Derry's famous city walls, and bounded on two further sides by a huge 'security wall' separating it from Bishop Street, a Catholic neighbourhood within the

Workman Gate, Springfield Road, before transformation

much larger Catholic Bogside. In the 50s, the population of the Fountain was two thousand, now it is down to a 10th of that number. The Fountain's cul-de-sacs can be accessed by the steep Wapping Street, now lined by abandoned and boarded up terraced homes, and on its other side by the pedestrian 'dog-leg' gate – scary because the exit is not visible from the entrance – directly onto the Bishop Street gate into Derry's walled city centre.

The Fountain and Bishop Street wall is the object of the Triax IFI funded peacewalls programme, which has two full time peace workers, Donna McCloskey and Sophie Blake-Gallagher, and two local community development workers in their first jobs, Rachel Mullan and Kyle Thompson. Rachel is from Bishop Street, and Kyle is from the Fountain, and neither had been on the other side of the wall until they started working for Triax a year ago.

Until five or six years ago, when community leaders put in teams to monitor the wall 24/7, there had been regular attacks, rioting and abuse at the pedestrian gate; now there is very little trouble. Nonetheless, when the peacewalls programme began, there was a lot of resistance. They have spent the first 18 months just building relationships and they have come a long way, says Donna McCloskey, the Triax peacewalls coordinator. "People talk about the 'Derry model', it's just about really hard work on the ground, knocking on doors, talking to residents, leafleting." Fountain residents are not used to accessing services or engaging with community programmes. Triax took 40 residents from the communities on a trip to Crumlin Road Gaol, and in December 2014 there was a shared-space Christmas and crafts market in a marquee on the interface. Now slow progress is being made on the programme targets. Grilles have been removed from and triple glazing installed in windows of houses opposite the wall, and Kyle and Rachel have worked with volunteers to paint the frontages of the abandoned terraces on the steep old street.

Just through the Bishop Street gate and inside the city walls on the left hand side, is the newly opened headquarters of the Holywell DiverseCity Community Partnership. Eamonn Baker from Towards Understanding and Healing, one of the nine organisations in the partnership, describes the lunchtime event he holds every Wednesday. The week before I met him, he had used the opportunity to present draft scenes from *The Fountain, a Musical* by local musician Roy Arbuckle, to which 66 people, including a good number from the Fountain, came.

The musical contains a song tribute to Bobby Stott, an UDR member from the Fountain shot dead outside his home in 1975. In the audience was Kate Nash, whose brother was killed on Bloody Sunday in 1972. The song was performed by actor Seamus Heaney, whose brother Denis had been an IRA member, also shot dead, by the British army in 1978. The performance was, said Eamonn Baker, one of those "magic moments" of resonance and connection. Kate Nash told the *Londonderry Sentinel* that the performance had been a poignant reminder of the suffering of both the people of the Fountain and their Nationalist neighbours. Songwriter Roy Arbuckle said that he hoped the completed musical would remind people of how prior to 1969 Derry was a more united community: "All around here, the city centre, Fountain, Bishop Street, all those streets were mixed streets, it was a shared space" (Kevin Mullan, *Londonderry Sentinel*, 4 Oct 2014).

Across the Foyle River, with its stunning Peace Bridge, which links the Catholic Westbank to the mainly Protestant Waterside, in the grand old St Columb's Park House, is another IFI funded peacewalls programme, and the coordinator is Kirstein Arbuckle, daughter of songster Roy Arbuckle. She has a Masters Degree in Human Rights Law from the Transitional Justice Institute of the University of Ulster. She left Northern Ireland for a few years to work among aborigines in Queensland, Australia; she started as peacewalls coordinator for St Columb's Park House in October 2013. She has four neighbourhoods and two interfaces: one between Protestant Tullyally and Catholic Curryneiran on the edge of town just off the main road to Belfast, a grim estate built during the 70s which became 'somehow' segregated by fences and a laneway; and a second, unmarked interface between Nationalist Top of the Hill, which overlooks the Foyle, and Protestant Irish

Street, the area beneath it and bordering the river. The project has four outreach workers, one in each area.

Kirstein Arbuckle has worked in a range of creative ways, starting a cross community choir for the four communities, and getting young people to decorate derelict houses and graffitied bus stops. Many of her IFI targets are completed, and she is now working on developing a learning tool that can be used in all interface areas.

Geraldine O Donnell is responsible for Community Safety at the Top of the Hill Community Forum. Born and bred in Top of the Hill, and with a "passion for community", initially Geraldine went to catering college, married and got "five children very quick", and started giving a few hours to community work. She returned to full time education in 2004 and graduated with a first class degree in social policy and sociology from the University of Ulster in 2007. In 2011, Geraldine gained full time employment as a community development worker for the Top of the Hill area.

Cross community dialogue started about five years ago, she remembers, when residents from Top of the Hill and Irish Street came together to decide what should happen after some lads from Top of the Hill petrol bombed a pensioner's house in Irish Street. It was portrayed as a sectarian attack. Geraldine and her work colleague Junior Morrison asked residents from Irish Street if they could go over for a meeting. "There were over 25 people there, and we explained to them that the same element that had petrol bombed them was also holding our own community to ransom by engaging in anti community behaviour." Since then, there has been all sorts of socialising, women's groups, cross community youth programmes and a shared history group. The women had an outing to the Dail and Glasnevin Cemetery in Dublin, and stayed in a hotel together – a number of them had actually worked together in the shirt factories, which were always mixed. They had gone separate ways during the Troubles but reconnected on the trip.

Although there are no physical walls or fences between Top of the Hill and Irish Street, there are six IFI programme interface sites, including the regeneration of the former school site, an abandoned house, sports facilities and a green space at Mountain View between the two areas. They received an all-Ireland Arts Council award for Re-Imaging Communities in November 2013 for the transformation of space by removal of sectarian flags and kerb markings and the installation of four Locky Morris silhouette sculptures, 'Short Cuts', depicting young people doing ordinary things as they walk in the street like eating chips and texting on their mobile phones.

The big key was the opening of the Peace Bridge, says Geraldine O Donnell, which has given pedestrian access from the area to the city centre across the Foyle. Like community workers everywhere, she bemoans the levels of poverty in Derry, which is a "low wage economy", where for many people it is "eat or heat". When Geraldine began volunteering in her local area, community work only treated the symptoms of disadvantage; however this has since evolved with many partnerships being established to tackle the root causes.

The longest unbroken peaceline in Belfast runs from the semi-rural streets behind the upper Springfield Road under Black Mountain all the way down the Springfield Road in one form or another (Clusters 2 & 3). Further down Springfield Road on the left is Workman Gate, across Workman Avenue which leads into Woodvale Avenue and Woodvale Park, where in August 2013 Sinn Féin Lord Mayor Máirtín Ó Muilleoir was attacked by a Loyalist mob when he visited to open a children's playpark. Across from Workman Gate, houses are built with only one window; below the gate a long mock-brick 'boast wall' with high mesh fencing above it runs down to Lanark Way. Here, there are heavy reinforced metal gates across the road; the military green wall turns and runs behind the lower Falls and Clonard Monastery down Cupar Way, via further security gates across North Howard Street, Northumberland Street, Percy Street and Townsend Street – which runs parallel and next to Westlink and another set of security gates, topped by barbed wire. The other side of Westlink and directly facing Townsend Presbyterian Church is the small section of wall in Brown Square Park believed by Frank Higgins to be the earliest wall.

All the way down the longest wall there are community, peacewalls and church programmes of various kinds, working independently and/or together to maintain the peace, build cross community relationships and ultimately reduce the gates and walls. There has been no serious violence on this interface for seven or eight years and now moves are afoot to transform or remove a number of the smaller barriers.

Workman Gate was, before its replacement in April 2015, an oppressive structure; the small pedestrian gate cut into it was open during the day and allowed glimpses from Springfield Road into the Protestant estate beyond. Workman Gate is opened just twice a year on the third Saturday in June and the 12th July for Loyalist parades to come through from Workman Avenue and march up the Springfield Road to the Orange Lodge. It was said to cost £1,000 to open for a quarter hour, requiring the removal of a welded bar each time. The new gate can be seen through and opens much more easily.

Next to and above Workman Gate is the former Springfield Road Methodist Church, now a community centre. Further up and opposite are the offices of InterAction Belfast, one of the earliest interface programmes. Started by former Loyalist paramilitary Billy Hutchinson and hunger striker Pat McGeown, its director is Roisin McGlone, one of Belfast's most experienced community workers. InterAction monitors the Springfield Road interface. Roisin works with cross community groups, facilitates dialogue between the community and PSNI, and amongst former paramilitaries. She has facilitated the discussions on the Nationalist side about the replacement of Workman Gate with a more attractive see-through gate, monitored by 24 hour CCTV. Opposite Workman Gate is E3, a new campus of Belfast Metropolitan College.

Further down, two churches straddle the peaceline and their ministers are actively involved in initiatives to open gates and transform the environment. New Life City Church sits on Northumberland Street, in a former warehouse – its front end in Protestant Shankill, its back end in Catholic lower Falls; the minister is Jack McKee, himself born and bred in the Shankill. Meanwhile Presbyterian minister Revd Jack Lamb serves Townsend Presbyterian Church on the bleak Townsend Street, which runs through abandoned wasteland including a site owned by the Maharishi and originally intended for a world-wide Transcendental Meditation Centre – until the recession cut funding support for the development.

The work of Forthspring began in 1997 when the congregation of Springfield Road Methodist Church had declined in numbers and a decision was made to reach out. An ecumenical partnership was set up among various Christian groups, including the Catholic Curragh religious sisters, who live on the Protestant side of the Workman Gate, and the mixed mid-Springfield residents' association – which later folded. Now Forthspring is independent, although it maintains links with the wider Methodist Church. It offers a range of services to the community including cross community work with women, disadvantaged young people, and childcare.

In June 2014, *Talking About the Troubles* was launched at Stormont, a book – the material also available online – of stories from residents on both sides of the peaceline which aims to arrive at a "shared but not agreed" account of the area's history since the 1950s. Under the ongoing EU-funded Five Decades Project, the book records stories shared in facilitated small groups: stories of daily life, of work and celebrations, of just carrying on – and also of the tragedies, losses and traumas, of being searched, of managing to get around – and of some surreal and convincing juxtapositions:

"I was sixteen at the time. It was the in thing to do. Bobby Sands was the first to die. Everyone came out for the hunger strikers. Everyone came out, nobody stayed in their house…

Because I was sixteen I couldn't get a proper cap for my tooth. I had a temporary one… On the way round we were talking that much and carrying on, the cap flew out. We all got down looking for the tooth, it was right in the front, you couldn't be seen without it, you would be scundered… My aunt gave me a bit of chewing gum to stick it in. We all went round to see the body. I can still see his face in the coffin. There was an armed guard at the top and bottom of the coffin, masked of course. I can still see his face in the coffin, the gauntness of it, the sunken cheeks; it really was a like a skeleton with skin on it (Forthspring 2014)."

During the building of E3, the well intentioned and well received new campus for Belfast Metropolitan College, an interface fence was "inadvertently" removed and a gate opened that had not been open in 32 years. This caused a sudden crisis – teenagers began coming through and "had a field day for a week" damaging cars. Catholic families began picnicking and flying tricolours in the grounds, intended to be neutral or shared space. It was, says one source, a "ridiculous situation. The college authorities had failed to take on board the access issues and how it would impact on both communities." A Loyalist community worker puts it more bluntly: "I could have choked them for their naivete. They wouldn't know the difference between an interface and an apple tart."

A multi-agency network group, described by one member as a "breath of fresh air", including representatives from both communities, Forthspring, the CRC, Department of Justice and PSNI was put together, to discuss the situation and offer the chance to build cross community relationships. The conversations have taken on "a whole life of their own", adds the source quoted above. Conversations have followed about a site which is part of the old Mackie's factory site, currently owned by Invest NI and planned for an Innovations Centre, as an incubation centre for business projects coming out of E3.

One local representative of a residents' group on the E3 network group – we can call her Jane – was indignant that plans for the shared space of the Innovation Centre, like those for E3, did not initially attend to access issues for the Protestant community. To avoid walking through Workman Gate, Protestants would have needed to walk down to Lanark Way and back up the Springfield Road, "a harrowing journey for any of our people", she says. The plans should have included separate access for Protestants. It has since proved possible to reopen an access route into the site from Workman Avenue.

Workman Gate,
Springfield Road,
transformed

Now that Workman Gate has been replaced, Jane says, "I hope to God the gates start to change people's minds". She has one adult daughter who is happy to walk through the current pedestrian gate and another who will walk a mile and a half around it – she was attacked there as a child "and still sees violence at that gate".

Jane works with young people on restorative justice and helped a cross community group to make the film *Breaking the Barriers*.

"It was very challenging for them. Some had never been outside the gate. We prepared them for it mentally, walked them through the gate, talked about incidents in the Troubles, and they met ex-combatants. One girl said: 'They are just like us'. It makes me feel sad that they have lived segregated territorial lives."

The worker believes there is a loss of confidence in the Protestant community, partly due to the lack of connection between the Protestant working class and the politicians, particularly the DUP, who "are all middle and upper class and have no connection to the grassroots."

Each cluster has its own story and stories to tell, both unique and echoing the themes and patterns from other clusters. In the immaculate new community centre in the heart of Ardoyne, Sally Smyth, coordinator of the Grace Women's Development Group, funded by the Department for Social Development through its neighbourhood renewal programme, attempts to respond to needs for mental health, isolation, employment search and personal development. The centre offers child care and family support, but she gets frustrated by the levels of poverty and her inability to address fundamental issues.

Grace has begun engaging in cross community work; they took 15 women away for a shared weekend with 15 from Glenbryn, the Protestant area behind the wall. Now they have been able to get funding for a cross community worker under the IFI funded Peace Impact programme. They would like to build a new shared space women's centre on a piece of land on the interface – and they are hoping that a gate could be opened allowing both communities access to the shops on Alliance Avenue.

Way across town, down in the Village, Angela Johnston is community and economic development officer for the Greater Village Regeneration Trust. Here, Donegall Road runs straight from Sandy Row all the way to the Broadway Roundabout and the controversial 'balls on the Falls sculpture' – actually the largest public art sculpture in Belfast, by Wolfgang Buttress, completed in 2011 and visible for miles around.

Here, the main interfaces are the roundabout, where it is hoped the new MacDonald's can be 'shared space', and Westlink, which divides this Protestant area from the lower Falls. The Village looks like a forgotten land, a grid of many old houses looking like a

50s film set, interspersed with the grim hulks – the old Ulster Weavers' site and several abandoned Douglas & Grahame menswear factories – ghastly debris and rubbish-strewn derelict plots of land beside the motorway. Like many Protestant areas it has its large vacant grassed area, where houses were razed some time ago, and some new housing.

This area has been free of violence the last two years, says Johnston, mainly due to the efforts of community workers. There are, she says, major social problems as a result of the Troubles. "It has always been a community in turmoil." She works on community safety issues, including interfaces, drug and alcohol abuse, anti-social behaviour and education.

Back the other way down Donegall Road, through the other side of Sandy Row, and close to city centre, is Donegall Pass and another isolated and depressed Protestant community of 620 homes, surrounded by the Nationalist areas of the Markets and lower Ormeau Road. Here, Elaine Mansfield, who has worked in community development in the UK and Northern Ireland for over 30 years, has been director of the Donegall Pass Community Forum, which is a partner in the cross community Cromac Regeneration Initiative (CRI), for eight years. Here, the interfaces are all carparks. People worry about going out of the area as they don't feel safe, says Elaine. Now the area is all smart new Housing Executive houses with gardens, replacing former slums, but as a result 70% of the population was lost along with the area's pubs, baker's, butcher's and other shops. The primary school has also closed. Donegall Pass is known for its Chinese restaurants, although the owners live elsewhere. In this area, says a local resident, "There's a Citizen's Advice building with no advice – because it's just admin – a police station with no police, a supermarket with no bread – because it's Chinese – and a school with no children."

Elaine explains: "People thought the ceasefire would be the end of our problems, but we are still seeing the legacy of the Troubles: health problems, heart disease, asthma, chronic lung diseases, smoking, drinking, children with problems, unemployment." In response, the Forum offers health advice, group work, history programmes, counselling, IT courses, community education and training.

Far away from the city centre, when I am heading to visit Ligoniel, the satnav dumps me on top of a mountain outside Belfast and then announces it has lost its GPS signal. Feeling 'scundered to a hundred', I eventually find the Ligoniel Improvement Association and its director, Maria Morgan laughs sympathetically, as I am not the first person to whom this has happened – although the incident also says something about how isolated and far away the community of Ligoniel feels. Maria Morgan, a veteran community worker, chair of the Board of Belfast Interface Project and a trustee of the Donegall Pass Community Forum and of the North Belfast Interface Network, says they feel very unsupported by the statutory agencies up here.

Ligoniel is an island Catholic community, which can be cut off at flashpoints at both ends of Ligoniel Road. There are new 'overflow' housing developments which have drawn occupants from all over Belfast. There is a major interface on Hazelbrook Drive which

Bryson Street,
Short Strand

sits above a sheer drop to a private Protestant estate, and where items can be thrown over. Glenbank Park is an interface with the Protestant area of Ballysillan.

The community forum was founded in 1974 by a number of concerned residents and professionals from both sides of the community. The association has no political affiliation and no paramilitary links; they are proud of their committed ethos and the highly skilled mixed staff and board. The association maintains a team of outreach workers and is connected with over 1200 young people. There are still regular attacks and fights, and on 12th July the Protestants bring their bonfire into the middle of upper Crumlin Road creating a sense of siege: "This is what we can do to you". Maria is convinced that much of the violence is orchestrated by "older and more serious people", fuelled by the ongoing conflict between the UDA and the UVF in Ballysillan.

During my research for this book, I discover that I have a distant cousin from the Short Strand; and of course Short Strand is where Frankie Quinn, this book's photographer, was born and lives to this day – so I develop a growing attachment to this particular neighbourhood. Theresa Murray Magee and I share a great great grandfather; our great grandfathers were brothers and were born in Seaford, Sussex, which is where the Cossticks come from. Theresa's great grandfather Edwin was sent as a customs officer to Strangford Lough in County Down, and her grandmother, Daisy Cosstick, was born there in 1894. Daisy was quite a character, and her story deserves its own book some day. Having had two children out of wedlock, she went on to have nine further children including Theresa's mother Yvonne with husband Robert Morton (of Morton's Flour in Ballymena). Daisy died and Yvonne and two of her sisters were

84

sent to a Catholic convent in Armagh, and became Catholics. Yvonne later gave birth to Theresa in an unmarried mothers' home on the Antrim Road, and Theresa was fostered with Veronica Murray in the old Vulcan Street in Short Strand – Veronica was actually the aunt of John White, the well-known Short Strand photographer, whose negatives are now held by Frankie Quinn and the Red Barn Gallery. Theresa married an electrician from South Belfast – John White gave her away – and moved to London in 1963, but still spends her holidays in the Short Strand with best school friend Kathleen Roberts.

Short Strand is the tiny and besieged Catholic enclave, within the larger area of Ballymacarret, which still suffers frequent attacks of bottle throwing and blast bombs by Loyalists and to which many journalists and film-makers head first. An area of just 1,000 homes and 3,000 people, it is almost entirely enclosed by walls and other barriers, surrounded by Protestant East Belfast with its population of some 60,000. It is also enclosed on three sides by main roads – on the west side by Short Strand, to the north by the Newtownards Road and to the South by Albert Bridge Road. To the East, the brick wall runs high all along Bryson Street and cuts across Madrid Street. "I come from Ballymacarret," insists Kathleen Roberts, "It was always Ballymacarret when I was growing up. It was the British army named us Short Strand."

It is here in the grounds of St Matthew's Roman Catholic Church, on the corner of lower Newtownards Road, that the latest fence – a retractable steel curtain – was installed with great reluctance by the Department of Justice in November 2013 at the insistence of the local community. Two weeks before my first visit to Short Strand, the mesh curtain was and remains closed, because of a disagreement between Protestant and Catholic communities about who had the right to close it, and because it takes a cherry picker three hours to shut it and therefore would not be much use in an emergency.

"The fence looks better closed", says Willie Ward, a respected local businessman in Short Strand and the parish priest's right hand man and spokesman. "Willie Ward! Willie Ward!" the children shout as we walk streets so safe that doors are left open and cars unlocked. Willie owns property, the supermarket and the Strand Bar, the area's one pub not blown up during the Troubles, where he does not allow discussion of politics or religion. This area suffered greatly during the Troubles, he says: there were over 50 deaths including of his own brother, murdered by local Republican paramilitaries. Willie comes from the largest family in the neighbourhood. His mother has 100 children, grand and great grandchildren. "There will not under any circumstances be removal of these walls," he says, "because of what we have suffered from Protestants."

Short Strand is the site of one of the conflict's most famous events, the Battle of St Matthew's, which helped to escalate the conflict in the early 70s and to fuel the wider sense of Catholic injustice and recruitments to the Provisional IRA. Kathleen remembers the night of 27 June 1970 well.

"I was 26, my daughter was 19 months old. We were one of five Catholic families living in the third house down in Austin Street, a Protestant street. It was a two up two down with an outside toilet we bought for £750, quite expensive, in 1967.

It was a cul-de-sac, so we were trapped. One of the Catholics on the Road, John Harman, had a sister who had married out of the faith and was living on the Shankill. She heard a rumour that they were coming over to attack Short Strand, so they let us know. The IRA on the Falls Road also heard the rumour, so there was busloads coming in to support the Catholic Defence League – they were the local group set up to defend our local church and each house paid £4.00 to them.

Some men came into our house to be able to see out of the bay window, and some men including Brian, my husband, and John Harman stood at the end of the street; one of them had a legal gun. I and my daughter were put for safety into John Harman's house further down Austin Street. Boom, the guns started and the army was firing rubber bullets at the church. In the morning we heard Henry McIlhone had been shot dead near the church – now the Historical Enquiry Team (HET) has ruled it was by Denis Donaldson."[1]

The Bryson Street wall was built during the 1970s and extended in 2003. Bryson Street had been a mixed street, with large, beautiful, privately owned houses, remembers Kathleen. She had a cousin who was put out of Beechfield Street and moved into Bryson Street, and was 'put out' again. The houses became derelict and there were continual attacks on St Matthew's, so the wall was built, starting at the church end of the street. "People were so frightened, they were relieved when the wall went up." The wall across Madrid Street was built relatively recently in 2002, when Catholics started moving into empty houses on the Protestant side, and extended in 2008 (BIP 2012).

It may be that Short Strand and East Belfast are suffering the most intense and consistent levels of violence in Belfast – still, when violence has abated at many interfaces. This, says Willie Ward, "is the most troubled parish in all of Ireland." He also notes the amount of cross community work that is going on. There would be some mixed marriages in Short Strand, and the area has welcomed a number of recent foreign migrants, including both a black and a white family from South Africa.

"Even when it's quiet, there are bottles of paint and urine, and blast bombs," says Willie. "No doubt the Protestants on the other side would say the same – although we do try to make sure the young ones don't get involved in community violence." There have been riots within the last few years, including a 'hand-to-hand battle' in 2012, after which the Department of Justice installed a secondary fence around the church and the Irish government gave £7,000 for upgraded CCTV cameras. There are grilles on all the grim presbytery's windows, and the priest's car is sometimes attacked.

---

1 Donaldson confessed in 2005 he had been a British agent, and was murdered in Glenties, Co Donegal, by the Real IRA in 2006.

The identity of Short Strand is strongly defined by the church; they have about 20% Mass attendance and the annual draw is supported by most people in the area. "We put a great deal of emphasis on education as the way forward, because we were excluded from jobs before and during the Troubles – the Protestants could always get a good job without an education", says Willie.

Short Strand has seen very hard times – now there are problems with alcoholism, anti-depressants and prescription drugs. The walls are a comfort blanket and unlikely to come down any time soon. But people are talking about opening a door into the empty Beechfield Primary School the other side of the wall, so that local youth can attend the boxing club started by Protestants in the premises. People feel much safer walking in and out of the Strand, and there are cross community groups. "I see a change, the work is being done, the small steps will build up to a bigger picture", says a local community worker. Two years ago the community forum brought people together for a story telling residential, families from both sides and former British soldiers: "friendships happened", she says. Kathleen Roberts participated in a 2007 cross community women's project among former pupils at Avoniel and St Matthew's Primary Schools. They met on Tuesday mornings, went on history trips including to the Ulster Folk and Transport Museum and the Battle of the Boyne site, researched the lives of Nelson Mandela, Bobby Sands and David Ervine, and produced a book of shared reminiscences called *Your Place or Mine*. "Listening is a powerful thing," notes Joan Carberry, the project facilitator, in her introduction (2007).

Bernie McConnell is director of the Short Strand Community Forum, which was set up in 1991, funded by Belfast City Council and brings together some 13 community organisations. Now there are 26 organisations and 17 staff, mostly local, are employed. With a budget of around half a million pounds a year, the centre delivers a comprehensive range of services, including playgroups, after school clubs, youth projects, and groups for senior citizens, special needs and cross community activities. This area is in the bottom 10% for deprivation: there are chronic housing problems, unemployment and a "ridiculous number" of people on prescription drugs for depression and their "nerves". There are people who don't leave their houses – trauma is a "transgenerational thing", she says.

Nevertheless, the fundamental poverty is not addressed – funding is just short term sticking plaster money. By the time the project gets under way, the funding is over and people are left angry and frustrated. She is on the board of the OFMdFM Social Investment Fund which totals £80 million and aims to tackle poverty and deprivation through improved community based services and facilities. East Belfast projects will include a new doctor's surgery and education, early years and employability programmes.

The Forum is involved in the Council's Youth Engagement Programme (YEP), working 1-2-1 with mentoring with young people at risk and their families. Acknowledging the ongoing problems at the interface, she says social media is greatly to blame and there are people on both sides who have not bought into the peace process. "Cross community is fine, but it's the ones that won't go to cross community we need to reach. There are people who seem normal and very friendly, but are filled with sectarian hatred, lack of understanding and intolerance." But it's not all bad news, adds Bernie O'Connell. There are young people locally with high educational aspirations and high flying jobs.

The other side of the wall in Protestant East Belfast is the office of Sammy Douglas, DUP MLA, who was born in Sandy Row, where "it seemed everyone on the street" joined the UDA, UVF or RHC. Sammy supported the Loyalist cause, mainly through work with Loyalist prisoners and political strikes. While he understands how many young men and women from Protestant and Unionist areas were caught up in the troubles, taking someone's life was a line he could never contemplate: "I couldn't have murdered anyone." He has spent the last 25 years working in social and economic regeneration in East Belfast and at times as a mediator in conflict resolution. A New Labour supporter "before the spin", he was a community advisor to Peter Robinson when he was MP, who persuaded him to join the DUP, and after consulting many people across East Belfast including from the Short Strand, Douglas agreed and went on to be elected as an MLA.

He is quick to note that violence emanates from both sides of the interfaces – people living in Cluan Place and Thistle Court areas would also feel under siege at times. "I have heard residents claim that some youth and community workers are community workers by day and wear hoods at night." With social media, a crowd can gather at an interface area in minutes. On one occasion when there were stones and bottles being thrown from the Catholic/Nationalist side of the interface at Madrid St, local paramilitaries asked him to mediate, so he went upstairs in an empty house to see from the window what was going on and reported back: "We've got a full battalion of the IRA here – it was six and seven year olds chucking golf balls over." Sammy says he supported the building of the Madrid Street wall because both communities requested it, but he has seen from it how "a wall protects but it also divides communities. It dehumanises the other side."

He admits the race hate issue has further complicated the picture in East Belfast:

"We still suffer from violence, division, racism – yet East Belfast was always a friendly place welcoming visitors and strangers. We would be dealing with race hate and intimidation cases on a weekly basis in the office here. I can understand why people are angry; they grew up in this place, they want a house here, they are on the waiting list, they might see foreign nationals coming in and there is a perception that they are being given preferential treatment by housing providers. And often there is a sectarian root to the behaviour."

As a politician, Sammy feels he can have more influence in getting things done for communities. He has been able to work with local residents, community and political leaders to get reinforced roofs and windows for houses in areas that have been petrol bombed. For many young people, he acknowledges:

"there's no hope, no future. Being in a Loyalist band is often central to their lives. They are cleaned up, in uniform, having a sense of pride playing an instrument, the crowds come out to cheer them on. The Northern Ireland Assembly has generated thousands of skilled, well paid jobs recently, but many young people from the most deprived areas won't have access to them."

Does Sammy see any end to it? "I would generally be an optimistic person, but 'hope deferred maketh the heart sick' (Proverbs 13:12). It's as if my hope is on hold, there are times especially when there are community tensions and strained community relations you do feel sick."

Cluan Place,
East Belfast

Revd Gary Mason was from 1999 until recently the senior minister at the East Belfast Mission on the lower Newtownards Road, now the site of the spanking new Skainos Centre. East Belfast has had more relatively recent confrontations than other areas in Belfast – in 2001–2002 when five Protestants were killed and locals remain convinced that the IRA was to blame; and the June 2010 attacks on Short Strand, which Revd Mason worked with Revd Mervyn Gibson and Sammy Douglas to resolve. Asked why it is East Belfast that is the persistent site of interface and interracial violence, he notes that due to its proximity to the shipyards, this is the largest Protestant neighbourhood, the bastion of Belfast Protestantism. While middle class people can leave, many working class people feel tied to the area, and for them territory and identity are terribly important. Perhaps it will become the next Twaddell, if parading issues are not resolved – and he adds that many Republicans do not understand the importance of the Union Jack to the Protestant community, so many of whom have served in the armed forces. "Their sons' bodies could come home from Iraq or Afghanistan wrapped in that flag", he says.

Ironically, the Skainos Centre was formally opened by First Minister Peter Robinson and deputy First Minister Martin McGuinness in December 2012, just as the flag protests were kicking off. Skainos and the East Belfast Mission were an offshoot of Forthspring, on the Springfield Road. Skainos means 'tent', and it was intended to be a place where difficult conversations could take place. Revd Mason sees the peace process as having different levels – and says there is a tendency to see things through an economic lens rather than a psychological lens. Despite its friendliness, Northern Ireland can be an aggressive and angry place, he says. Behind closed curtains and doors, there is aggression, abuse and bigotry.

It may seem that progress towards removing the walls has been painfully slow; sometimes it seems as though the projects are treading water or going up the down escalator. But, consciously or unconsciously, the IFI approach has been extremely clever. The IFI programmes are a good case study in why and how targets and outcomes do not create change in themselves. By focussing on specific targets – a given gate, wall, fence or other interface related feature, grilles on windows for example, or blighted land, or a derelict house, the programme has forced community groups to identify and address all the other issues which must be tackled before a given structure can be altered or removed. Community groups also learn that they may not be the people who have control over the many factors at play – and yet they are responsible to the funder for the change being made. They discover that negotiation and influence with a wide range of stakeholders are key elements in making change happen, and that relationships and conversations are the building blocks of change processes. For real change to happen, attitudes need to change.

They have also become more aware of the whole picture of regeneration needs for their communities. There is a new and emerging interface which presents both tensions and possibilities for these severely deprived areas, and that is the interface between community development and business development.

All the peacewalls programmes have needed to identify and face the massively complex challenge of making real change happen. There is the range of practical issues: the ownership of the walls, the need to fund changes or removals, the issues to do with bureaucracy, responsibilities and permissions. There are the complex social issues: the legacy of fear and insecurity, poverty, lack of confidence. There is the sometimes uncertain mandate of community workers themselves and the shadowy 'gatekeepers'; there are the negotiations with residents' groups. There is the elastic and amorphous dependency of the local grassroots peace process on the wider and higher political process – itself painfully slow. There is the specificity of the way all these factors play out in the dynamic of each unique interface.

All the peacewalls programmes have discovered that ultimately it is relationships and conversations that make change happen. And very often it is agendas for power and control, or simply bumbling incompetence, that can block it. Community workers have developed a shared understanding, learning from one another, about good practice: leafleting all residents, going door-to-door, convening small and large groups to present and discuss ideas and plans for the interfaces, aiming to persuade and change mindsets. Ultimately it is the actual experience of having a barrier removed, of being in a more normal environment, that is likely to alter the dynamic within a given community from the self-reinforcing 'vicious circle' into 'virtuous circle'.

Chapter Four

A MILE IN YOUR SHOES: TRAUMA, FORMER PARAMILITARIES AND YOUTH

"If I could be you and you could be me for just one hour
If we could find a way to get inside each other's mind
If you could see me through your eyes instead of your ego
I believe you'd be surprised to see that you'd been blind

Walk a mile in my shoes, walk a mile in my shoes
And before you abuse, criticise and accuse
Walk a mile in my shoes

And yet we spend the day throwing stones at one another
'Cause I don't think or wear my hair the same way you do
Well I may be common people but I'm your brother
And when you strike out and try to hurt me it's a hurtin' you" [1]

D URING THE WEST BELFAST Festival in August 2014, at St Mary's College on the Falls Road, there is an excruciatingly poignant exhibition, with the title 'In their Footsteps – Setting the Truth Free'. It was compiled to lobby the Irish and British governments for an independent mechanism to examine the legacy of the conflict. On either side of several corridors are neatly arranged 150 pairs of shoes, donated by families of victims. To see each one properly we need to bend or kneel. Each has one of the fuzzy snapshot images of the deceased that are a familiar feature of Belfast iconography; most have a typed or handwritten account of the victim's death and what is known of the perpetrator; like fingerprints, each pair is stamped with the weight and unique impression of its owner.

The display recalls the piles of shoes retrieved from concentration camps in Holocaust memorial exhibits. It also brings to mind the idea of 'walking in the other's shoes', the theme of a song sung by Elvis Presley and his Belfast doppelganger Jim 'The King' Brown. The song echoes a cliché of conflict resolution processes, no less applicable to Belfast than anywhere – the idea that reconciliation becomes possible when parties in conflict begin to 'walk in each other's shoes', and to see the world from the point of view of the other.

---

1 *Walk a Mile in My Shoes*, sung by Elvis Presley and Jim 'The King' Brown. Lyrics by Joe South (c) Sony / ATV Music Publishing LLC.

During my research on the walls and interfaces, three recurring themes emerged and became increasingly insistent. They overlapped and echoed with one another. To acknowledge each of the themes and their complex interrelationship requires making the compassionate choice to 'stand in the shoes of the other' and see the world from the other's point of view. The three themes are the high levels of conflict-related trauma in interface areas, the ongoing presence and role of former paramilitary combatants, and the problem of alienated working class young people. These are not the only issues at play in the complex system of the walls, but they are the ones that emerged and struck me most forcefully.

A key question for me was why, when there is no longer any serious violence around many of the interfaces, residents continue to object to their removal: a Department of Justice official recalls a fence that had no longer any role to play where the community was adamant it would not come down. A history of attacks there over 13 years ago was the driving force for the resistance.

Many people referred to or implied a certain 'stuckness' in the peace process now, over 15 years after the Belfast Agreement. Artist Rita Duffy explicitly refers to a "frozen numbness" in Northern Ireland, a central theme of her art. Others refer to the continuing impact of the flags protest and the 'toxic issue of the past'. Some complain of tiredness in their work for peace; others note that the necessary conversations, although they have not stopped, have slowed or faltered.

We saw the car stop, and a guy in a black leather jacket got out and pulled down his balaclava. I shouted "Jack!" and he turned around and was shot, and then fell down and was shot again on the ground. Then the guy turned and pointed his gun at me – click, click – he was out of ammunition. This was '82. Jack's mother asked me two questions, "Was he happy before he died? Why did he not shoot the two of you?"

During February and March 2014, Sally Smyth, coordinator of the Grace Women's Development Group in Ardoyne, referred over 100 individual people to the new Victims and Survivors Service (VSS) for assessment and treatment. "The legacy of the conflict is just as raw as when the conflict was happening," she says. Asked about how significant the levels of trauma are when it comes to difficulties in changing or removing walls and building cross community trust, she says: "All of it. Everything is due to trauma."

According to the Haass proposals:

"The various [political agreements in Northern Ireland] did not give society the tools or venues to fully grapple with the pain and anger that are inevitably the legacy of generations of violence and conflict. The paths made available over the years have not proven equal to that demanding task" (Haass 2013).

After many false and inadequate starts in policy, practice and delivery of resources, perhaps themselves evidence of communal denial of the reality and prevalence of trauma in Northern Ireland (Templer, PhD Thesis 2013), the Victims and Survivors Service (VSS) finally made its services accessible with, from January 2014, effective publicity and a minimum of bureaucracy. Between April 2012 when the new service started up, and the end of March 2014, there were over 3,000 expressions of interest.

There are many different reactions to trauma. Some people are naturally resilient or recover quickly. Others suffer delayed reactions. Others still suffer long term chronic symptoms. For some people, therapeutic interventions are helpful; for others their trauma is increased and complicated by the need to search for truth and justice. Grieving processes, says Sara Templer, may be interrupted by the unresolved search for truth.

The Irish word for Troubles, *Troiblóidí*, says poet Pádraig Ó Tuama, speaking during the 4 Corners Festival in January 2014, references bereavement. "Sorry for your troubles," say the Irish to one another on the occasion of a death. Some 3,600 deaths took place in Northern Ireland, and some 40,000 were injured during the years of conflict – not in absolute terms a hugely high number compared to other conflict situations, but amongst the highest rates proportionate to the size of the population. Almost 40% of the deaths took place in the five interface postcode areas of North and West Belfast, and a total

Serpentine Road

of a further 10% took place in the postcode areas for Short Strand, East Belfast, lower Ormeau and Whitewell (Fay 1999). Information gathered from 882 clients of the VSS, who responded to a survey of 1,000 who presented themselves between 1 April and the end of June 2013, shows that the postcodes of the greatest numbers of clients presenting to VSS correlates very closely to the postcode distribution of deaths during the conflict. Ninety-four percent of the VSS clients presented with one or more symptoms of trauma. The great majority of clients are coming to VSS in respect of incidents which took place between 1969 and 1998, with the expected peak in 1972, the year in which by far the greatest number of deaths took place. This correlates with research that suggests it can take 20 years or longer for victims and survivors to present themselves for treatment (Hansard, 9 Oct 2013).

According to the World Mental Health Survey, with a lifetime prevalence of Post Traumatic Stress Disorder of 8.8% (and 5.1% experiencing it at the time of the survey), Northern Ireland ranks highest in the world; and third or fourth in the world for the lifetime occurrence of any mental disorder (39.1%), anxiety (22.6%), mood disorders (mostly depression – 18.8%) and substance abuse (usually alcohol – 14.1%).

Furthermore, it has been estimated by the Commission for Victims and Survivors (CVS) that overall some 500,000 people in Ireland, almost a third of the population, were directly affected by death and/or injury – either as a victim, perpetrator, witness, family member or close friend. A relatively small number of them are asking for help; nonetheless, agencies and groups report being overwhelmed by the high and rising numbers coming forwards. In October 2014, it was reported that the VSS is receiving more than 500 calls a week, and more than ten people are approaching the service for help every day. Sixty percent have not been seen before. Meanwhile in June 2014, the budget was cut in real terms by 30% (*Belfast Telegraph* 29 Oct 2014). Having conducted extensive fieldwork in this area, Sara Templer reflects, "We are just scratching the surface". She writes to me later:

"It can be said that the language of victim/survivor has defined a sector within Northern Ireland's voluntary arena. As a result, when individuals now self-describe as a victim or a survivor, they are often identifying with this whole construct, and the baggage it entails. This is a point perhaps best understood in the negative: some people refrain from seeking help because they don't want to identify with this construct.

When I say we are 'scratching the surface' of the trauma problem, I mean that Northern Ireland is only starting to get to grips with the traumatic effect of the conflict in general terms. But I also mean that we should be aware that not all the people that have been affected will come forward to seek help in the way that it is offered. For ideological or personal reasons and just because they may not make the connection between certain things that have happened in their lives and their psychosocial wellbeing, some people will never seek support in a setting that defines them as victim/survivor. If we acknowledge this, we have to face up to the necessity of ensuring that public services in general are sensitive and responsive to signs of trauma – eg schools – particularly with regard to parent interactions – housing, hospitals, care for the elderly. A huge task, compounded by the context of financial austerity. Very challenging."

It is not unreasonable to suggest therefore that we are not only speaking of large numbers of individuals experiencing levels of trauma, but also of traumatised communities.

"In Northern Ireland, the level of casualties, the prolonged period of conflict and the marked divisions created in urban and rural landscapes, even after demilitarisation, make a strong case for arguing that residents have experienced collective trauma, trauma which extends beyond individual suffering to whole communities" (Herbert 2013).

Community workers interviewed for this book spoke of the high levels of depression, anxiety, chronic health problems, alcohol and prescription drug dependency they are dealing with on a regular basis. According to Mike Tomlinson of Queen's University Belfast, "All conflict experiences other than imprisonment are associated with a higher risk of poor physical and mental health, and most are associated with lower life expectancy" (*Poverty and Social Exclusion Survey* 2012).

The denial, repression and symptoms of trauma operate on a social as well as an individual level, writes Judith Herman (1992). Colin Graham recalls that British Prime Minister Tony Blair said in 1997 that it was time to forget the past. "Blair knew that the intention of the [Belfast] Agreement was to teach Northern Ireland amnesia." "Remembering was, temporarily, officially forgotten. Meanwhile, the 'present past' continued to press on the present consciousness of those living in the North, and as Stephanie Lehner points out, 'the temporality that trauma introduces seems, paradoxically, to remain forever 'outside history.'" However, "when trauma is pushed 'outside history' its voice seeks, continually, to find a way back, to be heard". This "awful dialectic of suppression leads to what Jacques Derrida described as a 'hauntology', a ghost which stalks that which represses it" (Graham 2013).

There is a widespread lack of understanding of transgenerational and communal trauma. In November 2014, Belfast website *The Detail* reported that anti-depressant usage in Northern Ireland far exceeds that in England and Wales – but questioned a link between these statistics and the Troubles because usage is also high among people too young to have directly experienced the conflict (*Irish Times*, 17 Nov 2014). Of course, high usage among younger people may be explained by the transgenerational nature of trauma.

"There has naturally been a strong concentration on individual pain and loss, often to the neglect of whole communities who have been victimised during the conflict. These were the communities that were least equipped to deal with the added burden because they were already the most economically and socially deprived" (Consultative Group on the Past 2009).

Speaking at a conference on 'Trauma in Northern Ireland' at the University of Ulster at Coleraine in September 2014, David Bolton, director of the Initiative for Conflict Related Trauma, said: "we have one hell of a psychological burden on this community that we have not addressed" and spoke of the "toxic impact on the community" combined with the effect on second and third generations. Theatre director Paula McFetridge says: "Trauma is like water, it will always find its way through."

John Paul Lederach says: "A group's identity is linked to what its members remember and keep alive" including "the collective memory of times they were violated by the other". The trauma "remains as part of the unconscious psyche of group identity and is passed down across generations." Therefore, trauma healing must be "understood and developed in collective and communal forms" (Lederach & Lederach 2010).

The three key symptoms of trauma are: firstly, hyper arousal – the survivor has persistent expectations of danger and is hyper vigilant, on permanent alert; secondly, intrusion – the indelible imprint of the traumatic moment; and thirdly, constriction – a numbness or frozenness, particularly of emotion. Survivors may also experience generalised anxiety symptoms and fears (Herman 1992). Geraldine O'Kane of Greater Whitewell Community Surgery says:

"For security, everyone sticks to where they are from. They give their children little freedom – they say 'don't be going here or there'. It's really hard for the mummies. Every mummy worries about the future for their children – 'I hope I can keep them alive'. They always had to keep the family as normal as possible, meals – breakfast, lunch, dinner – clean clothes, the house still ran. Then, when they are older, the women find they can't cope."

Andrew Sutherland of WAVE Trauma Centre, which has treated 3,600 clients so far and is experiencing increasing demand, notes that conflict related trauma is "not simply a collection of symptoms", but political violence is "laden with social meaning". The Northern Ireland experience of trauma is complicated by a number of factors: the political context; the level of political denial of the problem and failure to address it over several decades in a coherent and effective manner; the concentration of violence and its after effects in a small number of mostly urban areas. Political violence doesn't just affect the individual, says Andrew Sutherland, it affects their relationship to others and to society. Because they experienced the violence within these enclosed environments, there are continual reminders – anniversaries and memorials – and ongoing fear. They have less opportunity to recover. The levels of trauma being as high as they are, it is also likely that a significant proportion of those working with survivors – as group facilitators, and counsellors, for example – are suffering from denial and post-trauma symptoms themselves.

The walls are "the structures that remind us that the hostility, fear and anger of the past remain alive and continue to threaten the peace of people and communities on both sides" (CRC 2008). "The walls keep people settled in their innermost life," says Geraldine O'Kane, "The violence is fresh in their minds." "No matter how many peacewalls you put up, the Loyalist death squads still came in," says Maureen, from Ardoyne. "The biggest barrier for any community is fear. Fear holds back confidence and a positive attitude. The fear is of the past, it's very real, it's fear for my children. I would never walk past Twaddell camp."

Maureen's experience illustrates perfectly what cognitive therapist Brendan Armstrong, who also spoke at the Coleraine conference, describes as the "puzzle" of Post Traumatic Stress Disorder (PTSD). It is that the memory of a *past* event – and in the case of Belfast, often a series of events, or indeed, in the case of Ardoyne and other areas, the decades of dangers, surveillance and continual intrusion into people's lives and homes by the security forces – is projected into anxiety about the *future*.

The processing of the trauma, says Armstrong, creates not only the past/future "puzzle" but also the dilemma that the survivor's strategies for protection against and to control the perceived threat – which include hypervigilance, avoiding walking in certain areas, and the "frozen numbness" – are also likely to prevent healthy processing and moving on from the trauma. "Even normally safe environments may come to feel dangerous, for the survivor can never be assured that she will not encounter some reminder of the trauma" (Herman 1992). This has led, I suspect, to a level of communal trauma which plays out as endemic fear and mistrust of the 'other' community and leads to resistance to removal of the walls and interfaces. It is almost as if the walls are being 'held up' by the trauma.

Sara Templer has noted the use of 'victims and survivors' language. The relevant agencies use both words, but in common parlance one often hears one or the other used alone. Some believe that the language, mentality, experience of victimhood and associated feelings of powerlessness have become endemic in interface communities – it is, says Ravenscroft, "the basis for dependency on grants and grant-funded employment in interface areas." There has been, she says, "the construction of a communal identity as victimised" (Ravenscroft 2006). Feminists like Judith Herman tend to prefer the word 'survivors' because it emphasises a person's ability to overcome painful events and circumstances. "Healing is not a journey for the faint of heart", write John Paul and Angela Jill Lederach. "It takes courage, a process accurately characterised as heroic. With considerable insight many prefer the name survivor over the designation of victim to describe this journey" (Lederach & Lederach 2010).

Much of the literature about trauma focusses on the journey of recovery. If we accept

Alexandra Park

that communities as well as individuals can be traumatised, and taking a systems approach, can we extrapolate from what is known about the individual recovery process and ask whether similar processes can apply to traumatised communities? Just as we speak of individuals as victims and survivors, can we also speak about victim and survivor communities – and ask what would be the characteristics of a survivor community?

To begin with, there is the importance of empowerment. Herman says that "no intervention that takes power away from the survivor can possibly foster her recovery, no matter how much it appears to be in her best interest" (1992). This supports the prevalent notion that communities need to lead on decisions about the walls and interfaces.

The restoration of normality, says Herman, depends on public acknowledgement of the traumatic event and on some form of community action. This implies that public and political recognition of the suffering of particular communities is critical to enabling those communities to move forward. Symbolic gestures are also important. Herman notes the transformative power of the Vietnam Veterans Memorial in Washington DC, which has become a site of spiritual pilgrimage, a "sort of cathedral" for veterans and their families. The widely respected Eames-Bradley report recommended there should be an annual day of reflection and reconciliation in Northern Ireland and a shared memorial to the conflict (Consultative Group on the Past 2009).

The three processes for survivor recovery, according to Herman, are the journeys from, firstly, unpredictable danger to reliable safety; secondly from dissociated trauma to acknowledged memory; thirdly, from stigmatised isolation to restored social connection. Applied to the notion of survivor communities, this would affirm the value of current initiatives around community safety and the widespread monitoring of interfaces by groups of volunteers and with mobile phone networks. It would also affirm initiatives in cross community storytelling and explains the importance of local memorial sites to victims of the conflict that have sprung up in sectarian areas. Lederach says that the capacity is required to "recognise and build imaginative narrative that can link past and future rather than force a false choice between them" (Lederach 2005). Eamonn Baker of the Derry/Londonderry based group Towards Understanding and Healing notes that evidence shows that their work is effective "particularly where the programme is cross community and when participants have had the opportunity, perhaps for the first time, to hear the other's story". Geraldine O Donnell from Top of the Hill, a Catholic neighbourhood in Derry, describes how the 40th anniversary of the bombing of Annie's Bar, in which two Catholics and Protestant were killed, was marked on 29 December 2012, with Mass and a candlelight procession attended by both Catholics and Protestants.

Perhaps we can also speculate what the move from "stigmatised isolation to restored social connection" might look like if applied to traumatised communities. It might imply the transition from abnormality to normality for interface communities – that they become physically, economically and symbolically 'reconnected' to the rest of Belfast.

Recovery, says Herman, like a marathon, is a "test of endurance, requiring long preparation and repetitive practice" (Herman 1992). The Lederachs also speak of the iterative and repetitive nature of social healing. They ask the key question: "How do people with collective experiences of violence reconcile and heal from experiences that penetrate below and beyond words?"

Healing, peacebuilding and constructive change are not a straightforward linear journey from A to B. The Lederachs suggest that repetitiveness and circularity can be positive components of change – the sensation of repetition and "going round in circles" may not necessarily be negative. They also emphasise the enormous complexity of social (and personal) healing, which involves "many things happening at once". Social healing is best explored and understood at the "level of real-life, face-to-face relationships". As an alternative to the – prevalent – linear metaphors about change, they propose a "sonic metaphor" and suggest the journey of reconciliation emerges from a "mix of voices". Reconciliation as sound suggests the need for constant nurturing, circling engagement, mixing and remixing of voices and "the repeated deepening of meaningful conversation" (Lederach & Lederach 2010).

An empowered survivor may often make a conscious choice to face danger, says Herman. "As the survivor sheds her victim identity, she may also choose to renounce parts of herself that have felt almost intrinsic to her being." This echoes the way many speak about the walls and interfaces – they have become so much part of the landscape they cannot imagine Belfast without them. Yet to the visitor they almost always appear shocking, alien, even 'grotesque'. Could they be seen as the paraphernalia of communal trauma that could eventually be consciously discarded by survivor communities?

Frank Liddy was born on Cooper Street in the lower Falls in 1954, within the sound of Clonard Monastery bell. He had Protestant neighbours and all he knew was "certain times of the year, the neighbours stopped speaking to me. When the flags went up at the front, I went out the back." His cousin was murdered off the Shankill Road in 1972 – it was a huge funeral.

He and a friend, Mark, decided in 1976 to go to London and the night before they went they called into the Club Bar on University Road – "a safe place, home of hippies, students, rogues and charlatans." Mark got claustrophobia, so they left – Bang – Frank was the first into the dust and dirt and dark of the bar after the bomb went off. After he got home, his father took his clothes, covered in blood and flesh, and burned them right away. "I woke up the next day and thought, there has to be another way."

It was, he says, "fight, or flight towards a solution." And for him the solution was jazz and meditation. "Zen and jazz are one and the same: they help me understand." He became a Buddhist, and having seen the link between mental health problems and the conflict, trained as a counsellor and in 1991 started working with people with mental health problems, "a group of people tortured by voices who didn't have a voice." He saw the link between mental health and the Troubles. "People told stories. It was probably misdiagnosed PTSD."

He became a co-founder of the Black Mountain Zen Centre in Belfast, has been one of the faith chaplains to two Lord Mayors, Máirtín Ó Muilleoir and Nichola Mallon, and, with Revd Bill Shaw of 174 Trust on Duncairn Avenue, successfully promoted the proclamation of Belfast as a City of Compassion.

This book aimed from its conception to take a non-sensationalist approach; as a researcher I had no intention or need to be intrusive and I did not ask explicit questions about either traumatic experiences during the conflict or paramilitary links – however, when asked about their background or their involvement with the interfaces, many interviewees spontaneously shared such stories either on or off the record.

Paramilitary involvement often results from trauma and feeds into more trauma – there is an inherent link between paramilitary involvement and trauma. Sometimes people joined one of the paramilitary organisations because they had witnessed violence and wanted to defend their communities, and of course once they became involved there was a greater chance they would be involved in violence. A high proportion of former paramilitaries have suffered the effects of trauma, including poor physical and mental health – two thirds of the sample in one study were drinking at hazardous or dependency levels (Jamieson 2010).

"Like the victims, many of whom can never really forget and who live their everyday existence as a constant battle to transcend the past, ex-combatants, who might be construed as victims themselves, at least in different ways, are unable to put the past behind them because of the way post-conflict policy continues to marginalise them" (Brewer et al 2013).

Former paramilitaries continue to wield significant influence around the interfaces both for good and ill, by virtue of their former role. It may be difficult to generalise about them but they are a social phenomenon in Belfast of the last 50 years that is impossible to ignore. There are no reliable figures for the numbers of former politically motivated prisoners in Northern Ireland, but a number of estimates suggest there may be up to 30,000, some 90% of whom are now over 50 – they count as a significant proportion of Northern Ireland's older population (Jamieson et al 2010) and are highly concentrated in the interface communities (InterAction 2005).

Skegoneill Avenue

Some sources have suggested that paramilitaries have exploited the levels of fear, exacerbated by trauma, in interface communities in order to maintain control: "Fear has been used as a tool by both political and paramilitary groups to create and sustain territoriality" (Monaghan 2013). One interviewee tells me: "We all want paramilitaries to go away"; another says: "I'm not sure how useful it is to talk about paramilitaries anymore."

Nonetheless they remain a part of the complex dynamic of the interfaces. Some former combatants seem and would like to be seen to have transcended their pasts. A number are directly employed in community and peacewalls programmes and, for some, particularly Republicans, transition from activism on behalf of their communities as defenders and fighters to community development work has been seamless and has included getting professional qualifications and development. Ex-combatants were often in their early 20s when they went to prison, where they may have spent several or many years, and they used the opportunity to educate themselves, debate and reflect. They have built relationships with other former prisoners across the divide: "It's about talking to each other and getting to know where each other is coming from." A Springfield Road Loyalist is quoted as saying: "Because of the relationships and trust that has built up, I think this community would find it hard to fight each other again" (InterAction 2005). "The movement from involvement in armed conflict towards conflict transformation, community development and reconciliation is often a personal journey which frequently began in prison" (Persic 2004).

A senior PSNI officer says that ex-combatants have played a generally positive role in the peace process over the last ten years: "Would we have achieved the level of change without them? I don't think so." "Paramilitaries have an interest in the interfaces, and if you want to work at the interfaces, you have to make a choice", says one community worker. "The positive contribution of ex-combatants to the peace process has been largely underestimated" and deserves recognition (InterAction 2005).

However, during the time of research for this book, there was widely known feuding in North Belfast between and among the Loyalist UDA and UVF, some of whose members were employed in peacewalls projects – and indeed two were arrested and charged in 2014 in relation to a shooting incident (*Irish News,* 30 Aug 14).

The image that came to mind was the double face of Janus. Janus, in Roman mythology is a powerful God, usually shown with two faces – one looking ahead to the future, the other backwards to the past. Janus was the God of beginnings and endings, of change and transition, of gates, doors, doorways and passageways – in other words of liminality and threshold places. For sure he would be the Roman God of interfaces. "Janus presided over the beginning and ending of conflict and hence war and peace" (en.wikipedia.org/wiki/Janus).

Paramilitaries have this ambivalent role, they embody the spirit of Janus – suspended between looking forward and looking back. Some face absolutely towards the future. There are "some public, genuine and upfront paramilitaries", who as one community worker says, "have lasted, been true to their word, and got into community work without bullying, and they have become respected in the sector". Some former combatants have been actively involved in public dialogues and initiatives to dissuade others from following a similar path. Some have participated, for example, in 'From Prisons to Peace', an educational programme funded by Peace III designed for the Key Stage 4 curriculum for Citizenship Education (age 14–16). The programme includes text resources and panel discussions with prisoners and is intended as a "way in which political ex-prisoners could use their narrative to engage with young people to demythologise the conflict and encourage them to make a positive contribution to their communities." An evaluation conducted by OFMdFM discovered clear evidence of the positive effects of the programme, including increased levels of young people's awareness of the conflict; it also demonstrated that young people are interested and ready to engage with the controversies of the conflict. It had an impact on their attitudes towards the 'other' community and their intended levels of support for violence and political engagement. Its most effective element was the panel discussions, when well chaired, with former prisoners.

At the same time, some are unable to shed their previous behaviour – "it's hard to give up bullying if that's your culture". Paramilitaries are widely associated with criminality, thuggery, intimidation, drug dealing, and orchestration of ongoing violence and rioting by young people at interfaces. And some appear to be literally 'two-faced' – playing a double game – as one woman community leader says: "Some have learned to put on a front and present themselves as peacemakers."

This Janus-like nature is expressed when one Loyalist ex-prisoner says during a panel discussion for American students of conflict resolution: "Just because someone has a past doesn't mean they shouldn't have a future". In 2007, Bill Rolston wrote that the process in Ireland of DDR – demilitarisation, demobilisation and reintegration – had failed in a number of ways; there was no comprehensive and strategic attempt to reintegrate ex-prisoners in Northern Ireland (Rolston 2007). Former prisoners suffer continuing stigma and are "permanently excluded from certain occupations and activities" and this has "perpetuated their social and economic marginalisation" (Jamieson 2010). In 2007, a UK government working group set out to address matters regarding former prisoners and issued guidelines recommending that: "any conviction for a conflict related offence that precedes the Good Friday Agreement (April 1998) should not be taken into account unless it is materially relevant to the employment sought" (quoted in Carroll 2014). The Eames-Bradley report later noted that the guidelines were not being well used by employers and that former prisoners continued to be disadvantaged. The report recommended that the guidelines be "incorporated into statute and made applicable in the provision of goods, facilities and services as well as recruitment" (Carroll 2014). Jim Allister, the founder of Traditional Unionist Voice (TUV), led the campaign to block implementation of the 2009 Eames-Bradley report, on the grounds that payments should not be made to terrorists. It had recommended that a £12,000 payment should be given to the closest relative of every person killed during the conflict. Allister also promoted a Private Member's Bill to prevent former prisoners being employed as "special advisers" to ministers, which was passed in June 2013.

Attitudes in the statutory agencies concerned with the interfaces to former combatants vary considerably. Some civil servants, funders and bureaucrats say they need to be careful they are not supporting an ongoing military presence; others acknowledge that they have to work with former combatants but agonise about it. "They have a place as community leaders, but were they elected?" One civil servant expresses deep distaste: "They have brought nothing to the party. They should just go away. They are holding onto power and there is something not right about that." Theologian Dr Geraldine Smyth, Associate Professor in the Irish School of Ecumenics, notes that the underlying message of the walls and the murals to outsiders is "prepared for peace, ready for war". "From behind the walls, the prevailing view is that the boundary must be kept secure, strong," she says. "Where there is internal paramilitary domination, their interests dictate that the boundaries be kept 'hot', in order to maintain their power, under the rhetoric of 'protecting their culture.'" Jack McKee of New Life City Church says something similar: "Closed gates continue to give the paramilitaries a *raison d'être*. The gates continue to highlight and represent division."

Several church workers explicitly spoke of the importance of forgiveness. A Presbyterian minister and community leader said: "I made myself a promise; I would never worry about anyone's past. I work with all sorts." Another Christian community worker quoted Oscar Wilde: "Every saint has a past and every sinner has a future." There is a huge difference, he says, "between paramilitaries who are making a contribution and those who are engaging in criminality – in which case they should be defined as just that, criminals."

"The influence of paramilitaries is sophisticated," says one community leader. "It's about power and control – that's what our society is based on. It's all about wielding power." Paramilitaries often, particularly in Nationalist communities, held and continue to hold considerable status and respect as leaders, and this has been translated naturally into community building roles. Their role as – albeit unelected – community leaders is acknowledged – the shadow side of that appears to be levels of bullying, particularly of women and young people. They are credited with the influence to help deliver a peaceful parades season in 2014 or to "bring the city to its knees" with the flags dispute of winter 2012–2013.

A decade ago, InterAction on the Springfield Road produced a report on the interfaces which concluded that "to put it bluntly, ex-combatants are part of the problem and they must be part of the solution" (Persic 2004). They both reflect and help to shape the stresses and tensions of their communities, says the senior PSNI officer. "They have power in the absence of the landlords" – in other words, wherever and to the extent that there is a vacuum in elected legitimate leadership, that lacuna is likely to continue to be filled by former paramilitaries.

There is some anecdotal evidence of women community workers being bullied and intimidated by paramilitaries – primarily but not exclusively Loyalists. One experienced community worker says: "I have always worked with paramilitaries but will not work for them. There's a danger they create another division in an already fractured community". The reality of such behaviour is backed up by reports from the Women's Resource and Development Agency which suggests that in working class areas there is still widespread paramilitary control, "viewed as synonymous with male control", and that women are effectively silenced in their communities, also fearing that their sons will be recruited to paramilitary groups (Carvill 2013).

Eileen Weir of the Greater North Belfast Women's Network says that the community in Tigers Bay is not being properly consulted regarding the peacewalls and interfaces, and that community work, particularly in Loyalist areas, is being controlled by 'gatekeepers' – the term she prefers to 'ex-combatants'. Women, she says, have been forgotten – even though they had been involved in cross community work for the last 30–40 years, well before the peace agreement. She is working to get women more involved in community decision-making. She is working with groups of women in Tigers Bay and New Lodge in a project funded by OFMdFM to photograph and document the areas they want cleared up and issues taken care of, such as derelict houses, waste ground, mental health and antisocial behaviour. Things are changing, she says. Young women are getting more involved; they "don't want to be living behind walls", she says.

Academic Fidelma Ashe of the University of Ulster has written that peacemaking and non-violence were traditionally associated with women in the Northern Irish context; women have a long history of using their skills and creativity to engage in cross community dialogue and community activism. Meanwhile, the prisoners, through their engagement in resistance in prison, developed "strong analytical, negotiation and debating skills." They have taken on leadership roles in the community, leading to an "erasing of women's agency, skills and histories of community work" (Ashe, n.d.). In a further paper, Ashe and Harland note that there is a legacy of "militarised masculinities" and that the social conditions that shaped these masculinities have not been sufficiently addressed. They note the emergence of a "hyper masculinity" among young men, caused by their struggle to gain respect, independence and power through developing physical toughness, rather than building a career. They call for more critical analysis of the "complex dynamics of ethnic power and economic disempowerment" (Ashe & Harland 2014). At the CRC policy conference in June 2014, Paul Nolan, author of the Peace Monitoring Report (2014), raised the issue of "toxic masculinity", quoting the work of Carol Craig in Glasgow (Craig 2010) and pointing out that these issues are not unique to Belfast – although it could be argued that the significance of any social problem is magnified against the backdrop of post-conflict Belfast.

In October 2014, Briege Gadd wrote in the *Irish News* that there is "unfinished business in the whole peace process with regard to paramilitarism and in some cases the retention of the scaffolding of paramilitary control in some areas". There had been "a lack of a strategy or monitored plan for addressing the needs of paramilitaries" (*Irish News,* 23 Oct 2014). John Paul Lederach talks about "political transitions" and draws a parallel between the journey that paramilitaries have taken from combat tactics to political participation and the journey that policy in Ireland needed to take from a partisan RUC to a widely accepted and better integrated PSNI. Generally such changes take about ten years, he says, from recognition of the need to actual change.

Glenn Bradley, a former British paratrooper and Sean Murray, a former IRA member, who grew up 200 yards from one another on either side of the interface, spoke together of their friendship at the E3 meeting to launch the Anti-Sectarian Charter in April 2014. Responding to Dr Orna Young's challenge that "the narrative has been one of romanticisation of the conflict", Sean asked: "How do you remove romance from the discussion? There was no romance – we spent the best years of our life in prison."

Just as there is a link between the continuing presence of paramilitaries in interface areas and trauma, so there is a connection between paramilitaries and young people[1], and between trauma and young people. There is, says one community worker, "a fear of the past and a fear of young people now". This gives young people – at least as a social force – a level of systemic power that they are probably unaware of. This is what Revd Lesley Carroll refers to as the paradox of power and powerlessness. Those, including communities and young people, who feel most powerless exert a contradictory degree of power.

> ## Ronan
> There is no trouble any more… not really. There used to be 'round the corner at Torrens when the Protestants lived there but they don't live there anymore. The Peace Line is knocked down. Aye, it's knocked down now. There is houses being built there now. Well it's just like a big wall. They just knocked it down and they are building houses at the back of me, It is right behind me, that Peace Line, the Peace Line is not there anymore, like, It's all houses getting built like. Well the houses are not really done, they are only getting built now. They are nearly done like.
>
> There used to be trouble in it all the time, The Peace Line was took away about three years ago and there was nothing there and now they are building houses now because the people have moved away… Aye. So it's all-Catholic now. There used to be… there was a few Protestants living there, but they're like kind of old. But they have moved out now. It's all new houses now.
>
> Aye, they were put out like. Well, I wouldn't say they were really put out but there was always rioting and all. The Protestants lived on Torrens Avenue. We used to throw stones like, when we were younger. But we didn't do any big things to put them out. It was people in the area… all older people. I was only about 12 when they left. They weren't really told to get out. They just all moved out… they just couldn't take it anymore. They were getting their windows broken nearly every night. They couldn't take it so they just moved.

Young people – at least collectively, in groups and gangs – are often experienced as a problem at the interfaces. They congregate in abandoned and unkempt spaces near

---

1 All quotes from young people are from *Our View*, the Quaker Cottage project facilitated by Rita Duffy and Rory Doherty, 2010.

the walls; they lob missiles at one another and across sectarian frontlines; they throw golf-balls, cans and bottles – whatever is on sale at the off-license, as one witty resident in a TV documentary put it – over the walls. They can find any gap in the barriers, as Chris O'Halloran of Belfast Interface Project said, and flow through spaces like water. They harass older people on the street, could be using or abusing alcohol or drugs, and make the streets feel unsafe. Sometimes, apparently, they take taxis to pre-arranged riot venues.

No one can say for sure whether and to what extent the behaviour is actually sectarian. Normal and relatively harmless teenage gang behaviour takes on a more serious note against the sectarian backdrop of Belfast. Rarely is there serious injury or damage to property but police sometimes appear flummoxed and outwitted – they need to move fast to keep up with gangs apparently able to congregate in a flash and disperse equally quickly. Sometimes there is Romeo and Juliet behaviour – couples actually dating on either side of the divide. According to one Short Strand community worker, young people who were segregated at school are meeting and mixing at college and then splitting up in the evenings to throw stones at each other. The senior PSNI officer recalls stopping a group crossing from a Loyalist into a Catholic area and being surprised to find they were a mixed group of friends: "We were shocked."

Many people believe young people's behaviour is orchestrated – either amongst young people themselves, using Facebook and Twitter, or by older and more sinister paramilitary elements. When hard drinking and drugs are involved, when sectarian attitudes take root, when there is exploitation by older people and/or paramilitaries, then matters become more serious. If these young people are indeed "young trainee warriors" or a future generation of terrorists, then it is more serious. Similarly there is great concern when young people land in court and are convicted. There are justifiable concerns about creating another criminalised generation.

Holy Cross,
Crumlin Road

"Young people are being manipulated and abused by sinister people", said Sean Murray at the E3 Anti-Sectarianism Charter Launch. Dr Orna Young replied that if this was happening and if Twitter and Facebook were being used to recruit young people then the problem needed to be named and dealt with as a child abuse and protection issue.

Coleen

I live in Belfast, I am 16. I don't know what to say but… I now live in Grosvenor. I lived in Ballymurphy. I was born in the New Lodge but I was moved. I always moved about like. New Lodge, Springfield, Poleglass, Lenadoon, and then to me Granny's and then to Ballymurphy. I didn't even really realise it like, I was a kid. Dunno 'cos when we lived in Poleglass my Mummy swapped with my aunt and uncle because they weren't allowed to live in the Springfield no more. 'Cos my family were put out of the Springfield years ago, they weren't allowed in it.

I have had the most memories in Ballymurphy. I stayed in my friend's house one night and we went to bed, but like we woke up. Well here Mummy, my friend's Mummy, woke us up the next morning and said, like "There is a bomb downstairs". Someone planted two pipe bombs in, like, under the front door and she lifted them and didn't know what they were. Then her son came and told her and we all had to get out of the house and the whole street was closed down, and the cops and all and the big robot came.

There is concern over young people because of the coincidence, the 'perfect storm', of a number of factors: a school system which is failing some pupils, in particular poor Protestant boys; a post-conflict culture in which the threat of recruitment of young people to violent sectarian causes remains; the transgenerational legacy of trauma; a lack of appropriate leisure facilities and activities – due, for example, to modern health and safety, child protection regulations and sensibilities, and, since the recession a lack of funding. In impoverished areas there has also been a lack of education and employment opportunities.

Fewer than 20% of Protestant boys receiving free school meals are leaving school with a minimum of five GCSEs, versus 34% of poorer Protestant girls, 33.2% of Catholic boys and 43% of Catholic girls. While nine out of ten secondary schools with the highest proportion of pupils receiving free school meals are Catholic and nine out of ten of those with the lowest proportion are Protestant, eight out of ten of the top selective schools are Catholic and five of nine non-selective are also Catholic (Bell 2013). While 76% of school leavers living within South Belfast's poshest BT9 postcode area, which includes the Malone and Lisburn Roads, go on to higher education, versus just 19% from BT13, and 21% from BT12, the interface areas of North Belfast. Over a quarter of those in higher education go to study in Britain (Nolan 2014).

Sara

Even if people say don't live in the past, live in the present it is hard for me not to do that because there is so much that happened. It is not easy for me to try and just don't think about it, when clearly I have to think about it. What me and my psychologist try to work on is trying to get, you know a library… put all the pieces into order, like all the books in order… filing cabinets, filling them in, so that is what we worked on, but sometimes now and again one pops out.

I get DLA for PTSD, it is called Post Traumatic Stress Disorder, that is what my psychologist had put it under. I get a high rate of DLA for it and I just got paid for that, it was just under 300 pound.

I don't know who I am.

Well I am going on the drink tonight. I plan to get smashed tonight. I will be fine, it's just in the house, it will be safe. I don't get hangovers.

While overall unemployment fell slightly in 2013, youth employment rose by 5% to 23.8%. Northern Ireland has the highest proportion in the UK of those categorised as 'NEETs' – not in education, employment or training – estimated at over 20%. A study of 1,000 NEETs by the University and College Union found that 37% of them rarely leave the house and 39% suffer from stress (Nolan 2014).

Young people have also inherited the effects of trauma, and second and third transgenerational trauma has not been adequately addressed in Northern Ireland, many agree. There are disturbing statistics on mental health among young people – the highest rates of self-harm and suicidal thoughts are among 20–24 year old males, significantly higher than in the Republic of Ireland. Research by Professor Mike Tomlinson at Queen's University Belfast has linked the increase in suicide to the legacy of the conflict:

"the key finding is that the cohort of children that grew up in the worst years of violence, during the 70s, have the highest and most rapidly increasing suicide rates, and account for the steep upward trend in suicide following the 1998 Agreement" (Tomlinson 2012, quoted in Nolan 2014).

Meanwhile, all across the interfaces areas, community and youth workers are bending over backwards to reach and respond to the needs of young people.

Revd Bill Shaw of 174 Trust has been running a group for the last five years of young people from New Lodge and the lower Shankill who are now aged 14–16. "We intentionally move them around and try to make the walls and interfaces irrelevant – but we still need to drive them. One day we did try to walk and got awful verbal abuse from a Catholic guy. I had told them, 'you'll be ok', so it was disconcerting." The group plays football, and has also had workshops and conversations about flags and emblems and the murals. Seamus Corr also tells a story about a cross community football group – they always want the others dropped off first so they can see the others' areas. This, according to the CRC study of Young People at the Interfaces, is how Catholic and Protestant young people refer to each other – as the Others (Bell 2013).

Cliftonville Community Regeneration Forum has had intense engagement with young people, says Manus Maguire, and believes it has led to a significant reduction in violence on the Cliftonpark Avenue in recent years. Detached teams make contact and offer mentoring and coaching. A Short Strand community worker talks about the effective long term relationships they have built with young people. Suffolk Lenadoon interface project has engaged young people in art projects and the results can be seen decorating the walls of the PSNI fortress on Stewartstown Road.

In Greater Whitewell, Geraldine O'Kane has a range of programmes for young people. There is Achieving Personal Potential (APP), for up to 30 young people, which tries to help them think differently about their lives, and uses art and team building. There's another, mixed group of 12, six from Whitewell and six from White City, working with volunteers and the police. The relationships have helped on recent weekends when there has been trouble on the bridge. She has put on a cross community roller disco, for two age groups, 5–9 and 10+ "all having fun, that's what kids should be doing." On Black Preceptory Saturday, an Orange march that takes place through the area on the last Saturday in August, she takes 25 Catholic kids away for the day – the march creates great anxiety for them. On Thursday nights they have a "bitching night" – "at least someone's listening to them". "Who's looking after our young people?" she asks. "We haven't got it with our leadership – the biggest thing for them is getting on the sick, the Disability Living Allowance, or living on drug dealing and sitting up till three or four in the morning on their computers."

Roisin

I live in a street with a big peace line… I grew up in it. It's alright like, but when I was growing up, there used to be a big hole at the top of the wall. People used to come down and put bricks through people's windows in the street, and throw big bricks over the wall. Like, we used to do bonfires at the top of the street, and they used to come over the wall and break them down and stuff… light them for us… before we were gonna light them.

I just thought the peace line was a big wall. But, like, everyone else in the house is sectarian and all, except for me, cuz I've been going to groups like this for years. Mixing with people. They're all just bigots and racists. Like, my Da's the most racist person I've ever met in my life. He hates Protestants and black people… Muslims more than anything else. He's in the RA and thinks he's the shit. I've never met anyone who hates Muslims more, I swear. My brother and I just tell him to wise up.

Like, all my best mates and all have had bad things happen to them in their lives

---

too, and we all randomly fitted together. And me and my best mate are constantly getting stoned. I'd never sit on my own and get stoned. I'm dependent on it already. I've been dependent on it for about a year. Before that I was just smoking it because everybody else was. The costs… the only thing bad about it is that it costs me too much money. I owe about £140 next week. I love just going out and getting wiped out.

School told me I wasn't going to get a GCSE to my name, and they told me I was going to be pregnant by the time I was 15… but I've got 11 GCSEs and I'm still not pregnant.

This country… I want to leave it. I want to go over and do computer software design in New Zealand hopefully, if all goes well. I don't like Belfast. I don't like the history here. My Da gets on like… the worst thing that's happened to his life was living here, because it's just too much trouble.

Revd Lesley Carroll is minister at Fortwilliam and Macrory Presbyterian Church, whose congregation has encouraged a number of youth and community projects to flourish under its umbrella. Macrory Church sits right on the peaceline in Duncairn Avenue, with an entrance on either side. They employ three workers and two volunteers.

At Macrory there is cross community bike fixing project: "young people like working on bikes, as they use them to get away from the police." There is proposed development work for a state of the art kitchen – young people like anything to do with cooking. There are garden projects at Fortwilliam. Lesley Carroll commends her congregation for having been so enlightened and encouraging the work to happen.

They also have a partnership with the police, training them to have sensitive conversations with young people. One young man got involved with both the bike and garden projects and there has been a massive change in how he views himself – now he can see he is capable of achieving things. "He challenges sectarian attitudes in the group, and is training as a leader – some in the group can get an OCN in leadership skills – and now he has to make a choice about whether he is willing to join in the work with the police."

In 2008, Joseph Rowntree Foundation published a report on 'Territoriality in British Cities', based on research in Glasgow, Bradford, Bristol, Tower Hamlets, Sunderland and Peterborough. It concluded that territoriality was a part of everyday life, particularly for teenage boys and young men in their 20s. Motivations for engaging in territorial behaviour included positive aspects such as developing identity and friendships, but the behaviour often involved violent conflict. It emerged particularly "where young people's identity was closely associated with their neighbourhoods and they gained respect from representing them" (Kintrea et al 2008).

Agnes Street

These insights are echoed by the Youth Engagement Project, a multi-agency partnership run by Belfast City Council, which has received £1.1 million from Peace III over three years. The rationale for the project was to provide a practical and sustainable response to the significant problem of young people gathering at interfaces for arranged fights. The project participants are young people living in and around interface arcas, for example M1 – Westlink, Black Mountain, Ardoyne/Woodvale and Inner-east Belfast. The young people and their families have often been seriously affected by ongoing violence and conflict.

In Phase II, YEP works more intensively with youngsters who are most at risk of interface violence and crime. One hundred and forty-five young people have so far gone through the programme, which is based on one to one mentoring and support over a 16 week period. The programme is underpinned by strong community and statutory partnerships. Like almost all the programmes described in this book, future funding for YEP is in doubt.

If further evidence is needed to show a link between paramilitary violence, the experience of young people at the interface, and communal and transgenerational trauma, the recent report by Professor Liam Kennedy of Queen's University Belfast reports that between 1990 and 2013, a total of 167 children aged 17 or under were shot by paramilitaries – 94 by Loyalists and 73 by Republicans – and there were a total of 344 beatings of children – 166 by Loyalists and 178 by Republicans. These of course are reported crimes, the actual number is assumed to be higher. These attacks decreased significantly after the Belfast Agreement, and in 2013, the last year for which data so far exists, the numbers were nil for Republican beatings and shootings of children and three for Loyalist attacks – giving hope that this dreadful phenomenon is close to dying out. Furthermore, Kennedy reports "large but unknown numbers of children were subjected to torture, mutilation and psychological terror during the 1970s and 1980s".

"The typical victim of a paramilitary style punishment was young, working class and male, from either Protestant or Catholic background. He was likely to be educationally and socially disadvantaged. Those most at risk were men in their 20s. Some of the injuries were life altering, leaving permanent physical and psychological scars. A minority was executed. Among the victims sizeable proportions were children.

In the late twentieth century, Northern Ireland was home to waves of organised and violent child abuse, of a kind that had no exact precedents in the history of the Irish or British states. Some died, others were driven to suicide.

The punishment system generated its own automatic cover-up. Every victim understood that speaking to the media or authorities more generally could result in further attacks on them or their loved ones.

In the demi-monde of paramilitary control in Northern Ireland, they enjoyed and enforced silence and compliance. It is worth reiterating that vigilante justice produced enormous pain and suffering for both adults and children, to no productive end. It deformed bodies and lives. It visited its wrath on some of the poorest, most powerless and most disadvantaged in Northern Irish Society".

Professor Kennedy's report was launched on 10 November 2014 to mark the 25th anniversary of the UN Convention on the Rights of the Child (Kennedy 2014).

Chapter Five

MAVERICK MINISTRIES: THE CHURCHES

*"If our life in Christ means anything to you, if love can persuade at all, or the Spirit that
we have in common, or any tenderness and sympathy, then be united in our convictions
and united in your love, with a common purpose and a common mind... Always consider
the other person to be better than yourself, so that nobody thinks of his own interests first,
but everybody thinks of other people's interests instead. In your minds you must
be the same as Christ Jesus."*

Letter of St Paul to the Philippians 2:1–11

As AN OUTSIDER, I was initially and naïvely mystified by the lack of connection at the level of grassroots activism between the churches and community relations groups and workers. Sure, wouldn't everyone of good will be working together for peace? When asked the reason for the disconnection, community workers often cite the Hurd Principles and political vetting, but also the friction between the churches and political activists over funerals during the conflict.

During the 1980s, funding flowed freely into Northern Ireland and many services for children and families were delivered by community organisations. Significant amounts went into the Action for Community Employment (ACE) scheme in particular. On 27 June 1985, Secretary of State Douglas Hurd reported to the Westminster Parliament that:

"I am satisfied, from information available to me, that there are cases in which some community groups, or persons prominent in the direction or management of some groups, have sufficiently close links with paramilitary organisations to give rise to a grave risk that to support those groups would have the effect of improving the standing and furthering the aims of a paramilitary organisation, whether directly or indirectly... In any particular case in which I am satisfied that these conditions prevail, no grant will be paid" (Ó hAdhmaill 1990).

The next day, the Conway Mill Women's Self Help Group on the Falls Road received a letter announcing its funding was being withdrawn, with no explanation, no formal investigation and no right of appeal. Between then and 1990, some 26 groups lost their government funding, and an unknown further number were refused initial funding. Funds were diverted to church-based organisations, considered safer. "There was a feeling that the state needed the cooperation of the churches and the often more conservative voluntary and community groups in order to ensure social control." It was assumed at the time by the voluntary sector that the Conservative government had used the excuse of wanting to suppress paramilitary links and Sinn Féin connections in particular because it had great antipathy to community groups calling for social change and a "bottom up approach to the control and organisation of power in society". The effects of this policy were that the affected groups lost confidence, were shunned and marginalised, lost their ability to attract alternative funding, and in many cases closed down (Ó hAdhmaill 1990).

For example, Twinbrook Tenants and Community Association lost five ACE workers and had to close down its Welfare Rights Advice Centre. Meanwhile, the local church ACE scheme increased in size – seen as "safer, with no community base and no accountability in that community". Groups that received funding, including the churches, went to great

Alliance Avenue,
Ardoyne

lengths to distance themselves from anything or anyone with paramilitary links, leading to mutual resentment and suspicion by community groups of churches and vice versa.

Frank Liddy, of Black Mountain Zen Centre, was employed by the Twinbrook Association in the 80s until it lost its funding because it was perceived to be a front for the IRA. He recalls that Twinbrook's work included workers' and women's collectives, education and photography, and a project that linked young offenders with ex-offenders: "We would have been challenging the system on rights and benefits, and promoting social justice."

The transfer of ACE funding – which was substantial – to the churches exacerbated difficulties between the Catholic Church and local communities and resentments persist to this day. "ACE funding policy is a very blunt instrument, and the concentration of resources in clerical hands creates serious political imbalances within local communities." According to Morrow et al, the Catholic Church was a refuge for Catholics who did not support Sinn Féin, so handing funding to the Church widened the split in Republican areas, and rubbed salt into the wounds created over the conduct of funerals of those killed during the conflict (Morrow 1991).

Clergy were perceived by activists as using the occasion presented by funerals to preach against the violence and paramilitary activity. The Catholic Church was resented for not having given more support to the Republican cause, or in some cases for having failed to give pastoral care to bereaved families. Priests were in fact caught between their role of giving pastoral support and being seen to condone the violence. There was often friction between local leaders and clergy over paramilitary presence and paraphernalia at funerals.

Fr Tom Toner (later Monsignor), who died in November 2012, was parish priest of St Agnes' on the Andersonstown Road in West Belfast at the time of the tragic sequence of events that began in Gibraltar on 6 March 1988, when three unarmed IRA operatives, Mairéad Farrell, Seán Savage and Danny McCann, were killed by the SAS. Fr Toner presided at Savage's and McCann's joint funeral, which took place at St Agnes' on 16 March. It was immediately after that funeral that Loyalist Michael Stone killed three mourners and wounded 60 in a grenade attack at Milltown Cemetery where the Gibraltar three were being buried. Fr Toner also presided at the funeral of Kevin Brady, one of those killed at Milltown, three days later on 19 March, and it was at that funeral that the two off-duty British army corporals, Derek Wood and David Howes, strayed into the funeral cortège and were dragged out of the car, taken into Casement Park and beaten and shot to death. That series of events has been described as a 'nadir' in the conflict.[1]

Here is the full text of the homily preached by Fr Tom Toner on Sunday 20 March, the day after the soldiers' murder. I reproduce it as a tribute to Fr Tom Toner, who is in some ways the earliest inspiration behind this book, and who seems rarely far away during the writing of it, because it shows powerfully the complexity of the dilemma faced by clergy – and the anguish they experienced – who loved Ireland, but not as much as they loved the Gospel.

Homily Sunday 20 March 1988, 12 noon, St Agnes'
The strangers in today's Gospel came and said to the disciples: "We would like to see Jesus."

Two words are foremost in my mind today – one is the name of Jesus and his Gospel. The other is murder.

Last Sunday here I spoke about murder. At the funerals here on Wednesday night I again referred to murder. All in the light of the Gospel and the name of Jesus.

Let me tell you now that I have been subjected to the most virulent abuse for

---

1 Shortly after, Fr Toner invited me to come to Belfast and write the story of St Agnes' Parish and the sequence of events after Gibraltar, which was published in *The Tablet* on 21 May 1988.

using that word and even for using that Name. All day yesterday from lunchtime till I took the phone off the hook at midnight I took a verbal mauling over the phone – sometimes from Catholics, mostly from Protestants, some from anonymous callers, some from most reasonable troubled souls. I got many bitter letters from England. Even within my own circle I was told I could have chosen my own words more carefully.

This is not easy to take but I assure you, my dear people, that I will continue as conscientiously as I can to help you bring the Gospel of Jesus to bear on events which touch us.

About Gibraltar I would not change a word – I might add a few but I wouldn't change any. In Gibraltar people acted outside the rule of law and killing outside of the law is murder, whatever the identity of the people killed and whatever their intentions. I told you here at this Mass that people were shying away from the truth about Gibraltar, that there were two multiple murder plots there but that only one had been carried out. I pointed out that one of these murder plots was in the name of Ireland and therefore in your name and in mine.

Now, if we do not back off the truth about Gibraltar, my dear people, let us not back off the truth about what happened in our parish yesterday. Let us not flinch from bringing the light of the Gospel of Jesus to bear on those events. Let us try to let Jesus touch us through the reality of his own death and the deaths in our midst yesterday.

We had foul and bloody murder committed in our parish yesterday.

Our Parish is seen as dripping in the blood of the murdered. And one thinks of the mob baying for the death of Jesus: "Let his blood be upon us and upon our children." Whatever the identity of the people killed and whatever their intentions[2] – to use the same phrase as about Gibraltar – these were savage murders and stand condemned with all other murder.[3]

In the calls I was getting yesterday some of the blame for these murders was being placed personally on me and on you, the people of St Agnes'. In that context is well to reflect that the Milltown Cemetery murderer was at Mass in this church with his gun and grenades.

I bring to the altar this morning the pictures of the half-naked battered bodies that I saw lying in the waste ground; you bring the TV pictures of savage behaviour, some of you bring eye witness memories of that savagery. We bring these and all the feelings and reactions that accompany them to our Eucharist where we commemorate the battered body on the Cross of Jesus. We bring to the altar our shame, our fear, and any guilt we feel for what was done in our parish. We bring too

---

2 At this point, it was not known who the soldiers were or why they were where they were.

3 Fr Toner's own emphasis.

the hatred, anger and rage that caused people, Catholic people, to behave as they did.

"We would like to see Jesus". We must look for the face of Jesus.

I said somewhere that it was hard to find the face of Jesus here yesterday. But I did find it – in the dead bodies that were sacrificed on the altar of hatred, revenge and fear. I found his face in faces of women who wept at the memory of what they saw at Casement Park and I thought of the words of Jesus to the women: "Weep not for me but for yourselves and for your children." I found it in the drawn face of the priest who tried to prevent murder and ministered to the dead.[4]

There was a parody on the Stations of the Cross out there, even to the stripping of the victims. The 10th Station will never be the same for me again: "Jesus is stripped of his garments."

My dear people, what has happened to us? What have we got in our midst? What can we do?

Firstly, we must not run away from the truth. We must not try to condone or excuse in any way these murders. We acknowledge there was great fear and rage as a result of the Cemetery murders, but let no one suggest that fear and rage justify murder any more than feelings of lust justify rape.

Secondly, we must pray. We must atone for what was done in association with our parish worship. What could be more appropriate than to pray the Stations of the Cross every day till Easter? – to bring the reality of the Cross before our eyes, to make sure that our consciences are not blunted by emotion or propaganda, to keep before our eyes the stripped body and the battered face of Jesus, and to reflect on his kindness to those who killed him.

The strangers came and said they would like to see Jesus. The only Jesus we can show them today is in the same Gospel passage, the Jesus who said: "Now my soul is troubled; Father, save me from this hour."

As a result, therefore, of persistent tensions between the local church and communities, to a large degree any broad potential for effective collaboration at grassroots level to promote social change, act against poverty and deprivation, and further the peace process was not realised. "Serious discussion about the relationship of Christianity to intercommunity relationships have been limited" (Morrow 1991). Johnston Price of Forthspring says: "The churches' response to the communities has been one of abandonment. It's a class thing rather than sectarianism. The church didn't know how to cope. It was left to certain individuals and groups. There was bitterness towards church people."

---

4 Fr Alec Reid, CSsR.

These days, there are few signs of engagement by churches at institutional level across the interfaces. The institutional church appears to be more concerned with bolstering its shrinking congregations than with bridge building. Church activity is limited to "small prophetic initiatives" such as the 4 Corners Festival and carried out by a diffuse band of heroic characters, sometimes referred to as mavericks, with little connection amongst one another and little support from their own denominations and fellow ministers.

Against the background of a divided religious, social and political context in Northern Ireland, ecumenism has also had little relevance. Sometimes referred to as a 'dirty word', conjuring up, as it does, images of doctrinal and liturgical debates, ecumenism was a source of suspicion. Ecumenism these days, says Revd Lesley Carroll, is therefore less about theological debates and more about what kind of witness is being given. There is, she says, an attempt to be in the public square and promote one city and one people. In this context she notes the Lord Mayors' multi faith chaplains; an idea begun by Sinn Féin Councillor Máirtín Ó Muilleoir and continued by the next Lord Mayor, Social Democratic Labour Party (SDLP) Councillor Nichola Mallon.

A number of other factors in the wider context help to explain the ambivalent position and the "inertia", as Revd Lesley Carroll terms it, of the churches today. The churches lost credibility and authority during the years of conflict, due to their failure to take a courageous stand either independently or more importantly together at the leadership level. They are widely seen to have abrogated anything other than minimal responsibility – although some of course would dispute this. They spoke out against violence but did not do enough to promote the peace. To this day, churches are completely absent in promoting integrated education – understood to be the *sine qua non* for desegregation. This antipathy to integrated education is not new. In 1923, Lord Londonderry, Charles SH Vane Tempest Stewart was minister of Education and proposed a non-sectarian education system and "in a rare show of unity all churches objected to it" (Hatch 2013).

The Catholic Church was further damaged by the decline of its moral authority over contraception, divorce and remarriage, and in particular the child abuse scandals – during which the Irish bishops are thought to have failed to respond effectively. In October 2014, Ian Elliott, the former Chief Executive of the National Board for Safeguarding Children in the Catholic Church in Ireland is quoted as accusing the Irish Bishops of "minimal responses and empty gestures" in their approach to the abuse of children by clergy (*The Tablet,* 24 Oct 2014). Meanwhile, the Protestant Churches also lost authority particularly in interface areas. Protestant worshippers are fragmented across many denominations and individual churches. The Shankill has a church attendance of just 3% across 40 individual churches and congregations. Some of them survive only because of their commuter populations, who drive in on Sundays for nostalgic reasons from the suburbs to which they fled during the conflict. The mainstream denominations are thought, like the Unionist politicians, to have abandoned the working classes.

John Paul Lederach says that the churches have struggled to position themselves in the conflict and post-conflict Northern Ireland: "they have had a narrow and dogmatic viewpoint, defining inclusion and exclusion. They are limited in their ability to act effectively because of the narrowness of their boundaries." This is reflected in something Bishop Harold Miller says: "We have to be very careful that we don't benefit from being in segregated areas. A shared society will make our edges more fuzzy."

Overall, writes Professor John Brewer, "the institutional church is facing a crisis of legitimacy that is affecting its moral authority in Northern Ireland, which is potentially very threatening". He goes on to say that there has been a significant increase in "religious independents", those who have no religious affiliation or who refuse to state it, from 11% in 1991 to 17% in the 2011 census. There is also a rise in "small, independent charismatic and conservative evangelical churches", particularly among those who reject the labels of Unionist or Nationalist (Brewer 2014).

Jim 'The King' Brown, who grew up in New Lodge and now lives on the interface fence at Hazelwood Integrated Primary School, grew up Catholic but became a born again Christian and has been a regular attender at Evangelical Churches. He and his wife have difficulty thinking whether the majority of their friends are Protestant or Catholic – and says he "does not have a sectarian bone in his body". Jean Brown, who grew up in Suffolk and married a Catholic in the 60s, spent many years in a kind of anguish over church membership, until she and her husband joined a small Evangelical Church in East Belfast. These stories echo John Brewer's assertion that "disaffection with the old identity politics" is driving the rise in religious independents.

Bombay Street

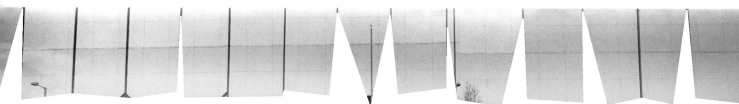

Jonathan Hatch writes in his thesis on the peacewalls that he had noticed that "it would be actually quite easy to practice Christianity in the Irish context without any particular notice paid to social realities or commitment given to a particular outworking, particularly in regard to post-conflict social transformation" (Hatch 2013). One might equally suggest that those whose main concern is the social reality of post-conflict Belfast could and do spend the majority of their time and effort without attending to the presence of the churches.

Hatch concludes in his thesis that the clergy he surveyed did not engage with or see the need to engage with the reality of the barriers; clergy do not see the walls as part of their remit. This chimes with some of my research – I certainly met one priest who said, when I asked him about the massive peacewall cutting through his parish, "I don't like to think about that". In fact, there are a number of churches active on the interfaces once you learn where to look, and a range of ways in which they are engaging with the peace process.

Some, like New Life City Church on Northumberland Street and Revd Lesley Carroll's Presbyterian Church of Fortwilliam and Macrory, balance their community outreach role with maintaining a worshipping congregation. Some, like the former Springfield Road Methodist Church, now Forthspring, and the 174 Trust on Duncairn Avenue, have morphed entirely into community organisations, although they retain some official church connection and their work is driven by a Christian ethos. Some churches retain traditional congregations, while their ministers are personally active in cross community church and other initiatives, like Revd Jack Lamb of Townsend Street Presbyterian Church, Fr Martin Magill of Sacred Heart Roman Catholic Church in Oldpark and Fr Gerry Reynolds and layman Ed Petersen of Clonard Monastery.

Townsend Street is a wasteland of carparks and abandoned land, including a large and debris-strewn site owned by the Transcendental Meditation Guru Maharishi Mahesh Yogi. The site was bought to house a world-wide centre for meditation – until the recession struck; this was one of many abandoned ambitious building plans for Belfast.

Revd Jack Lamb is minister of the huge church that sits directly on the peaceline, next to the ugly barbed-wire topped gate, and overlooks Westlink, which cut right through the parish. Revd Lamb is an active participant in civil society, regularly seen at networking events and a member of local groups in dialogue with Belfast City Council over improvements to the interface, which is also due to have an artwork installed.

The vast church was built in the 1870s to accommodate the influx of shipbuilding and linen workers from the countryside. Now he has a congregation of just 50 adults – plus 15 or 20 children – at least half of whom are driving in from the suburbs. The church boasts fine stained glass windows, one by Wilhelmina Geddes (Faith, Hope and Charity, installed in 1913 from the Tower of Glass Studio in Dublin) and some of Jesus – said to be unusual in Presbyterian Churches though I am later shown another one in Crumlin Road Presbyterian Church.

Jack introduces me to a lay worker, Jim, who tells me he was brought up by his mother to say he was Christian, not Protestant. "The working class Loyalist has more in common with working class nationalists than with unionist politicians," he says.

Not far from Townsend Street is Clonard Redemptorist Monastery, famously the home of the late Fr Alec Reid, one of the conflict's most active and prophetic priests, and Fr Gerry Reynolds, now aged but still devoted to the cause of church unity and reconciliation. Clonard, in the lee of the Cupar Way wall, still attracts large congregations and continues to be an oasis of integrity, tranquillity and spirituality in the heart of the lower Falls. It has thrived partly because the Redemptorists, like other religious orders, have always been freer to plough their own, frankly more courageous and sometimes more political (with a small 'p') furrow than the anxious and overly cautious diocesan church. Clonard employs Ed Petersen, who facilitates the Unity Pilgrims, who join with Protestant congregations on the other side of the peacewall for their Morning Services.

Ed Petersen is from New Jersey, came to Ireland to study theology and met his wife, who is from Belfast, and now works in ecumenical peace ministry alongside Fr Gerry Reynolds at Clonard. He believes the relationships being built through the Unity Pilgrims are becoming even stronger and developing into real friendships. "The importance of the work is to say that we would never want divisions among Christians to be what they were at the outset of the Troubles." The Christian vision, he says, is of a "united kingdom", and he stresses the importance of the connections being built across the walls. "We need to free people to be reckless in their generosity towards the other community", and asks: "what would an act of real generosity look like?"

Among the Unity Pilgrims are Christian Brother Finian and the Curragh Community of Workman Avenue. Brother Finian lives in a community of four religious Brothers on the Crumlin Road – he is a member of Unity Pilgrims, also attends weekly bible study in a Shankill Road Methodist Church, and is the Catholic presence in the multi-denominational Dock Café in the Titanic Quarter. "Cross-community is my middle name," he says.

Workman Gate, recently replaced with ornamental gates, lies just below the Springfield Road Methodist Church, where Forthspring is based. The gate blocks access from Woodvale and Workman Avenue onto the Springfield Road; within it is a pedestrian gate open 7.00 am to 7.00 pm. The first house inside on the left is uninhabitable and owned by the Orange Order. Further up, also on Workman Avenue, which is considered to be a mixed street as a few Catholic families live on it, live two Roman Catholic sisters of the Sacred Heart of Jesus and Mary.

The Curragh Community was started by a Dominican sister, Sr Noreen Christian, in

Workman Gate, Workman Avenue, before transformation

1992, because she believed someone should be living on the peaceline. She lived there until 2003 when Sr Bridget came and was joined three years ago by another sister who prefers not to be named. They are on the board of Forthspring, and host various women's and community groups. They are also members of Clonard Unity Pilgrims. Every last Saturday in June, the Whiterock parade passes in front of their home and through the gate – the sisters go shopping in the morning and then go inside and close the doors and the window blinds. Their house and car were regularly attacked, apparently by Nationalists coming through the gate, who presumably believed Protestants lived there, until Sinn Féin made a public statement deploring the attacks.

Springfield Road Methodist Church was in decline. There was the option to close the church or do something radically different – a courageous decision was made to reach out, and 17 years ago Cornerstone, Clonard, the Curragh Community and the mid-Springfield Residents Association – which later closed down – got together to form Forthspring. It is a shared space with a range of services to the community. It hosts a community planning group, engaging with local residents, politicians and statutory agencies. Johnston Price says: "Set piece meetings are a bit tired and predictable; building relationships creates a much more interesting conversation."

Johnston Price, who joined Forthspring five years ago, believes that the peace process is currently "managed but not transformed"; things are "kind of stuck". Transformation can't take place until the toxic issues of flags, parades and the past are dealt with. Local actors, he says, are "connected and positioning themselves for the political process – it compromises the space for doing things differently".

Back down the Falls/Springfield Road interface lies Northumberland Street, which is bisected by heavy military gates. With its front door in the lower Shankill and its back end in the Catholic lower Falls, in a large former warehouse, is New Life City Church, led by Pastor Jack McKee. The church, one of Northern Ireland's sixty-five Elim Pentecostal congregations, has about 200 worshippers, 80% of whom are Protestant and 20% of whom are Catholic and other minorities. "It's time for the gates to be open and the walls to come down", he says.

Pastor Jack has been actively working to get the gates open and now they are open 10.00 am to 3.00 pm on a Sunday in addition to being open daily from 7.00 am to 7.00 pm. Until that time, Catholics were putting themselves at risk by climbing over the gates on Sundays or taking the long walk round via the Shankill Road.

"In 2011, Christmas Day was on a Sunday and I contacted Department of Justice Minister David Ford and asked him as a token gesture to open the gates on Christmas Day – and threatened to hold the services at the gates and bring the media in unless it happened."

Born and brought up himself on the lower Shankill, he says he has experienced regular intimidation from both UDA and UVF paramilitaries. Neither Sinn Féin nor the Loyalists want the gates open, he says: "The closed gates continue to give them a *raison d'être*, they continue to highlight and represent division". After Minister David Ford visited the church last year and the Department of Justice improved lighting and CCTV at the gate, "two key people from the Shankill and the Falls were photographed for the front page of a local paper, saying it will be the residents and community who will decide when the gates are open".

Eighty-five percent of the work of New Life is community outreach. There is a comfortable café, and there are programmes for special needs, personal development, preschool playgroups, sports hall, young people and women's groups. Church members have actively campaigned for change. Last Lent, they witnessed for 39 + 1, the days of Lent plus Good Friday. They walked around the walls and interfaces carrying the Cross, and held prayer vigils in a number of interface areas including Carlisle Circus, Lanark Way, and on the Crumlin Road between the protest camp at Twaddell Avenue on the one side and Ardoyne on the other side. "We stood on what we considered neutral ground between these communities for 2–3 hours a day every day and during those days there wasn't a single incident."

Over in North Belfast, Fr Martin Magill is parish priest of Sacred Heart in Oldpark; his parish is divided by the 'yellow wall'. With a Master's Degree in Ecumenism, and fairly recent into the parish, he has reached out to community workers on both sides of the walls – his habit is also to worship in a Protestant congregation somewhere in the city every Sunday. He and Revd Steve Stockman of Fitzroy Presbyterian Church are the leading lights behind the 4 Corners Festival which gets bigger and bigger every year.

4 Corners began as a creative and contextual way to celebrate Christian Unity Week in Belfast. It offers a series of events across the city to encourage Christian leaders, worshippers, politicians and ordinary people the chance to travel beyond their local areas and comfort zones to meet and listen to one another telling stories, formally and informally.

In a memorable event from the 2014 programme, four church ministers came together for a session of personal faith sharing with an audience of 200 people in Belfast South Methodist Church chaired by Professor John Brewer. Asked to reflect on the 4 Corners theme of "is Christ divided in this city?" Bishop Harold Miller recounted how at the age of 20, in 1970, he was told for the first time that his grandfather, who had died 50 years previously, was a Roman Catholic. Through charismatic renewal he learned that Catholics were his brothers and sisters.

Revd Norman Hamilton was Presbyterian minister in Ballysillan at the time of the 2001 Holy Cross dispute – he and Fr Aidan Troy, the Passionist Roman Catholic priest at Holy Cross, talked and prayed together every day during the dispute. "What the Lord did was to force me into a public relationship with a high profile member of the Catholic clergy."

Revd Dr Heather Morris, at that time serving a one-year term as President of the Methodist Church in Ireland, is an "evangelical and ecumenical Methodist". She noted the importance of relationships and asked: "are we afraid to speak words of forgiveness and reconciliation because we know we haven't lived them in the past?"

Fr Ciaran Dallat, assistant priest at St Peter's Roman Catholic Cathedral, described himself as "Catholic through and through". He asked, "the question is not whether Christ is divided, but why are we separate? I just don't get it." Bishop Miller said, "We need to consistently describe this as one community and not two communities – could the churches dare to paint that vision? Could we dare to paint a picture of a shared future?" The theme of fear reverberated through the discussion. A woman in the audience said: "I got married in 1969; I have experienced fear since 1969. We need to find a way to drive it out. How can we claim that freedom?"

The most controversial event of 4 Corners 2014 was the conversation between Brighton IRA bomber Pat Magee and Jo Berry, daughter of Sir Anthony Berry, who was killed in that explosion. Small but violent Loyalist protests took place outside Skainos, the East Belfast Methodist mission, where it was held. Skainos was daubed with graffiti, and attendees, some of whom might never have been to East Belfast before, had to run the gauntlet of aggressive protesters and police in full riot gear. To bring a convicted IRA terrorist into East Belfast was seen as extreme provocation by some local residents – but also served as a useful lesson to those of us who might have been naïve about the level of sectarian sensitivities in Belfast.

Skainos is a stunning building of brick, wood and glass; as the meeting began there were riot police at all entrances and the room was lit with the flashes of petrol bombs. Jo Berry started by recalling that she sought a meeting with Pat Magee for several years – they were both at different times participants in the discreet dialogues that took place during the

1990s at Glencree Centre for Peace and Reconciliation. Their first meeting lasted over three hours; Pat explained his reasons for joining the IRA and planting the bomb. "At some point he stopped being a political person and we became two human beings", Jo said. Pat Magee said: "I felt disarmed by this woman's willingness to listen to me. I went into the conversation with a political obligation that turned into a personal obligation."

Fourteen years later, and after over 100 public conversations in Ireland North and South and around the world, it is still difficult, they say. "We can't change the past but we can change the future," says Jo. Pat Magee says, "We in the IRA came through the conflict believing we were on the side of the angels. In the middle of it, you can't help but have a reduced view of the world, and a narrow view of the people you are in conflict with – it's demonisation." He breaks off. "I am trying to expand my awareness, trying to understand these people out there." He is referring to the rioters outside the hall.

In the room, when they have finished, a woman stands up and tells the story of her husband, Patrick Brady, a milkman, who was shot dead in retaliation for the Brighton bomb. She says: "tonight I have to get rid of the thorn in my head. He was gunned down by someone from East Belfast." Another man stands up. "I was a Loyalist prisoner in Long Kesh at the age of 19. I lost a lot of friends. We said at the time we were responding to Republican violence. I honestly think now there was a better way forward." Another man stands up. "I am a former Loyalist leader and survivor of a bombing. I had to come tonight – it is the 38th anniversary of my being blown up. My question is about guilt. How do you deal with it day to day in your black moments? Hurt and anger and guilt don't go away." Pat Magee responds, "You carry the ghost of the past with you. I don't know if you ever get to the point where you leave it behind." Jo Berry responds:

"I have learned that anger and pain can be transformed, every time I am listened to. There is the potential to move on, even if there isn't closure. It turns into the passion for change. It would be wonderful if political leaders could understand what the other community needs. Abraham Lincoln said, 'Do I not destroy my enemies by making them my friends?' I now see Pat as my friend, beyond any label."

The Skainos event, says John Brewer, was brave – and showed that the 4 Corners Festival was trying to be more than a middle class South Belfast phenomenon. Revd Gary Mason, senior minister at Skainos at that time, afterwards defended to the local community the decision to allow Pat Magee onto the premises of the East Belfast Mission in the "Loyalist heartland" of East Belfast and said his reason was simply: "I do not want any more Patrick Magees." He hoped, he said, that EBM could be the place

"that took a risk in listening to an IRA bomber who maybe, just maybe, will speak into the lives of young Republicans … The words of dialogue, however difficult, are never as loud or as damaging as the bombs that have bloodied this place for decades."

Over in North Belfast, Revd Bill Shaw, who received an OBE in the 2011 New Year's Honours List for his services to the community, has presided over the remarkable and award winning transformation of the Presbyterian Church on Duncairn Avenue, around the corner from the high green Brucevale Park security fence, into an arts and community centre.

Bill Shaw grew up in city centre Protestant Sandy Row and became an architectural technician. In his mid-20s, he had a call to ministry and offered himself to the Presbyterian Church going on to serve in Portadown and then in Shankill. He described himself as a "card-carrying Calvinist, with a very conservative understanding of

Alexandra Park

scripture". "I was in Portadown through the worst of the Drumcree protests of the mid-90s, asking myself fundamental questions about my ministry. I had no interest or involvement in politics."

In the Shankill, he "very quickly realised that very conservative patterns of ministry weren't working – it was an area of multiple deprivations versus a middle-class church. I saw the sickness of sectarianism. It was ministry to people who were too nice, who didn't see themselves as sectarian."

Bill Shaw saw the post of Director of the 174 Trust advertised and applied just before Easter 1998. He took up the post three weeks later and in the euphoria of the 1998 Agreement. Duncairn Presbyterian Church, by then firmly in the middle of the Nationalist New Lodge, had closed as a church in 1994; the Trust's work was all social outreach – coffee shop, drop-in, meals on wheels, and ACE scheme. His brief as director was to encourage the locals to use the building; he wasn't entirely sure how to go about that. He signed up for a two year community development course at the University of Ulster. He started an AA group which meets 365 days a year; people came looking to start an Irish Language primary school, which now thrives in classrooms behind the church. Linda Ervine, sister-in-law of the late Unionist politician David Ervine, took the idea for Irish language classes from there to Skainos in East Belfast. 174 Trust also supports 80 families with special needs across North Belfast and runs a cross community youth group. They also host a monthly prayer group for North Belfast clergy.

174 Trust has been redesigned and rebuilt, and reopened in early 2014, with an artist's studio, offices, and as a conference and music venue. Its striking rose window has been described by former Lord Mayor Máirtín Ó Muilleoir as the best stained glass window in all of Belfast.

Of the peacewalls, Revd Shaw comments that despite the 2023 commitment:

"we have an executive with a vested interest in keeping them up. It's benign apartheid. The dynamic around social housing is that the Protestants want to move out – orange flight – and the Catholics want to stay. If the walls were down, people could live wherever they wanted to, and Catholics would move further into Protestant areas."

Bill Shaw is working with Frank Liddy and a small group to promote Belfast as a City of Compassion, on foot of Karen Armstrong's Compassionate Cities initiative (Appendix 1). The Charter has also been endorsed by John Paul Lederach – compassion, he says, is a value that has not been widely enough promoted. Launched on 2 June 2014, on the last day of Lord Mayor Máirtín Ó Muilleoir's term, later endorsed by Belfast City Council, it aims to transcend the religious and political divide, and is intended as a "lightning rod to bring together people of good will", which they hope will lead to "action and change" in Belfast.

A question I found myself asking during the South Belfast church leaders' session was, do the churches realise the power and potential they have to make change happen? What is their responsibility to do something, and what is holding them back?

Bishop Harold Miller responded to that question during a phone interview later:

"Aspirationally, if it were possible for the churches, including the evangelicals, to speak with a united voice, it would be very powerful indeed – the challenge becomes greater the wider the group. A number of institutions speaking together becomes more powerful, but it takes longer to achieve because of the internal processes. It's not ill will."

Even during the 50s and 60s, Revd Gary Mason of Skainos has written, "the churches were not courageous in dealing with the underlying religious sectarianism that fuelled the conflict". There were toxic theologies and centuries of the teaching of "religious contempt". Professor John Brewer says: "During the Troubles, church leaders showed exceeding cowardice and lack of courage." They "couldn't agree on what peace meant, gave minimal encouragement to the mavericks, and absolutely failed to associate the church movement to peace". Furthermore:

> "the churches unintentionally benefited from the Troubles because the violence helped maintain remarkably high levels of religious identification and practice as a form of identity formation and defence, in a conflict that had a religious form despite a political substance" (Brewer 2014).

Dr Geraldine Smyth notes that the churches are caught up in the day to day business of keeping the churches open and the show on the road. At the institutional level, they don't know what to do. One key responsibility of bishops and church leaders, she says, is "to publicly encourage prophetic initiatives on the edges and between the churches, so that they are not constantly giving into fear", a fear that is she says "endemic" and a "curse". Otherwise, "if the only language of the institutional church is fear, rather than courage, trust and love, where is the gospel witness in all of this?"

Professor Brewer says that ecumenism successfully linked itself to peace, reconciliation and community relations – for example through the activities of Corrymeela, Cornerstone and other groups – but the nature of the post-conflict problem is quite different. Ecumenism in the sense of interfaith dialogue is irrelevant to the legacy issues emanating from the conflict. The churches however do have real expertise and resources they could contribute to a public debate on the residue of anger and need for healing in Northern Ireland. They should indeed, he says, have been leading that debate since the Belfast Agreement. However, if middle class well-meaning people will not touch paramilitaries, the opportunity to lead or join the debate will not occur. Paramilitaries are part of the mix. Middle class Protestants, says Professor Brewer, "would rather hug a Catholic than hug a Loyalist."

Ecumenical initiatives tend to be well meaning middle class people who agree with one another, they are not very successful at speaking with strident people, dissidents or Loyalists – they are not able to engage in the kinds of conversation that are necessary to move the peace process along. 4 Corners, he says, is good because it is not just middle class people from South Belfast. Revd Lesley Carroll echoes his sentiments: 4 Corners are able to take risks, she says, and bring together people who might not have come together otherwise. Her own commitment, she says, is to "look for ways to bring people in – it's very difficult but we need to be able to craft a public debate that allows people to share respectfully". The relationship aspect is critical, she says.

Gladys Ganiel, a lecturer at the Irish School of Ecumenics in Belfast, who is also on the 4 Corners committee and writes a blog called 'A Church without Walls' (http://www.gladysganiel.com/) quotes Ephesians 2:14–15, which speaks of the division between Gentile and Jew. "For Christ Jesus is our peace, who has made us both one and has broken down the dividing wall of hostility… So that he might create in himself one new man in place of the two, so making peace." She aims to create a more "creative form of Christian unity in a city in which "there are walls everywhere, including metaphorical walls".

Professor Brewer says that the institutional churches have evacuated the public sphere, have failed to own up to their responsibilities for the past and are not leading on key issues of truth, justice, memory and forgiveness. Geraldine Smyth agrees:

"The churches need to be more active in promoting reconciliation, forgiveness and justice. Why are we not hearing more from them? Churches, interchurch bodies and all Christians need to be standing back and asking, what intervention can we make?"

John Brewer asks if there is a possibility that civil society and the churches could start to work together on educational disadvantage, unemployment, anti-social behaviour, and drug and substance abuse. "Is it possible that a class politics can be developed in Loyalist neighbourhoods to deal with social and infrastructure issues, rather than 'flags'?" Only, he says, when people start to vote on class, rather than ethnic tribal basis, will the real issues be addressed.

At Crumlin Road Presbyterian Church, which sits with its back to the Shankill and faces the abandoned Hillview Retail Park and the Flax Street gates, Revd Jack Drennan has been the minister since 2003. He has been making valiant attempts to reach beyond the borders of his own deeply conservative Loyalist community – a community with which he strongly identifies, since he grew up in its midst, but in which he also represents a broader and Christian vision. He was born on the Antrim Road, and his grandparents had shops in the Shankill. Having lived away from Northern Ireland he wants to stand with his people and at the same time not blindly accept their point of view. Fr Martin Magill's parish of Sacred Heart actually lies within his own parish boundaries; he took a group of church leaders to visit there, and invited them back for St Patrick's Day.

Revd Drennan has nominally 150 families in his parish, although a smaller number actually attends services, and he doggedly pursues the development of the church community. He feels the church has let people down and they have voted with their feet. Getting people involved is very difficult, but he is pleased that they have partnered with ROC – Redeeming our Communities – a Christian group working in partnership with churches and community agencies in the UK for "kinder, safer communities". They leafleted 600 homes, and 60 people attended a meeting; as a result they have been able to set up a youth club for primary school children.

He was invited to the consultation for a new nursing home planned for land next to the Catholic Holy Cross Church further up the Crumlin Road. They had "basic questions" which weren't answered. Would the home be neutral? How were Protestants supposed to access the home, given the walls and interfaces? How would it have a Christian ethos and yet be non-denominational? The questions weren't answered and he has heard nothing further. He recognises the valiant effort at consultation and inclusion by the developers but was left bemused. "We just wanted our questions answered", he says. "Protestants like to see things worked out."

Going against the grain of the Shankill, which "is neurotic, everyone feels under siege from government and nationalists; they are pulling the wagons into a circle", Jack Drennan deeply believes that the "salvation of the church will be people from outside". He wishes middle class people would settle in the area. On Sunday mornings there is an outdoor market in the empty Hillview Retail Park which draws people from "all over the city, the country and the world". The church gives out refreshments, and in the last six months two African families and an Ethiopian have joined and been welcomed.

In a consultation of the congregation on what changes were needed a few years ago, the outcome was that the church should "become good neighbours", and this is what he has been trying to do, reach out in all directions, a Sisyphean task: "It's all about process, and Presbyterians are not good at process." He concludes: "From a Christian perspective, I see the weakening of the church as a good thing – like the Jews in the 8th century BC, Christian Church is being sent into exile."

The first time that Bronagh Lawson, of Creative Change, carried out 'Lament', a walking meditation, with her American artist collaborator, Sue Ellen Semekoiski, it was during the East Belfast Arts Festival of September 2012. She was quite surprised that 17 people came along, including a Catholic priest – it was Fr Martin Magill – and a Presbyterian minister. The event was along the lines of using art, spirituality, meditation and walking to effect healing in traumatised communities. The pair repeated the performance in Ardoyne at the Twaddell roundabout in July 2014.

Bronagh Lawson was brought up in the Church of Ireland but now describes herself as a free spirit. Her background includes 13 years in cross community work, with which she became disillusioned. Since 2011, she has attended services at 340 places of worship, a "myriad", representing all faith traditions. She chooses the places randomly; there is, she says, no definitive list of places of worship and she doesn't necessarily think about

Springmartin Road

what denomination it is, she might try to figure it out once she's inside. She is drawn sometimes to places where there has been some recent news or political event. Lawson takes photographs and notes, collects newsletters and service sheets, and makes a record of each visit. This is, she is sure, an artistic intervention. These ephemera were exhibited in four churches during the February 2015 4 Corners festival.

After 20 years in Belfast, the experience has completely changed her view of the city, she says.

"There's so much focus on the division and sectarianism. Very rarely do people focus on the light and positivity. We see a lot of religion as cultural expression rather than faith. It doesn't matter where you go, in terms of faith communities, there are people trying to do something. They are trying to keep a bit of light in an area."

It has made her, she says, very hopeful. She believes that, despite everything, the churches could be part of a solution to Belfast's future. "There are people who don't go near the church because it is just so hard, but I think that could be the key. There's a whole body of people – if they joined forces and moved beyond traditional barriers, all sorts of things could happen."

For thirty-four days, in October 2012, pedestrian gates in the two barriers across Flax Street were open allowing people to walk through and experience *Ambulatorio*, the temporary artwork created in the space between by Colombian artist Oscar Munoz. The event took place without any incident and helped people reimagine having the gates open again after almost 30 years. It is directly credited for enabling plans to open the gates again and transform the space.

Ambulatorio in Spanish means 'triage centre', the space in a hospital where the initial assessment of an accident and emergency patient happens. It is therefore a place of initial reception and response, a very temporary passing through, a place of encounter, a preamble to healing.

Ambulatorio was a product of collaboration between the artist and Draw Down the Walls (DDTW), "designed to imagine a city without walls", which brought together the North Belfast Interface Network, the Lower Shankill Community Association (LSCA) and the Golden Thread Gallery. It began when Peter Richards, director of the Gallery, was invited to pitch an idea for the Cultural Olympiad as part of the overall plan for the 2012 London Olympics and decided to involve DDTW.

Oscar Munoz visited Belfast for extensive discussions with DDTW and the local community. He had made previous works to do with exploring, conflict, healing and memory and adapted an idea he had already used in an exhibition In Calle, a deprived town in Colombia. The Flax Street gates, which lie in the urban wasteland between the old Crumlin Road flax mill and the vacant Hillview Retail Park, were chosen as the site. Munoz insisted that a pedestrian gate be cut into the second security barrier. Local residents also asked that the gate in Columbia Street be open for the duration of the project.

The artwork consisted of 130 jumbled up square tiles of aerial photography of North Belfast, sealed with toughened but cracked security glass and made locally. They were installed as a temporary floor in the 50 × 20 foot space, but the graffiti and weeds were not removed. "Oscar insisted on leaving as much as possible of the wild growth. The space had a very odd feeling, of being in the past, of being slowed down, of a 'space between times'", says Ruth Graham of Golden Thread Gallery. Mixing the tiles up would have 'desegregated' the space, if only artificially. "The idea was," says Ian McLaughlin of LSCA, "that you could walk anywhere in Belfast." Visitors might have found the views unidentifiable, but locals were quick to recognise landmarks or even their own street or house. There were a number of invigilators from the Shankill, Ardoyne and the Gallery, and daily rituals for passing the keys and opening the gates.

About 2,000 people came to see the artwork, presumably including many who would not normally be visiting an interface area, and some 740 just used it as a throughway, not even looking at the art. People began to use Flax Street again as a short cut to get to bus stops on the Crumlin Road. It is a site full of memories of particular deaths; according to Ruth Graham, one man who had lost a close relative at that spot said that visiting *Ambulatorio* had given him closure. It was, she says, "art as process and as intervention". It stimulated a conversation about what might happen if the gates were open, although it was inconceivable, says McLaughlin, that they would remain open at the end of the project. Nonetheless, two years later, *Ambulatorio* has shown how art of international standard can be respectful of both context and community, and may have the potential to be genuinely transformative.

Art on the interfaces takes many forms and serves many functions, both explicit and implicit. There are the murals, used for sectarian and paramilitary propaganda, to campaign for war, peace or justice, as history lessons, as memorials to the dead in the conflict, to define territory or alert outsiders. Graffiti ranges from the crude spray painted sectarian acronyms up to sophisticated and colourful 3D cartoons created by funded youth groups. There was a mural on an overpass in East Belfast with lyrics from punk song *Teenage Kicks* by the Derry band the Undertones, painted in 2004 to commemorate the death of DJ John Peel. When it was painted out by the roads department, there was uproar and a Facebook page got over 7,000 likes. £6,000 was allocated to a community project for its replacement. On the walls of Stewartstown PSNI station there are images of peace and love made by Lenadoon teenagers. There are the craft-metalwork signs which often mark the frontiers of or entrances to segregated interface areas – messages of welcome and warning. There are well-meaning but decayed attempts at art and sculpture, like the curious six foot high boulder with tin fishes tacked to it and a dilapidated mosaic base in the no-man's land by the Manor Street yellow wall, intended to represent 'regeneration'. There are the artworks along Cupar Way, all horribly disfigured by the tourists' narcissistic need to record their fleeting visits.

Hundreds of thousands of pounds is currently being spent on art installations and projects by the Arts Council and Belfast City Council, with or without community consultation – and there are often cheap and tacky bits of ill-thought out decoration and graphic design which serve only to highlight the poverty and squalor they fail to disguise. Consciously or unconsciously, all these attempts to spruce up the grim surroundings of the interfaces raise the question of the function of art in a difficult social and political context.

In an article for *Anthropology Matters*, academic Bryanna Hocking observed and recorded the process by which the *Hewitt in the Frame* Cupar Way mural, celebrating the life and poetry of Belfast-born poet John Hewitt (1907–1987), was produced. Funded by Peace III, it reflected, says Hocking, "the competing policy goals shaping the state's relationship to the walls". She observed several art and poetry workshops between the Greater Shankill Partnership, the East Belfast artists' collective Creative Exchange, youth and community groups and primary schools to enable Creative Exchange to make a Hewitt-themed multi-panel mural that would "contribute to the vibrant expression of the Shankill and its people" (Hocking 2012). While she found that some of the youth

Cupar Way, lower Shankill

workshops were notable for their anti-sectarian tone and content, others were didactic – "we are trying not to do flags" – or included only fleeting references to the poet and his works. In the end, the Hewitt mural was unveiled in December 2010 with a sparsely attended ceremony with no local residents present; within months the mural had been graffitied, and Hocking was not confident it had achieved its stated aim of contributing to a "shared cultural space".

Less than a year later, Hocking carried out a dozen in depth interviews with Shankill residents, most of whom could see the Cupar Way art from their windows. The residents had mixed feelings about the art, although "few had a clear sense of what the art was about or what it was meant to accomplish". At best, some had a vague impression that the wall art was about peace. Some said it was a waste of money or they never looked at it, although some said it did generally represent the community and its history. In particular, the art did little or nothing to ameliorate the residents' negative associations of the walls with the conflict, their "ever present fears", their memories of the violence and the British observation posts, and of feeling "cut off from former friends and family who lived in the Catholic community on the other side of the wall". None of the residents, even those who were vaguely aware of John Hewitt and his poetry, were aware that a mural in his memory had been added to the wall within the previous year.

In a conference held at Ulster Museum on the theme of 'Art of the Troubles: Culture, Conflict and Commemoration' on 6 June 2014 (held to accompany a major exhibition on the same theme), many key and relevant rhetorical questions were raised:

What is the role of popular visual culture in fostering plurality, peace and stability?
What interventions are necessary to promote change and transition in the post-Haass era?
How do visual arts work to dismember reified memories and reconfigure alternative futures?
What lessons can be drawn from other post-conflict and deeply divided societies in promoting reconciliation through visual art?

Actor, writer and director Tim Loane said that the only function of art is to "create a moment of distraction, to divert and distract, rarely to confront". "The arts don't reshape, they reinforce, spoonfeed people within their own ghetto." Community art offers inclusivity at the price of excellence – and "the concept of arts as a tool for reconciliation is led by bureaucrats not artists". It is naïve, Loane suggested, to believe that art can lead to reconciliation in Northern Ireland: "What is missing is art as shame."

Other speakers suggested that art can help people to see things from the others' point of view, or that it can cajole and confront. It can allow for different versions of the truth to stand alongside each other. Comedian Nuala McKeever asked: "We think we are challenging, but are we just describing and sanitising?" "Our attitudes contribute to keeping the acceptable level of conflict going", she suggested.

Rita Duffy grew up in a Catholic family in Stranmillis; her father was from the Falls Road and her mother from County Offaly. Duffy was sent by her mother to attend St Dominic's School on the Falls Road throughout the Troubles, and grew up feeling like an outsider, both there and as a Catholic in Stranmillis. Dissatisfied with the fine art department at the University of Ulster in 1981, who seemed unaware of the Hunger Strikes or the fact that "the whole city was burning", Duffy made a decision that she would make art about where she was.

Her women's Last Supper scene, with the secular title *Banquet*, is a huge photo-mural attached to the Cupar Way wall, where it is now elaborated by a myriad of tiny additions made by the black taxi tourists' marker pens. Like all Duffy's art, it has been meticulously researched and designed, and weaves feminist, political and historical themes. Characters sitting behind the table are dressed from the costume archive at the Lyric Theatre and Duffy's own or their own wardrobes. They include a Christ figure who was one of the participants in Rita Duffy's Quaker Cottage project and whose family were 'put out' by paramilitaries, a genuine local protester, Mrs Pankhurst, Rosie the Riveter, and girls from the local school dressed in uniform or as a Harland and Wolff worker or a doctor. The Director of the Shankill Leisure centre came as herself. The characters were photographed separately and Photoshopped behind the table, which is strewn with objects representing peace and war. There are slabs of raw meat, a teapot dressed in a balaclava, the scrubbing brush from Mairéad Farrell's cell in Armagh Women's Prison, clocks to show how precious time is, a skull – *memento mori* –, toy soldiers, and a weapons box filled with oranges.

A number of Rita Duffy's earlier paintings and drawings feature the walls and British army observation towers – sangars – explicitly. In *Banquet* (1997) a dining table and chairs is shown surrounded by walls; in *Plantation* (1997) it is a small field. In *Crown Cake* (1996) and *Coronet* (1996) women are seen emerging from 'dresses' or 'cakes' whose skirts are ringed by observation towers. In *Speirbhean* (1997) – literally 'sky-woman', a celestial spirit or a muse, but also 'fair lady' or perhaps Our Lady Queen of Heaven – the hem of the dress worn by a woman in an ecstatic reverie is pinned down by observation towers. Woman is shown as 'hemmed in' by the walls, yet rising above and beyond them, acutely aware of the intrusion and surveillance that was the norm during the British army occupation of interface areas.

Rita Duffy's work has returned again and again to the effects on Northern Ireland's people and society of the conflict. In *Veil*, exhibited in the 'Art of the Troubles' exhibition, Rita Duffy set out to explore the "internalised pain and grief that Northern Ireland is saturated in because of the decades of violence". The six sides of the six foot high sculpture are made from prison doors she reclaimed from Armagh women's prison. Enclosed within are glass teardrops and the structure stands on a bed of salt.

Duffy recalls standing in a Post Office queue behind a man whose head had obviously been scarred by some sort of explosion. She went on to paint a series of "lead heads", people seen from the side or behind, in which she has carefully cut and then restitched a panel from the canvas, which she covered in metal. This is to suggest "great vulnerability and a feeling of insecurity". "A stark reality encompassing pain, fear, grief, numbness and solitude." (As an aside, almost 10% of the injuries recorded by the VSS in its survey of 1,000 clients were brain injuries.) The paintings allude to the medical process of trepanation, the act of cutting a hole in the skull to release built up fluid from the brain. Trepanning dates back to the 14th century, she says, and curiously was invented by the monks in Ballyconnell, Co Cavan, where she now has her studio, as a way of dealing with mental illness.

In the exhibition of these portraits, each one is accompanied by a painting of an iceberg the exact size of the cut out panel. For Duffy, the Titanic is the predominant metaphor for the conflict – except it is the iceberg rather than the ship she thinks should be attended to. The iceberg represents the "frozen numbness" she believes is the emotional legacy of trauma in the country, a pressure that needs to be "released". The frozenness of ice is "one way to describe the pain after war", she says. The iceberg of course also represents danger and hiddenness, the whiteness and shape of an iceberg repeatedly echoed in Duffy's work – even in the handkerchief peeping from the pocket of Lord Mayor Tom Ekin in her official portrait. A recent series of 'cloth paintings' was shown in Limerick City Gallery of Art in 2014, in which handkerchiefs allude to the unshed tears of a post-conflict society and also evoke the white handkerchief held aloft by Fr Edward Daly as the fatally wounded Jackie Duddy, the first victim of Bloody Sunday, was carried away. In further complex layers of meaning, the white cloth is echoed again in her images of wedding dresses, in sheets and tablecloths held, stretched and folded by women, within them the warp and weft of the linen threads, in turn an image of Belfast's linen industry and of Protestant and Catholic – at the same time inseparable and integrated and running at 'cross purposes' to one another, *thricheile* 'through other' – confused or a bit of a mess, she explains.

Duffy has spent years researching and exploring the phenomenon of 'frozenness' in art and literature, and talks not entirely frivolously of her plan to tow an actual iceberg to Belfast as a way to provoke discussion around the legacy of trauma. The concept has resurfaced in *Thaw*, Duffy's astonishingly inventive 'product line' made for a pop-up shop on the Falls Road during the 2014 West Belfast Festival, Féile an Phobail. The cleverly named and labelled products range from Billy's Baby Carrots "succulently sectarian, tenderly triumphalist, and simply supremacist among vegetables", to B Special Honey, "two teaspoons a day will boost the immune system, prevent illness and war", to Ulster Vinegar, "produced through a historical process of pain, anger and grievance". Most delightfully, a T-shirt which shows Gerry Adams' face surrounded by mandarin oranges – 'gerrymanderin' – was removed from sale in the shop after a complaint by Sinn Féin. The *Thaw* products and concept merge an incisive wit with a profound commentary on the systemic damage inflicted by the Troubles. There is, she says, in post-conflict Belfast, a need to "thaw" and "interact in a more emotionally intelligent way".

The work of the artist, she says, is to find new interpretations, to "open up the narrative", to approach issues obliquely and sometimes with humour, and to search for ways to explore the issues of feminism, politics, peace and war. She does believe in art as "a spiritual force for change".

In *Our View*, published in 2010, Rita Duffy and youth worker Rory Doherty documented the lives of 21 young people from North and West Belfast involved in the Teenage Project at Quaker Cottage, a cross community centre on the interface on the slopes of Black Mountain.

Using drawings, transcribed interviews, anonymised portraits and photographs from disposable cameras given to the young people, the process took place over a number of weeks in 2009 and 2010 and included a residential workshop in which they shared their stories. The project produced an exhibition and a book – extracts are included in Chapter Four. The aim was to give a small group of individuals "the opportunity to speak and be heard". "The project was structured around the ancient processes of storytelling and drawing, as a means of self-evaluation and personal growth" (Duffy & Doherty 2010).

The personal stories are testaments to chaotic lives; the young people tell of being shuttled from one place and relative to another, or in and out of care; of their affection for their family members combined with frustration or disapproval of their parents' behaviour – usually involving alcohol abuse. The teenagers know they are being sold short in life, but there are few signs of bitterness. They tell stories of their struggles and ambitions at school, of their friendships and their own cavalier approach to drugs, alcohol and driving, all often against the banal backdrop of interface life, with its persistent rhythm of violence and conflict, writ both large and small. They tell of their hopes and dreams and above all their own will and ability to survive.

In November 2014, I met four of the young people at Quaker Cottage to ask how their lives have changed since, or even because of, being involved in the *Our View* project.

Quaker Cottage appears impossibly suspended on a side of Black Mountain, with the complete panorama of Belfast spread out below it. Accessed by a perilous pothole-strewn lane, bordered on one side by the green graffiti-daubed Finlay's site interface fence, Quaker Cottage has offered a magical other-worldly respite space for conflict damaged and weary mothers, children and teenagers for decades. On the wall of the teenagers' room is a double life-sized Romeo and Juliet mural of a Protestant boy and Catholic girl, hand-in-hand, storming through the city and kicking down the peacewalls. Quaker Cottage is shown on the hills which, as ever, overlook the interface areas and the birds in the sky have one wing painted in red white and blue, and the other in green white and orange.

'Juliet' is actually in the room now, one of the three lively young women and one young man who were part of the *Our View* project five years ago. They remain anxious to preserve their anonymity – and of course they are not necessarily entirely representative either of the group of 21 youngsters who participated in the project.

None of them could remember much, if anything, initially, about the project – and they were somewhat reluctant to revisit it; they had an overwhelming sense of having moved on. As they began to recall details, they remembered doing timelines of their lives, and of telling their stories and sharing them in the residential workshop during a snowy spring at Corrymeela. Part of the reason they couldn't remember much was that telling and sharing their stories, they said, had enabled them to "let things go" and move on. Three of them had moved out of their families, and that has been transformational. Katie went to university in England and came back to become a social worker and live in her old interface area – but "because I am different, everything is different." Richard moved out to live in South Belfast and says things are completely different; now he lives his life on his own terms: "I got to the point with my family where enough was enough."

They also remembered their fears that their stories would be identified. As Juliet says, they would be "mortified, scundered". Sarah, the third young woman, recalls having been in an English class in school and her horror when the teacher pulled the book out to start reading from it, terrified it would be her story she would choose to read out. It wasn't.

Juliet is now in tech, studying to be an administrator; she looks forward to a normal future. Sarah went to university and is now a youth worker, and although she doesn't live at home, sees her family regularly. She would never, she says, say the things she said about them in *Our View* now. Katie is also "scundered": "I was an angry wee person, why did I say those things?"

They can see now how an outsider would be shocked by the circumstances of their lives, but, they all agree, to them, coming from housing estates, that was normality. They didn't know "what was going on", Richard says. Katie says she has learned a lot from becoming pregnant and realising she doesn't want her child to go through what she went through as a teenager: "It was all mental health problems, anxiety, depression and grass-smoking." So, some of what they experienced was relatively normal – perhaps at an extreme end – of teenage angst and alienation; but some of it was due to the conflict. "There was huge tension in Belfast. We used to call it Stressfast – and it's still going on." Katie credits the *Our View* process for a number of changes in her life. She changed her career path from business to social work, and her friendship group changed. "I literally woke up one day, went into school and didn't see those people any more. I floated around for a while until I found people I wanted to associate with."

They also agreed that Quaker Cottage had been a huge help to them – it was a place they kept secret and considered private. All had come for years, even from as young

Wolf End Drive/
Squires Hill, Ligoniel

an age as seven. They also agreed they were happy for extracts from *Our View* and the interviews with them now to be published in this book: "It will show we have moved on."

The question that cannot be answered definitively, of course, is whether participation in the *Our View* project had a positive effect on them – ironically it may be the very fact that they can't remember much about it that suggests that it did. It and Quaker Cottage gave a stability and a space in their lives to articulate, to dream and then to move on. Sarah recalls: "It helped me to open up. I remember coming here all the time, sitting around and talking, it was chilled and relaxed." Richard says: "Quakers encouraged me, gave me more confidence." "You open your eyes," says Katie, "get a bit wiser. Cop yourselves on." The young people also stressed the value of the anti-sectarian atmosphere at Quakers – they think the walls should come down, there is no point to them, they "block you out" – apart from Katie, who believes the city is not ready for it, not this generation or the next.

The fact that they remain hyper-alert to the embarrassing awfulness of their stories signals a warning to all those engaged in the facilitating, recording and disseminating storytelling, that it matters where it goes and how it is seen. It is also further evidence to funders, if evidence is needed, that impact is often difficult if not impossible to measure. The real beneficiaries of the *Our View* project, indeed, may be the children of the participants.

'Kabosh' means the explosion caused by the violent collision between two opposing forces, says Paula McFetridge, artistic director of Kabosh theatre, who has produced or facilitated a number of dramas on or about the interfaces.

Those You Pass on the Street is an hour-long play, and like all plays produced by Kabosh, a fictional story performed by professional actors in non-theatre spaces. Commissioned by Remembering Through Healing, under Peace III funding, written by Laurence McKeown, it tells the story of the wife of a murdered RUC man who goes to Sinn Féin to ask for help with anti-social behaviour. One of the venues was Townsend Presbyterian Church on the peaceline in the lower Shankill, and Paula McFetridge, the director of Kabosh, facilitated a post-show discussion among 20–30 locals, many of whom had never been to the theatre and were there because the Revd Jack Lamb had invited them. One member of the audience broke down, saying he had not communicated with his family for many years and had found it hard to get help; and two people admitted they had themselves gone to Sinn Féin for help. The show was also performed at 174 Trust and in Barron Hall on the Antrim Road. Many of the audience at the shows were aged about 45–50, reckoned McFetridge, a generation that feel a "great sense of frustration, abandonment and loss".

The West Awakes were five short dramas which accompanied the Coiste political walking tour on the lower Falls, with investment to enhance these existing tours from the NI Tourist Board. Then a request came from the Shankill to do a similar project there, and Finn Kennedy of Kabosh worked with a community group for five months on four dramas – but only one was set post-1969. They didn't want to explore the contemporary conflict in the same way.

McFetridge describes her purpose as "giving voice to unheard stories". *Wonderwall* was performed just once with a mixed group of 15 young people from the lower Falls and Shankill. Kabosh was looking for ways to get young people from both sides to look at the peacewall and what it meant to them. The playwright, Rosemary Jenkinson, worked with the young people and created the play about a trial to decide whether the wall on North Howard Street should be removed. Funny, authentic and quite acerbic, the play was performed by the young people themselves.

From Wonderwall...

Music: 2001 A Space Odyssey. Casey in slow motion, like an astronaut on the moon,
  puts a foot across the gates.
Roisin That's one small step for man, one giant leap for mankind.
Ciara To boldly go where no girl has gone before.
Casey And I see the windows of the houses on the other side, starin blackly back
  at me, the low whistlin of the breeze through the long grass of no man's land
  tauntin me, the flags there shakin their heads at me, don't do it, don't do it.
Casey steps back.
Ciara Good girl ye.
Roisin You big wuss. It's easy, c'mon. *(grabs their hands)* You put your left foot in,
  you put your left foot out, your left foot in and you shake it all about.
Ciara *(going along with it out of amusement)* You big spa.
Roisin You do the hokey-cokey and you turn about. And that's what it's all about.
  Whoah, hokey, cokey-cokey… Sure what's to be scared about?
Ciara Everything.
Casey History.

Characters in the play include a judge who is irritated because she is not being paid as much as she would have been on the Saville enquiry, a tourism director who wants the walls to stay up because "conflict tourism sells", a police officer who wants them up because they "cause riots" and he gets overtime, and residents who don't show up because no-one thought to invite them – and are therefore presumed *in absentia* to want the wall down. In a sub plot, two young lovers, the girl a Catholic from the Falls and the boy a Protestant from the Shankill, arrange for a taxi to bring her to him – but she insists that it stops away from his house in case people realise she has crossed over. Then she finds she

Superheroes wall,
Sliabh Dubh, Upper
Springfield Road

is wearing a T-shirt with a Gaelic motto on it in very small writing, so they will know she is a Catholic anyway. In the end the vote is equal for and against, and the judge decides with her casting vote that the wall will stay because "it is too early for our generation to forget the past". But the young lovers bring a bulldozer along and knock the wall down anyway. This is what Aaron, the Protestant boy, has to say earlier in the play:

"And I'm thinking of them in the court, all shades of shady shite skittering out their ancient gobs, and the hate bred into them like the fight into pups, and I'm thinking we're different, we don't have long memories, sure the amount of blow and yellas I neck I can hardly remember yesterday let alone the nineties. And we still get blamed – sure I was on one of them cross-com dos last month up to Derry and they told us it was our fuckin fault for Bloody Sunday. Our fault that the Paras went paranoid, like. But our generation had nothing to do with the Troubles, neither side of us. And fair enough, I said to the community worker, if our forefathers did bad things in the past, but on the positive side did you know it was the Prods who invented Guinness."

Frankie Quinn was born and raised in Short Strand. He wanted to be a chef; his dad wanted him to go to sea. He was bought a camera for his 16th birthday – the MacAirt camera club had been set up by photojournalist Buzz Logan in the local community centre, one of four – the others were in Shankill, Lenadoon, and Springmartin. The centre lost its funding in the wake of the Hurd Principles, but by then Quinn was already hooked. After O levels, he started work as a darkroom technician at Collins Photographic under the 1983 Youth Training Programme. Now he runs the Red Barn

Photography Gallery, just off Royal Avenue in the city centre, which holds important archive collections.

Frankie Quinn began photographing the walls early and "pushed himself a bit" to produce his first collection of *Interface Images*, which he published in 1994, and a second collection and book, *Streets Apart*, in 2008. He was fascinated by the walls and interfaces, which surround Short Strand, and which affected his life daily: "they are constantly evolving", he says. They have had a negative effect on both communities; they are "a short term solution to a long term problem". He used his photography to give an insider's view of the effect of the walls on Belfast.

In 1981, during the Hunger Strikes and at the same time that Rita Duffy was making a commitment to creating art in context, Ciaran Mackel was completing his architectural practice examinations. "The emotion and violence of that period and its legacy impacted on the development of my own architectural voice and influenced a view that embeds architecture in the realm of power and politics," he has written (Mackel 2012).

Ciaran Mackel's fascination with the walls and passion to contribute to their removal began with the rebuilding of Bombay Street, which was notoriously burned out by a Protestant mob on 15 August 1969 in one of the early and most dramatic conflagrations of the Troubles. Forty-four houses were burned out and 170 in all were beyond repair. Mackel's father was also an architect and was one of a group who committed to working with local residents to rebuild the street. The new houses were completed in June 1970. Mackel has vivid memories of watching the process as a teenager and of visiting churches to help collect the funds for the rebuild. This was: "a story of self-sacrifice, self-reliance and self-realisation [which] remains an outstanding example of community activism" – the story has recently been retold by the activists themselves in *From Ashes to Aisling: Belfast Gaels and the rebuilding of Bombay Street* (2010).

Over the years Mackel has realised that the peacewalls were a "fundamental mistake" and also pointed to the wider problem in Northern Ireland of sectarianism. There are 87 hectares of void space around the 30.5 km of peacewalls, he says, creating a "landscape of neglect" and a "symbol of restricted horizons" which have "been disinvested of capital by all of us who should have known and cared more". In recent years he has lobbied the Council to include the interface areas in its planning schemes, and pay more attention to the need for "connectedness" across the city, something he is more hopeful about once planning powers are given to Belfast City Council in April 2015. "The issue of dealing with the walls and void spaces is critical to how we deal with the concept and built reality of a truly cohesive, connected, shared city." Mackel's architecture practice is called ARD, which stands for Architecture, Research and Development; *ard* in Irish also means high, or height, or ambition – and his ambition is to make a difference in the city. In 2008 he set out to implement his belief that architects should give *pro bono* time on a research project, and he decided to forensically document all 88 physical peacewalls. Working with interns and colleagues in his practice, he completed his record of the walls between the Falls and Shankill, and in Duncairn Gardens:

> "We have photographed and drawn each section of the wall in increments of 6 metres – that is in the known dimensions of the ordinary building blocks of the older terraced streets of the city. We have also begun the process of gathering the statistical data on each wall that will tabulate the dates of construction, the materials of the structure, the ownership of each wall, the group to whom responsibility for maintenance and repair – or demolition would fall, the insurance issues, the government body with responsibility for the maintenance/repair team, the names and contacts of existing community contacts and groups, the ownership of all adjacent lands. Our intention is to gather all the facts of the structures and void spaces. Our view is that such information will afford us the opportunities to present the material in exhibitions and conferences and to offer that material as a means to engage with others to begin the process of removing the walls in the city… We understand our work as inventory that notes the material quality of the structures and records the layers of work over time (Mackel, 2012)."

Socially and politically aware architects see Belfast as a whole, as a complete spatial system. They are as interested in the empty spaces between buildings and roads, and the relationship of elements to one another, as in any individual building itself.

Agnes Brown and Tony Stevens of Urban Innovations have been working with Jennifer Hawthorne of the Housing Executive through BRIC – Building Relationships in Communities – a Housing Executive initiative to encourage greater levels of integration in the Northern Ireland housing sector – to help communities reimagine how the walls might look, and how the interface areas could be transformed. Ornamental see-though gates with a heart-shaped 'Hello' feature, yellow brick paving and landscaping are some ideas that Urban Innovations have offered, as well as lowering walls and replacing them with more attractive designs. They have offered designs for all 19 walls owned by the Northern Ireland Housing Executive, and have worked more intensively with community groups at Black Mountain, on the Crumlin Road, and on the Falls/Shankill interfaces. They themselves are a complimentary pair: Tony is very "left brained, creative and weird," says Agnes, while she is quite practical.

They were able to create a different dynamic when facilitating community groups as they were not part of the political or bureaucratic structures around the walls. They were able to make quite radical suggestions and ask direct questions. Urban Innovations asked communities to think more creatively about their areas; it was left up to them to turn the plans into reality and get funding or investment to make the plans happen. They put down real proposals and pictures. They showed communities what the neighbourhood looks like now on both sides of the walls using Google Earth, and they used 3D visualisations to suggest what the future possibilities might be. They ask communities what their visions for the future are in 5, 10 or 20 years– "they say they want better jobs, education, they want tourism, they want visitors". Communities want the places they live in to be places that people would want to visit. Urban Innovations are "innovative, quirky and very provocative", says Jennifer Hawthorne of the Housing Executive. "Something magical happens when you put creative people into communities – they helped to create healing and relationships in cross community groups."

Mark Hackett is also an architect and co-founder with Declan Hill and Ken Sterrett of Forum for Alternative Belfast (FAB), a not-for-profit Community Interest Company which campaigns "for a better and more equitable built environment in Belfast". FAB notes that in the last 40 years, the population of Belfast has declined by over a third, significantly increasing the number of people commuting into the city by car – "the inner city areas have been decimated by the impacts of road infrastructure, low density housing development and the proliferation of car parks."

'Shatterzones' have been created along empty arterial stretches including Divis, Shankill, Clifton Street, Crumlin Road, the Inner East roads (Albertbridge and Middlepath) and York Street. Road schemes and carparks encourage the city centre to be accessed primarily by car, mainly in the interest of the more affluent commuting population from the surrounding metropolitan area. In 2010, FAB's 'missing city map' was launched by Lord Mayor Naomi Long, showing the vacant sites that surround the city centre, the legacy of a shrinking population and lack of responsible urban planning. FAB campaigns to "restitch" and reconnect the city, and for planners to build homes and schools to reattract people to live in the centre of Belfast.

Mark Hackett notes that security considerations and the cul-de-sacs, barriers and gates locked at night have affected the "permeability" of the city – the ability to get through and out of city areas, making the streets feel unsafe, particularly in working class areas, both for walkers and drivers, especially at night. Lengthy stretches of road, for example the Springfield Road or Duncairn Gardens, become "tubes", because the side streets are blocked off by gates and walls, making everyone feel instinctively uncomfortable. For Hackett, the urban design failures are "more about poverty and class than segregation"; planners have "sleepwalked into a broken city divided by class". Like Ciaran Mackel he hopes that devolution of planning powers to city councils will bring a more enlightened approach to planning in Belfast.

Seen as a whole, the range of artistic interventions, mixed as they are in their quality and confused as they are in their motivations, raise more questions than they answer about the role and place of art in the conflicted social, economic and political context of Belfast's interface areas.

In the 1970s, writes Declan McGonagle, Director of the National College of Art and Design in Dublin, art in Northern Ireland "was not positioned or understood, generally, as a means of negotiating reality, as a means of dialoguing and as a reciprocal rather than a rhetorical process". Art's involvement was marginalised as 'community arts' and political engagement was also held on the fringes of mainstream art practice. As we see in the emergence of practitioners like Rita Duffy and Ciaran Mackel, it was in the late 70s and early 80s that "a dynamic started to develop around reciprocal relations between art and context" (McGonagle 2008).

Dr Daniel Jewesbury, a lecturer in the School of Media, Film and Journalism at the University of Ulster, is writing a book about the 'cultural geography' of Belfast and poses a number of questions about the role that art plays or is meant to play in a supposedly post-conflict context. In a genuinely post-conflict situation, he says, the main function of art is normative, to underwrite a predominant model of social regeneration – but the question is whether Belfast is in fact in a post-conflict phase. In community art projects, local people are asked to participate in choosing between designs and themes for art works. The art often ends up representing 'new beginnings', or generic themes like peace, love and hope. "It becomes a kind of shorthand for a 'moral economy'". However, if Belfast has not genuinely arrived in a post-conflict phase, but in fact, as some would suggest, the conflict has simply morphed into another configuration, then this type of art ends up feeling uncomfortable and occupying an ambivalent space – it ironically accentuates the lack of progress made, rather than being able to celebrate the road travelled. In fact, it is very hard for artists to respond to the reality of this phase of the conflict.

There are, says Jewesbury, all sorts of questions about how communities are involved in community art, and how they use the space in which they live. At the interfaces, therefore, art ends up, too often, in ironic self-mockery: trapped between representing clichéd and aspirational hope of a thus far unrealised peace and prosperity, encapsulating the difficulties of authentic community engagement, and attempting authentic political and social commentary. The function of art should rather, perhaps, be to ask "what haven't we done?"

With the intention of directly confronting some of those questions and cleverly bridging art, architecture and activism, a new Twitter feed appeared, on 21 November 2014, under the name 'Interface Architects' (@Inter_Arch), and within a week had 50 followers, 100 by 1 December and over 300 by the New Year. The feed consisted of photographs of walls and interface areas, with single words and brief phrases superimposed on them – deliberately presented in Futura font: "BELT & BRACES"; "THE FUTURE WILL NOT BE TERRITORIAL"; "LANDSCAPE PAINTING" – over a photo of the graffitied Alexandra Park fence. The feed also shared information, links to documents and quotes about the peacewalls. Its author is architect James O'Leary, originally from Cork, now based in London. He grew up seeing the nightly news from the North, which became a "mythical place" for him. He first visited Belfast in the early 90s, aged 18 and "frightened out of my life". O'Leary works with his wife, Kristen Kreider; they make performance, installation and time-based media work in relation to sites of architectural and cultural interest (http://kreider-oleary.net/). O'Leary wanted to investigate a site with "embedded political complexity", and has chosen the Belfast interfaces, which continue to scandalise him. The Twitter feed is both an artistic and a campaigning intervention; it is "graphic agitation",

Bryson Street,
Short Strand

aiming to be a form of "visual activism", to "document the current realities of the interface areas and to propose future alternatives". Over time, he hopes to create a coalition of people involved with the walls, to work with communities and help to address what he sees as a "poverty of imagination" that currently exists about how the space around the walls could be transformed.

In an interview recorded at the time of his 2014 Royal Academy retrospective[1], German artist Anselm Kiefer said: "Art is spiritual – it makes a connection between things that are separated." Kiefer was born in 1945 in the Rhineland, at the end of World War II. Despite also saying that artists have no social responsibility, he explicitly tackled the legacy of the Nazi regime in Germany – including shame. His work is also explicitly concerned with transformation and transcendence. In a graphite drawing, *Ways of Worldly Wisdom*

---

1 http://channel.louisiana.dk/video/anselm-kiefer-art-spiritual

(1977) a scene of rows of military crosses entitled "Verdun" is scrawled across as if the artist is trying to obliterate the picture. In other paintings the image of a ploughed and furrowed field, sometime barren, sometimes with signs of new growth, suggest the cycle of decay and rebirth of Germany. In a watercolour entitled *Everyone Stands Under his Own Dome of Heaven* (1970), the small figure makes his Nazi salute in a barren and empty field, under a blue dome of sky and solitary delusion (Soriano 2014). History, said Kiefer in the interview, is agile, like a sculpture. It can be reformed and become less catastrophic – implying that the artist through his or her work helps to reshape history, and make it less catastrophic.

At the CRC policy conference in June 2014, Denis Bradley – the influential former priest and co-chair with Lord Eames of the Commission on the Past – said that, speaking from his current experience as a therapist, what was required was to "face the unknowable within our society". In his thesis on the peacewalls, Jonathan Hatch quotes the theologian Walter Brueggemann: "Human transformational activity depends on a transformed imagination." The arts play an indispensable role in helping to transform a society's imagination. At its best, art surfaces for discussion the undiscussables, the nine-tenths of the iceberg below the surface, the denials and invisibilities in society. At their best, the arts and architecture help to surface, if not necessarily to answer, the questions raised by the continued existence of the peacewalls.

Chapter Seven

A PHOENIX CITY: BUSINESS AND TOURISM

"Spreading investment into North and West Belfast is not merely a question of raising the level of skills but of creating an attractive city, where the best and brightest want to work and live. Interfaces may seem to offer safety, but they scare away investors, visitors and shoppers."

Duncan Morrow, CEO of CRC, 2010

COLIN WALSH, CEO OF Crescent Capital and president of the Confederation of British Industry (CBI) in Northern Ireland, has a dream – or, that is to say, he sometimes daydreams about burying Westlink. His fantasy echoes the 'Big Dig', the Boston Central Artery project in which an elevated section of US Interstate 93 was replaced by 7.8 miles of highway, of which about half was buried in a tunnel. The project had significant benefits for traffic flow, business, employment and health in the city, and more than 300 acres of new parks and open space were created, including 30 acres along the old roadway. Of course, says Colin Walsh, it "cost squillions" – $14.6 billion in fact (versus the $2.6 billion original estimate). As with Westlink in Belfast, the Central Artery had cut off key neighbourhoods from its downtown areas, limiting the residents of Boston's North End and Waterfront from being able to participate in the economic life of the city.

This massive intervention, one supposes, can only ever be a daydream, although the costs are not so ridiculous when you look at some of the numbers associated with the costs of a divided Northern Ireland or its unsustainable economy. "The historical cultural barriers between the two communities are slowly coming down. And the sooner they do, and the sooner the physical barriers come down as well, the sooner the floodgates of private investment will open," said New York Mayor Michael Bloomberg in May 2008 (*Irish Republican News*, 8 May 2008).

A systems view of the walls would be incomplete without exploring some of the economics and commercial aspects of the interface areas, including business investment and tourism. At the risk of repetition, there is a £10 billion gap between government expenditure and revenue raised in Northern Ireland. In 2011–2012, total expenditure was £23.8 billion and total revenue collected was about £14 billion (which actually represents only 6% of UK GDP). Public sector employment stands at 30% of all employment in Northern Ireland and 40% in Belfast, compared with about 19% for the UK as a whole. The unemployment rate of 6.7% is greater than the UK average rate of 6.4%, and the proportion of economically inactive is 26.6% compared with the 21.9% average in the

UK. "The bottom line is that Northern Ireland, in common with other regions of the UK, needs to up its game in terms of dynamic domestic enterprise and sustainable economic and social development. The current funding approach and dispensation is not sustainable" (Healy 2014). Economic indicators have improved in the last couple of years, but Northern Ireland lags consistently behind the rest of the UK[1].

Colin Walsh is not generally in favour of interventions to manipulate economic growth in the interface areas: "too much intervention is not sustainable and is distorted," he says. He was surprised, however, when an evaluation of 13 Crescent Capital investments revealed that about a third to 40% of them were located in Areas of Special Social Need in Northern Ireland, meaning significant knock-on benefits for those areas in terms of employment, use of local services and so on.

He cites two examples from West Belfast: Andor, a high tech digital imaging company, and APT, a software company. Andor moved into Springvale Business Park, one of Mackie's old sites, in 1997 and currently employs 400 people, 250 in Belfast, of whom a third to a half are from the local community. The reason some of the fledgling businesses in which Crescent invests end up in deprived areas is that Crescent is, as Walsh puts it euphemistically, "economic with the amount we give them", and so they are motivated to look for good value premises and end up in cheaper neighbourhoods.

One current challenge for economic growth in Belfast, Walsh says, is communicating with schools about what kinds of jobs exist and what skill sets are required. Andor is working with E3 and other colleges to encourage courses to provide local young people with the required skills. CBI is starting a pilot scheme in integrated schools to put employers into classrooms and "let the dog see the rabbit". In the financial year to end March 2014, Invest NI created 10,800 jobs from a mix of foreign and indigenous companies; in the first six months of 2014–2015, 10,000 jobs had already been created. This is, Walsh says, "thirty to forty large employers who have a crystal clear idea of what jobs are needed".

Development, says Colin Walsh, tends to be tidal – in other words, it tends to extend out from the city centre and retract depending on the health of the economy. In 2008, shortly before the economic crash, Brendan Murtagh was able to write that Northern Ireland was experiencing "sustained economic growth, net in-migration, and rising house prices, reflecting a buoyant post-conflict economy" (Murtagh 2008). By 2007, unemployment had dropped to 3.9% and there was a booming need for office space. Rates of segregation had stabilised, wrote Murtagh, and there were signs of gentrification and the generation of new mixed religion neighbourhoods.

---

1 PWC Northern Ireland Economic Outlook September 2014

Meanwhile, Belfast had been "quarterised" in the fashionable French sense of *quartier*, to create new "inauthentic zones of navigable and safe places" for tourists, investors and moneyed residents. Difficult territories and pasts were sanitised, with the Quarters hinting at an alternative and social context. Murtagh can't resist lampooning the central place of the *Titanic* myth in the iconography of the 'new Belfast': "The fact that the ship, itself, never actually made it anywhere seems to be a minor point of detail." Nonetheless, there was "deeper exclusion of those in old spaces largely untouched by the peace dividend and economic modernity". It was, he said, a "twin-speed city – those with education and skills doing well; those without resources are increasingly corralled into 'sink estates', stratified by poverty, segregation and fear" (Murtagh 2008).

Murtagh places the turbulent development of Belfast in a wider context. The Irish conflict echoed the "uncertain, contested and sometimes over-stretched peripheries of empire". In these areas, he said, where "acculturation was weak and the locals less persuaded", imperial control was often insecure and would lurch between the tenuous and the brutal. Towards the end of empire there were, for example, the nasty wars in Algeria and Indo-China, the Amritsar Massacre in India, and the brutalising scandals of the repression by the British of the Mau Mau in Kenya, and the Black and Tans in Ireland. "Nothing disgraced the empires so much as their leaving", concludes Murtagh (Murtagh 2008).

It does not strike me as unreasonable to describe Ireland as having been "on the periphery of empire". As a somewhat British person who has travelled often to and widely within Ireland since 1977, I am still perplexed by the widespread ignorance in Britain of Ireland in general and Northern Ireland in particular. Although in geographical terms barely a stone's throw away, the psychological distance from London to Dublin or Belfast is huge. There are of course hundreds of years, and the last half century in particular, of excuses, if no good reasons, for Britain to want to ignore or be in denial about the realities

Alexandra Park

of life for its nearest neighbour. I knew little of Ireland until I went to live in New York in the early 70s and made lifelong Irish and Irish American friends. In my school history lessons, Ireland was defined simply as a 'Problem' – always with a capital P – and as far as I can tell from current news coverage, that is what it remains to this day in the minds of politicians and most of the general, even the educated public.

The point is sometimes made that the 'problem' of the peacewalls is more generally viewed from an economic point of view than a social one. As theologian Geraldine Smyth says: "I find it very interesting that most of the drive to get the walls down is coming from the politicians and the business community." On the other hand, summing up an Assembly debate on the cost of division held on 8 December 2014, Stewart Dickson MLA (Alliance) said: "We often think of the consequences of the legacy of the post in terms of the human and social cost, and we should never underestimate that, but the financial costs are quite often forgotten."

The debate followed a motion brought by Chris Lyttle MLA and the Alliance party to require the Executive to conduct formal audits of their budgets and publish their assessment of the financial cost of division, a resolution which was accepted by the Assembly. The debate referred back to the 2007 Deloitte report, which said the cost of division could be up to £1.5 billion a year. Chris Lyttle told the Assembly:

"We need political stability and community cohesion to generate the sustainable economic development that we require to improve living standards and achieve the full potential of everyone in Northern Ireland. In a globally competitive economy we need to avoid additional costs for our service industry and ensure we attract visitor numbers and highly skilled labour to Northern Ireland" (Hansard 2014).

The research for this book has suggested that Belfast interface areas are among the most deprived economically and socially in Northern Ireland and the UK. By whatever means you explore or examine Belfast's working class areas, on foot, by car, on Google Earth or using, for example, Mark Hackett's 'missing city' maps, you become aware of the number of bleak tracts of land, empty plots, derelict factories and public buildings. Some of the blight has been caused by depopulation, decline or movement of industry, and some by the deliberate use of land for security or 'no man's land'. Some lies empty as a result of the recession, which had a disproportionately negative effect on interface areas. One couple I interviewed moved into a house backed by the peacewall on Glenbryn Avenue. They bought the neat, new house at the top of the market for £125,000 in an estate of private housing which was subsequently abandoned half completed when the developer went bust in the recession. Mention the potential for private and commercial investment and people will often refer to the Gasworks development in lower Ormeau, which included the Halifax call centre, insurance companies and the vehicle tax office, and promised employment to Ormeau Road and Donegall Pass which never materialised.

Belfast City Council has moved to make the necessary legal changes to have social clauses inserted in procurement contracts for council-funded schemes such as the regeneration of Girdwood, which require job fairs (one of which took place in December 2014), opportunities for apprenticeships and business startups to be offered.

It is generally agreed that the peacewalls constrain economic development of the city and country in general and the interface areas themselves. This may be partly because they restrict all sorts of mobility, but also because certain areas, or even Belfast in general, are perceived to be still dangerous and unattractive. Increased economic investment – more direct employment and training, more service delivery – must be positive, for one reason at least: schools and housing remain stubbornly segregated, but commercial companies cannot discriminate in employment and therefore workplaces must be desegregated.

Clearly, as the Assembly debate shows, in the minds of politicians and policy makers there is a direct link between economic development, segregation and the peacewalls. The IBM Smarter Cities Challenge report on Belfast (2014) says of the peacewalls: "the impact they have on relationships, labour markets, the inefficient use of services and facilities, significant urban blight and poverty are all characteristics of dividedness." The report also concluded that "generally those living in the most segregated communities, where disadvantage is highest, are likely to have low skills levels and be unemployed, claiming welfare benefits". Evidence suggests that some individuals forego employment opportunities in areas they perceive to be dominated by the other community. "This further isolates and marginalises communities in areas already seriously disadvantaged by underinvestment, poor levels of health, educational under achievement and environmental dereliction." Furthermore, the "diseconomies of segregation" are borne disproportionately in these areas (IBM 2014).

In the Assembly debate, Stewart Dickson MLA quotes a recommendation by the Deloitte report in 2007 that new health centres be located in places acceptable to and accessible by both sides of the community. Because Deloitte and its recommendations were not accepted post-devolution by OFMdFM, four health and wellbeing centres were built instead of the two or at most three that were actually required. "In short, additional health facilities have been built to accommodate division… It is a disgrace to think of the millions that have been, and continue to be, spent propping up a dysfunctional system" (Hansard 2014).

Yet as we saw earlier, removal of the walls is not automatically connected to desegregation. That is presumed to be a separate and surely even more challenging matter. For example, and it is often quoted, the Shankill Leisure Centre is only 200 yards from the Falls Leisure Centre, but on the other side of the peacewall and at the other end of Northumberland Street. In the event of the Northumberland Street gate being permanently opened and the interface walls removed – remembering that the Cupar Way wall was the first to be erected and is almost certain to be the last, if ever, to come down, could local residents be persuaded to use just one leisure centre? And if so, which one would it be? In the case of Alexandra Park, which currently has 'two of everything' –

Clandeboye Gardens,
Short Strand

playparks, benches, outdoor gyms, etc – could park users be persuaded to manage with just one set, saving on purchase, maintenance and replacement costs? And if so, which would it be, the green or the orange? The more general point perhaps can be made that Belfast requires holistic thinking.

Removing the peacewalls is not a magic bullet for improving the NI economy or even the interface areas themselves.

Seamus O'Prey has been CEO of Ortus Business Development Agency since 2005. Ortus has three elements: property, business services and foreign languages, and has its headquarters in one of its business parks, next to New Life City Church on the Northumberland Street peaceline – they used to hold the contract for opening and closing the security gate. Ortus is one of a number of Local Enterprise Agencies in Northern Ireland, and several in interface areas including Townsend Business Park on Townsend Street, the Argyle Centre, North City Business Park, Work West, East Belfast Enterprise Park, and Ormeau Business Park. Ortus was founded in the mid-80s by a group of "visionaries and courageous people", including the late, popular priest Fr Matt Wallace, John Carlin, the Dean of Business at Belfast Met, and University of Ulster Professor Ken O'Neill. They raised a million from the Local Economic Development Unit (now Invest NI) and other loans, and began by building a row of shops with a 'proper' bar, a bank, a newsagents', a bookmakers', and larger industrial units. It aimed to offer just what people needed – most bars then were actually shebeens, and most people did not use banks, they used the 'tick man' for loans and hire purchase; next to a bar has always been the best place for a bookmakers.

In those days, the streets between the lower Falls and Shankill were very dangerous. Now Ortus is a successful and established social enterprise with a turnover of £7–8 million; profits are reinvested back into the community, and they are proud of being financially autonomous with no grant funding. Ortus Business Park has 140,000 square feet of rentable space, and there are 83 businesses including Suki Tea and EFP gym equipment, and many sole traders. Rent is subsidised for local tenants. There are 700 employees across the 83 businesses in balanced numbers across both communities. Flex languages employs 990 freelance interpreters and translators, covering all world languages and most dialects, doing over 1400 assignments a month. The business services company helps small businesses and startups, and now Ortus is the first enterprise agency to have a city centre presence, offering a completely free service.

Despite the location, they have never had any bother from the conflict or from paramilitaries. Business tenants are happy to come to the interface as long as it is well looked after. Ortus make sure that any broken windows in the business park are repaired immediately. The Ortus headquarters are a neutral space and can offer discreet space for cross community dialogues. They avoid political involvement. O'Prey engages with political parties just around business and economic development; politically active people can't sit on the board. He is feeling positive about the future and about making major investments: "the prognosis is good as long as the likes of us can do our job and not get pulled into sectarian politics." Ortus also put £100,000 into the design concept behind the Innovation Centre planned for the Upper Springfield Road.

Seamus O'Prey was brought up in the St James area on the Westlink interface and still lives on the Falls Road. He had parents who insisted on an education; he studied law and worked in retail and as a community worker before going into social enterprise. Although their approach to business in the interface areas is very different, there is at least one thing on which Colin Walsh and Seamus O'Prey agree, and that is that the schools and colleges need to be preparing children and young people with relevant, marketable and up-to-date qualifications, including in particular up-to-date IT coding languages.

Tourism is also critical to the economy of the interface areas. Belfast now has some 1.7 million out of town visitors each year, and almost a quarter of them visit the walls and other conflict related sites. Many visits are by the traditional black taxi tours, buses or walking tours led by former prisoners in West Belfast and the Shankill. The tours are given by guides who identify themselves as Republican or Loyalist and who unapologetically tell the story from their own point of view, although some tours hand over to 'the other side' mid-way through. The tours feature the walls, the memorial gardens, point out scenes and tell the stories of particular shootings and bombings during the conflict. The taxis always stop at Cupar Way and part of the ritual is for tourists to deface the art works with their signatures and other graffiti with marker pens handed out by the taxi drivers.

Belfast Black Taxis are one of the longest established black taxi companies and ran the 'taxi buses' or 'people's taxis' that served West and North Belfast during the conflict when there was no official transport. Tourists began looking for tours *ad hoc* and seven or eight years ago they established the Taxitrax brand; about a quarter of the 200 drivers have done World Host training and give the tours – which have to be billed as 'living history' – they can't call them political tours. They do about 2,000 tours a year.

Two of the three taxi drivers I met, let's call them Seán, Gerry and Jack, are among the 10% of Belfast Black Taxi drivers who are former prisoners. Seán has been a driver since 1993, has a diploma in Tourism and says giving the tours is a "joy". His passengers have included visitors from Southern Ireland, Europe, Americans with Irish heritage, and British, including former soldiers. He remembers one South African woman who was amazed by the peacewalls – though she also comes from a segregated country.

Seán became a driver because there wasn't a lot else out there, there was discrimination against former prisoners. He has personally never felt stigmatised or marginalised; he was, as he puts it, a former freedom fighter, a political prisoner. Gerry is a former prisoner who lives on a peaceline behind Conway Mill in lower Falls. He is one of a network of excombatants on either side of the wall who talk on mobile phones and face-to-face to defuse any violence at the interface. People seek out Taxitrax, he says, because of the history of the association. People are told up front it is a Republican tour but the drivers have agreed that the important thing is to tell the truth and not use the tours for propaganda. Jack became a taxi driver about six years ago and "has never looked back". Brought up on the lower Falls, although he has since moved, he remembers being caught in the three-day curfew of 3–5 July 1970, and the death of his friend, shot on the street by the British army in 1972 for being a suspected petrol bomber. He recalls walking home after work from North Queen Street to the Falls in the mid-70s, at the time of the Shankill Butchers – there were five men coming towards him and a woman crossed the street to meet him, took his arm and walked him straight past them. "She saved my life", he says – now his tours take in both the Shankill and the Falls, but he always starts in the Shankill as he would not want to be driving there at night time.

Generally, tourist agencies have been rather coy about encouraging the 'gawk' factor or what is described by Lennon and Foley as "fatal attractions". Visit the Welcome Centre on Donegall Square in city centre, and if you dig around you will find flyers for bus and taxi tours. Yet on TripAdvisor, in spring 2015, six of the ten most highly rated 'Tours & Activities' in Belfast are taxi tours. The third most popular is 'A History of Terror', given by Mark Wylie of Dead Centre Tours. Of the 'Top things to do' in Belfast', the first of 156 is Crumlin Road Gaol, the Peacewalls rank at number 47 and the Titanic Belfast comes in at number 4, clocking 600,000 visitors a year.

The Peacewalls, Crumlin Road Gaol and Titanic Belfast all qualify as 'dark tourism'. Having developed the 'Titanic Experience', Belfast in fact exploits and has made a huge success of what has been "somewhat arbitrarily" defined as the chronological starting point for dark tourism, the sinking of the tragically fated vessel.

Dark tourism is an essentially postmodern phenomenon, with the following definitive factors: firstly, it depends on media, global communications and modern technology to generate the interest. In the case of the *Titanic*, the films of 1958 (*A Night To Remember*) and 1997 (*Titanic*) stimulated world-wide fascination with the shipwreck. In the case of Troubles-related sites the immediacy with which the highly televised Northern Ireland conflict entered people's living rooms led to a curiosity and made Belfast, therefore, to some degree a pilgrimage destination for tourists from other conflicted areas, diaspora Irish, those of Irish heritage around the world and for former British soldiers. The second feature of dark tourism are its spinoffs: the focus on tourism as 'education', and therefore interpretation, and also 'commodification' – the opportunity to develop a saleable tourism product, the 'experience', the tours, the T-shirts, the oven mitts. The third definitive factor for dark tourism is that the experience – and it is always an 'experience' – induces "anxiety and doubt about the project of modernity". The phenomenon causes existential questions and perplexity. Thus Revd Chris Bennett of The Dock, the Christian café next to the iconic Titanic Belfast building, says that visitors often find themselves, to their surprise, asking themselves profound questions – about who lived and who died in the wreck, about human hubris and the role of the divine due to the captain's famous remark that "only God can sink this ship", and about people's expectations about the invincibility of modern technology. In the case of the walls and interface areas, visitors are shocked and baffled by the fact of sectarianism and division in what is supposed to be 'civilised' Western Europe, and ask themselves questions about the nature of security, safety and conflict and peace.

Signing the wall on Cupar Way is highly recommended and a part of the curious ritual as if, faced by the incomprehensibility of the wall, tourists feel the need to do something, however meaningless and futile. The TripAdvisor messages have a curious tone of moral obligation:

"Found it fascinating, would encourage anyone and everyone to write on the wall a nice and peaceful message and sign it."
"If you are there, sign the wall."
"Make sure you bring something to write with."
"Try to fit this into your schedule so that you can sign your name on the wall."
"It afforded my wife and I an opportunity to reflect on our world as we now have it, and on the kind of world we would love our children to grow up in. We made personal pledges to do our part and contribute to the peace of the world".

The question of tourism and the interfaces has been and remains controversial. To begin with, there is the question of how local people and residents react to being looked at, or having strangers visiting their areas. There was for a while a tour company called 'Belfast Safaris' – perhaps the title alone suggests why it did not last too long. Someone threw a stone at me at the St Matthew's fence in Short Strand from the other – Loyalist – side of the road, and a woman walking past me stuck her tongue out as I was photographing Workman Gate on the Springfield Road. Communities and residents themselves seem ambivalent about tourism. On the one hand, some say they don't want to be stared at from the top of a bus – such tours have been described as "pandering to curiosity which does not rise far above voyeurism" (Rolston 1995) – but others, when asked what they want for their communities, say they would like to live in areas that people would like to visit – they are very conscious of living in places that look terrible – or even of wanting to encourage tourism, providing the buses stop for tea or to shop. The Attitudes to Peacewalls report found that 81% of the general population and 67% of those living near the walls believe that the walls send out a negative message about Northern Ireland. Thirty-eight percent of the general population and 53% of local residents believe the peacewalls are a tourist attraction; there is a significant difference between Protestant residents, 65% of whom believe the walls are an attraction, versus 47% of Catholics (Byrne, 2012).

In 1995, the year after the ceasefire, Bill Rolston noted in an article called 'Selling tourism in a country at war' that in 1993 there had also been 1.7 million visitors. One of them would have been me. I first came to Northern Ireland, arriving alone by car and ferry, in September 1977 and afterwards returned at least once a year. I never remember in any way feeling frightened or personally threatened by the conflict. Instinctively I understood it had nothing to do with me. I felt quite comfortable going anywhere. And as far as I have known, no tourist was ever personally attacked or injured in any way. As far as I knew, the first non-nationals to be killed were two Spanish and an English schoolboy on exchange visits to Donegal, in the Omagh bomb. (I have recently been corrected – I now understand a Nigerian was killed in 1980 when a bomb exploded prematurely on the Belfast to Ballymena train.) I was always amused by stories of American tourists in bullet proof vests, and I had a number of friends who would drive around the North from Dublin to get to Donegal.

Rolston suggests that there were three ways to approach selling tourism in a war zone. Firstly, ignore it and offer a glossy approach, with sanitised accounts of the past, packaged as 'history'. Secondly, point out that Northern Ireland isn't as bad as you think – which was almost certainly true. Or, thirdly, acknowledge that people have come to view conflict at first hand and use "the opportunity to harness this curiosity factor".

The easiest solution is to 'not mention the war'. This is an excerpt from an email response to my questions from the Northern Ireland Tourist Board:

"…Political tourism is a sensitive issue wherever it takes place, and Northern Ireland is no different from other regions in this regard. Northern Ireland has a rich and multi-faceted history and culture which has the potential to be an asset in the development of Northern Ireland's tourism offering. However, past conflicts have left a legacy which reflects communal division and is manifest in many aspects of life. This includes tourism, where it is clear that aspects of cultural and political tourism related to Northern Ireland's recent history run the risk of being politically sensitive or causing offence. The view of the Northern Ireland Tourist Board is that the interest of visitors into Northern Ireland's political history must be handled sensitively. Many individuals, groups and communities have suffered – physically, psychologically and economically – and it is therefore essential that any tourism activity which touches on these aspects of Northern Ireland's history must be undertaken with the utmost sensitivity.

Crumlin Road

In addition, the marketing of political tourism, and any other support for it, must be balanced both in tone and quantum, reflecting the perspectives of all parts of the Northern Ireland community. Equally importantly, nothing should be done in the name of government, or funded by the taxpayer, which would appear to justify, idealise or glorify acts of violence, or eulogise those responsible… While there are reasons why political tourism might legitimately be encouraged, this is always subject to essential boundaries and limits which reflect the experiences and which respect the feelings of the many people within our communities."[2]

The NITB quote illustrates the tension that can arise between "competing imperatives of a commercially driven projection of a positive sense of place, and a more

---

2 Email dated 19 November 2014 from Policy and Insights Manager, Northern Ireland Tourist Board.

complex, community driven self-fashioning in the wake of a long history of conflict" (Topping 2014).

Academic Sarah McDowell aims to "question the motivations behind the commodification of conflict 'heritage' in peacetime Northern Ireland". She covertly participated during 2005–2006 in 11 tours by local councils, prisoners, taxi drivers, and community groups. She concludes that such tours have "reified and formalised divisions through their single-identity work". She notes that external perceptions and 'global recognition' are, especially to Republicans, very important and suggests that political tourism "places tourists in a more politically active role than traditional forms of tourism permit". Tourists are invited to see for themselves, make a judgement, and take that back to their own communities with them. She takes particular issue with the bus tours, in which visitors are "driven through areas to gaze upon fractured communities, never interacting with those who have lived through the conflict". McDowell is critical of the fact that some tourism initiatives have been grant-funded in order to assist with conflict transformation but in fact were "instrumental in sanctifying divisive, sectarian landscapes". McDowell goes on to critique the West Belfast Festival, Féile an Phobail, which began in 1988, the year of the Gibraltar murders and their aftermath, as a strategy to present West Belfast in a more positive light. It has become a hugely successful festival, albeit one with an unapologetic Republican ethos and a wide, indeed catholic, celebration of language, music, history, arts and faith. The festival was, she said, "linked inexorably to commemorating a Republican narrative of the Troubles," and proposes West Belfast as an "alternative Republican state". This form of tourism, she concludes triumphantly, "can be read as a manifestation of the conflict by other means" (McDowell 2008).

Dark tourism is defined as "the phenomenon which encompasses the presentation and consumption by visitors of real and commodified death and disaster sites" (Lennon & Foley 2000). It is rarely the prime motivator for choice of a destination, but once in a given place, many will pay a visit to the sites of death and tragedy. 'Phoenix tourism' follows on from dark tourism, and is the process of rebuilding, remaking and reconciliation in a post-conflict setting.

Lennon & Foley's analysis places dark or conflict tourism within a widespread global and modern/postmodern context and phenomenon. Such tourism is an inevitable consequence of global media and communications technology, which have led to a "collapse of time and space". Experiencing news events, and reflecting on them, in their own homes, brings people to the "intersection between the global and the local" (Lennon & Foley 2000). Media and films which dramatise and glamorise tragedy, death, conflict and violence – and which also confuse fact and fiction – have also made it inevitable that tourists will want to make a sort of modern pilgrimage, with its own pseudo rituals such as the signing of the walls, to sites to which they have developed some sort of real or imagined personal attachment. I noted the popularity of Godfather tours on a recent visit to Sicily. What could have comprised a more kitsch experience than visiting the villages in which a fictionalised Hollywood version of a very real and present danger, the Mafia, is cheerfully commodified by the local population?

This is Lennon & Foley's point: the popularity of dark tourism is an inevitable consequence of "the way we live now". They suggest there are three phases of external interest in a tragedy or conflict: in the first place, it is considered appropriate only to show grief, respect and floral tributes. In the second phase, memorials are constructed but it is considered unseemly to offer interpretation at the actual site of the event. The third stage, which takes longer, is acceptance of the site as an "experience" which can be interpreted. Controversy over tourism at troubles-related sites, therefore, can be explained by seeing that, for many years, Belfast has been 'between' these phases and is perhaps just only now being accepted as being in the third phase.

Féile an Phobail is an example of what is called 'phoenix tourism' by which a community aims to transform itself through 'festivalisation' and other means. The evolving ambition of the festival to "reflect a global as well as a local community is evident in its engagement with Belfast's ethnic minorities and international artists". In the transition from dark tourism to phoenix tourism, Féile thus represents the celebratory potential of the 'glocal' (Topping 2014).

Although Dead Centre Tours do not usually take in the interface areas, their approach is instructive. Mark Wylie prides himself on the "really honest" approach of the tour company, which takes visitors on a walking tour of Belfast City Centre, where there are no physical reminders or memorials, to the sites of eight or nine incidents, some now almost forgotten but some infamous, such as the Abercorn restaurant bombing (4 March 1972) and Bloody Friday (21 July 1972), which took place between 1971 and 1976. The tour offers a non-partisan and unbiased approach with a strong reconciliation theme, thus consciously embracing the principles both of dark and phoenix tourism. They have spoken to community representatives to minimise any negative reactions to the tour; nonetheless, Visit Belfast refuse to promote the tour because of their perception that the tour might cause offence, he says. Many types of culturally curious people, mostly from English-speaking countries, Scandinavia and Asia, take the tour. Mark Wylie is also invited to give it to special groups including school children and foreign diplomats. One tour was given as a birthday present for a 70 year old. He has come to believe that in a secularised world, people are much more comfortable confronting death when they are away from home and out of their comfort zones. (As an aside, that space in people's lives is known as 'liminal space' – threshold space, or the space between things, a time when people are particularly open to reflective thinking.) In Belfast, Wylie says, there is a curiosity about how such a war – and he chooses that word deliberately – could have taken place in a Western European country. They offer a very honest, but not macabre presentation of events, but also stress how far the city has come in the intervening decades.

Mark points out that most tours of peacewalls and murals are partisan – history is always told from the point of view of the victor and in Northern Ireland there was no winner – so tours are one weapon in the ongoing conflict over who is right or wrong.

It appears that some official approaches to conflict tourism may be maturing, perhaps with the passage of time. Belfast City Council has accepted that it needs to embrace conflict tourism and the new strategy will have the theme of 'Beyond Peace' as one of several key pillars. Research in Europe and Scandinavia has shown a clear interest in Belfast as an example of post-conflict society and in "the story behind the story". The strategy will point to the potential for tourism to bring economic regeneration to the communities, and will encourage tour operators to "professionalise but not sanitise" their presentation of the narratives.

They will also focus on building the capacity and infrastructure of interface areas to welcome more tourists, by, for example, greater use of airbnb.com. The council tourism office aims for growth to involve communities and be community-led, which would respond to Chris O'Halloran of Belfast Interface Project's suggestion that community groups be given space to inform visitors to interface areas about the work that they do. Belfast City Council also hope to actively attract peace conferences to the city, and engage local businesses in tourism development.

Crumlin Road Gaol is a fine example of dark and phoenix tourism, and of how public and private investment can work collaboratively with one another and local communities to regenerate neighbourhoods and help people to reframe their perceptions of conflict sites and neighbourhoods.

The Grade I listed prison closed only in 1996 and after a £14 million restoration has drawn 250,000 visitors in its first two years as a tourist attraction to 18 November 2014.

Alliance Avenue, Ardoyne

The 13 acre site is owned and managed by the Crumlin Road Gaol Regeneration Team at OFMdFM, while the visitor attraction and conference centre are operated commercially by Belfast Tours. Nine hundred events have taken place in the gaol and conference centres during its first two years, including concerts, a couple of weddings, a 50th birthday party, charity and cross community sleepovers, and the Ultimate Strongman Giant competition, held in August. Two former prisoner groups, Coiste and Epic, have brought in groups of young people, holding discussions about their own experience in addition to the official guided tour.

Plans for the future include continued restoration of listed cottages on the site. The lottery millionaire Peter Lavery will open a whiskey distillery in A Wing of the old prison, which will also showcase the history of whiskey making in Belfast and include a corporate hospitality suite and is due to open in December 2015. An old Victorian sangar, next to the Mater Hospital in the corner of the site, is also being restored and will be open to visitors, who will be able to see from a webcam installed on the roof the view the British army would have had during the conflict.

Local communities were widely consulted in the planning of the scheme, and the OFMdFM team meets several times a year with a local community forum. The site remains sensitive, however, and illustrates some of the ambivalence and tensions that remain around tourism and the interfaces. John Loughran of Intercomm says that the restoration of the gaol as a new shared space shows that Belfast is "open for business" and that progress is possible. The gaol, he says, can be the catalyst for the regeneration of the whole area. Michael Culbert of Coiste, the Republican ex-prisoners' collective, notes their disappointment that management of the gaol was given to a commercial company from outside the area and that the tours are "politically sanitised". He would have preferred that former prisoners from both sides be able to give tours and share narratives from their own points of view.

Development of the gaol site is part of a grander vision for the development of a 'cultural corridor' from the centre of Belfast to the Gaol – just a 20 minute walk – and ultimately from the Titanic Quarter further up the Crumlin Road, which could take in the renovated Carlisle Memorial Methodist Church at Carlisle Circus, the Carnegie Library on Old Park Road, and of course the Crumlin Road Courthouse, if, as and when it is eventually redeveloped.

According to TripAdvisor, the Gaol is now Belfast's most highly rated attraction. Indeed, the Queen enjoyed her visit so much that she mentioned it in her Christmas 2014 Message: "What was once a prison during the Troubles is now a place of hope and fresh purpose, a reminder of what is possible when people reach out to one another."

Chapter Eight

CONCLUSIONS: RESPONSIBILITY, RELATIONSHIP AND RISK

"We see a haphazard approach compartmentalised into the spaces of violence. We have failed to push for an acknowledgement that coming out of violence is a massive endeavour. We need to invest in creating spaces for dialogue."

Participant, Moving On Conference, 2004

THIS BOOK WAS MOTIVATED by my passion for understanding how change happens in complex situations, and specifically by curiosity about how change would unfold in the complex web or system around the peacewalls and interfaces in Belfast. Here, at the end of the book, we can ask: what do we notice about what has changed in the two years since the Northern Ireland Executive Together Building a United Community (TBUC) commitment to remove the walls within ten years was made in May 2013? And then, what are we learning about how change is happening in Belfast? And finally, of course the $64 million question of whether and when the walls can or will come down?

Although this book has intentionally steered clear of the higher level political process, we note the importance of the Stormont House Agreement reached just before Christmas 2014[1]. The Agreement is significant both for its content and its process. It approves the devolution of Corporation Tax, which could substantially improve business investment in Northern Ireland. It recalls the recommendation made during the 8 December Assembly debate that there should be "an audit of departmental spending to identify how divisions in society impact on the delivery of good facilities and services, and then to consider how best to reconfigure service delivery consistent with a shared future". It makes a direct reference in paragraph 67 to the "establishment of a compact civil advisory panel" to advise the Executive. Most importantly, the Agreement commits the Executive to ensuring that victims and survivors of the conflict have access to high quality resources and to implementation of a comprehensive Mental Trauma Service, within the NHS and working closely with the Victims and Survivors Service and other relevant organisations.

The Agreement says that responsibility for parades should in principle be devolved to the Northern Ireland Assembly, and it provides for the establishment by June 2015

---

1 As we go to press, the Stormont House Agreement remains imperilled by Sinn Féin's objections to the welfare reform proposals. However, the Agreement's lessons remain relevant and we live in hope.

of a commission on flags, identity, culture and parades to report within 18 months. The Agreement has thus relieved some of the pent-up tension that has been building, particularly since the December 2012 flag protests and the foundation of the Twaddell protest camp in summer 2013. Whether the mechanisms it has put in place are adequate to resolve the tricky issues of flags and parades remains to be seen – but it is likely that it will at least release some of the 'stuckness' that has held back progress on the interfaces.

Overall, the Stormont House Agreement is a step forward from the stalled Haass process, a further semi-colon in the ongoing political and peace process in Northern Ireland. It has received a cautious welcome at grassroots and confirms the iterative nature of the peace process – no silver bullet, no magic final solution, just a little further on in an agonisingly slow two-steps-forward, one-step-back journey. From the statutory agencies' point of view, the Stormont House Agreement allowed a budget to be agreed, and therefore averted a financial crisis and eased concerns about how the interface work will be paid for. Because the Agreement did not directly address the issues around flags and parades, community tensions will remain. Perhaps most importantly, the Stormont House Agreement showed that the five parties could sit in a room together for 14 weeks, and come to a measure of agreement. Of almost equal interest was the role played behind the scenes by the Make It Work (MIW) campaign, an informal coalition of civil society leaders who accompanied the process.

John Paul Lederach's preferred metaphor for the peacebuilding arena is a spider's web. In this book, I aimed to explore the web or complex system around the peacewalls and interfaces, in the context of the challenge to change implied by the 2023 commitment. I have tried to offer a snapshot of a dynamic but incomplete change process, as it has unfolded over a two year period from the May 2013 promise, and summarise as much as possible of what is known about the walls from the varied perspectives of the people and groups within the system. Of course the picture of the world of the walls and interfaces I have drawn is not complete – how could it be? It is also shaped by my own 'gestalt', the jumble of influences, skills, and prejudices, conscious and unconscious, that I have accumulated in the last sixty-plus years.

The Germans have a wonderful word: *Reichtshaberein* – the 'need to be right'. There seems to be an awful lot of that about in Northern Ireland. As Paul Nolan writes in the Peace Monitoring Report, "the war of the narratives has replaced the war of the weapons. Each side not only insists on the validity of its own narrative but also on the lack of validity of any other narrative." I have, however, attempted to avoid asking questions about who is right or wrong, or to make claims about being right myself. In a classic complexity theory text, Margaret Wheatley says:

"There is no objective reality; the environment we experience does not exist 'out there'. It is co-created through our acts of observation, what we choose to notice and worry about… If we truly embraced this sensibility, conflicts about what's true and false would disappear in the exploration of multiple perceptions. We could stop arguing about truth and get on with figuring out what works best" (Wheatley 1999).

I have assumed that each person's perspective on the walls is valid and determined by their own history and position within the system – their own 'gestalt' or whole experience – both conscious and unconscious. I have, in unattributed words which went past me one evening on RTE Lyric FM, tried to "listen to everything all at the same time in order to hear the grand composition".

Margaret Wheatley has written:

"Instead of the ability to analyse and predict, we need to know how to stay acutely aware of what's happening now, and we need to be better, faster learners from what just happened… We need to become savvy about how to foster relationships, how to foster growth and development. All of us need to become better at listening, conversing, respecting one another's uniqueness, because these are essential for strong relationships."

This is why I have simply, within a limited time frame, asked as many people as I could, questions about what is happening now around the around the walls and interfaces from their point of view.

I would like readers to participate in drawing their own conclusions – what difference does it make to them, whoever and wherever they are, and for whatever reason they have read this book, to listen to the voices of a variety of people who are, by choice or circumstance, concerned with and about the interfaces and peacewalls? What resonates with them? What interests you enough to raise it in conversation with those around you?

There were, during my research, themes, phrases and refrains which echoed and reverberated, and it is the task of this final chapter to try to articulate and summarise those. Some were repeated from different sources and in different contexts during my research. Some were single phrases or words which took root in my own thoughts and niggled away at me. One is the repetitive demand for more leadership, and for a better connection between the communities and the various levels of political leadership. Another is the debate about whether Northern Ireland is in a post-conflict or reconstruction phase, or whether it is still in conflict, and what difference that makes. And related to both these questions is the critical role of funding in propping up the peace process as a whole.

Bundled into the question about leadership are issues about the relationship between top and bottom – Stormont/Westminster and the communities (with the Irish and

Beechfield Primary,
East Belfast

Westminster governments in the mix as well) – and also about responsibility. Just whose responsibility is it to determine the path and pace of change? Leadership is perceived widely to be weak because the five power sharing parties can rarely arrive at consensus over anything, because the two dominant parties are continually at loggerheads, because of the perception of a lack of statesmanship at Stormont: the Executive seems incapable of modelling strong visionary leadership that puts the interests of the majority of the population and its most vulnerable members first. "We are managing the peace very badly because of the lack of leadership", says one civil servant; "Belfast needs real political leadership", says another. On the 20th anniversary of the IRA ceasefire, Nancy Soderberg, a foreign policy adviser to President Clinton, called the Northern Irish political parties' inability to respond to the Haass initiative "an abysmal abdication of leadership" (*Irish Times* 28 Aug 2014). That the parties to the Stormont House Agreement arrived at a significant measure of consensus may begin to alter that perception. After the Stormont House Agreement, US Secretary of State John Kerry was able to say: "This is statesmanship, pure and simple, and leadership by all parties to break a political impasse."

Communities are clear that the kind of cohesion that is being looked for at community level needs to be modelled and symbolically represented at the highest levels of leadership. The corollary of that is that any lack of cohesion at the highest levels is experienced and mirrored at the grassroots, or indeed, as one community leader said, "magnified toxically" at local level. The other consequence, as we have seen, is that any vacuum in leadership is susceptible to being filled locally by unelected leaders, including former paramilitaries.

During the 8 December Assembly debate, Steven Agnew MLA said: "We politicians cannot take down the peacewalls, nor should we. Communities have to lead that process, facilitated instead of hindered by politicians, as is often the case." Perhaps that statement contains within it a confusion about the role of leadership? Nothing relieves the politicians of their responsibility for leadership on the issues around the peacewalls; but they are in principle in charge of their leadership style. The potential danger of this particular collusion or collision of factors – namely on the one hand, communities being given responsibility for leading on transformation of the walls while on the other there is a disconnect between communities and political leaders – is firstly an abdication of political responsibility for the interface areas, and an abdication of the need to recognise and address at the highest strategic level all of the critical issues affecting interface areas, some of which have been surfaced in this book: the legacy of trauma, the role of former paramilitaries, young people, funding, the need for joined up thinking. Secondly that abdication of responsibility and the unchallenged meme that 'communities will lead on decisions relating to the walls' may be placing an inappropriate level of responsibility onto the shoulders of communities.

There are a number of problems with the idea that communities are solely responsible for decisions relating to the walls. Firstly, questions are sometimes raised about *whether* communities are genuinely being consulted and the role of gatekeepers, an issue strongly raised during the CRC 16 December 2014 conference. Secondly, there is the question of *how* communities are being consulted. Literacy rates are said to be exceptionally low in some interface areas – one figure of 25% has been quoted, casting doubt on the value of written and postal questionnaires. Some say there can be intimidation by the 'gatekeepers' during door-to-door consultation. The third problem with over-emphasising the responsibility of communities is that their viewpoint, due to a number of factors, is necessarily limited. They lack the ability, as has been said, to be 'meerkats' and to look up and over the walls. Their vision is limited by trauma, and by being in enclosed communities and too close to the walls themselves. Helping local residents to broaden their view and see that the walls are not just their business but have implications for the whole region is a responsibility of the peacewalls programmes and community leaders.

A number of interviewees said they thought communities should be challenged more and encouraged to think in terms of taking a risk. Between April and December 2014, there were 605 reported incidents of assaults, anti-social behaviour, petrol bombs and other low level violence at the interfaces. The question is, would this number increase or decrease if a barrier is removed or transformed? How do the numbers vary according to specific location? To what extent do the interfaces themselves and the blight around them invite the destructive behaviour? There is the associated dilemma, as the PSNI source said, of whether you can build cohesion with the walls there. Many people assume, according to another meme, that it is the 'walls in people's minds' that need to be removed first, but he admits that it could be argued that in order to move forward, the walls need to come down first. The question of risk raises the question again of leadership. One official said, during a CRC conference, "what would change the whole dynamic would be politicians taking risky decisions" to which the instant riposte came: "OFMdFM don't do risk".

The work of the communities is to no avail unless it is balanced at the top. "Strong leadership is required to embrace the many unpalatable realities of the day" (Heatley 2004). Another source noted that "politicians are not learning from the peace process." In other words, politicians are not paying rigorous enough attention to what is going well at community or other levels.

For John Paul Lederach, genuine change is "located at a deeper level of the complex web of social and relational histories embedded in the context of the conflict" and it requires:

"The capacity to imagine ourselves in relationship;
The willingness to embrace complexity without reliance on dualistic polarity;
The belief in the creative act;
Acceptance of the inherent risk required to break violence and venture on paths that build constructive change."

At the same time, Lederach sounds a cautious note: "If you want to learn something of what genuine change means you must listen carefully to the voices of people who have suffered greatly and who are slow with their belief that things are in fact moving in the right direction." This is what Lederach has come to understand as the "gift of pessimism", which, he says, is not an obstacle and is not the same as cynicism (Lederach 2005). Here, surely, is a classic both/and challenge – how to hear, understand, and value the caution of traumatised communities at the same time as valuing the need for risk to break through cycles of violence.

On 29 November 2014, former BBC *Newsnight* presenter Jeremy Paxman included two thoughtless and patronising paragraphs in his *Spectator* column about an overnight visit to Belfast he had made, sparking a salvo of indignation in Northern Ireland. Paxman made disparaging, tasteless and too-clever comments about the new Belfast: "Whatever the loss of life, that iceberg did the city a huge favour," he wrote. The reaction showed how sensitive the city is to how it is perceived elsewhere. The editorial comment in the *Belfast Telegraph* was longer than the original paragraphs, and referred to something which is rarely explicitly mentioned: "As someone who covered our Troubles during the early years of his career he must realise that the region has a lot of catching up to do in rebuilding not only infrastructure but also civic confidence." There was a similar reference by Education Minister John O'Dowd, speaking during a stuck moment in the Stormont talks, when he said: "The gridlock will only be broken when the British government realises that the need in Northern Ireland is higher than in the other regions and that the transition from our past to our future is going to take longer" (*Irish News* 18 Dec 14). And, he might have added, cost more money.

In 2007, writing about the failure of Northern Ireland to adequately reintegrate its political ex-prisoners, Bill Rolston wrote that "this failure was emblematic of a wider failure, the lost opportunity to erect a robust programme of reconstruction in Northern Ireland. In fact, the concept of 'reconstruction' was studiously avoided by the British government, the Northern Ireland Office and the EU, as if to concede the concept was to imply that somehow Northern Ireland could be seen as being like a failed or failing states like Afghanistan or Somalia." Specifically with reference to former prisoners, Rolston continued: "What ex-prisoners needed was not reintegration narrowly defined, but a robust programme of reconstruction and a recognition of the skills and political wisdom they had to take a lead role in that reconstruction" (Rolston 2007).

The implications of that insight are manifold. By "a robust programme of reconstruction" Rolston meant an explicit recognition by the Westminster government

Ligoniel

and the Stormont Executive that Northern Ireland is in a post-conflict phase and requires policy, strategy, structures and budgets to reflect that recognition. In her submission to the UN Consultation on Truth, Justice, Reparations and Non-recurrence in May 2014, Revd Lesley Carroll made a similar point about the inadequacy of the response to victims and survivors. The Belfast Agreement of 1998 needed, she said, to "be followed up with other agreements and discussions to reach the point at which Northern Ireland began a journey into something new". She continues: "There are countless peacebuilding organisations but as 80% are sustained by external funding they are driven more by funders' requirements than by strategic and shared vision." There is, she concludes, "need for a wide ranging strategy to address both past and future".

The job that needed to be finished, to recall Bill Clinton's phrase in Derry in February 2014, includes, therefore, not only the incomplete agenda of the Belfast Agreement, and the ongoing issues that have continued to wash up in its wake – flags, the past and parades – but also the establishment of a platform for the future which acknowledges the depth and breadth of the work to be done. Peace agreements, says Lederach, "tend to hide the reality that the conflict has not ended". They may address the "more visible and destructive expressions of the conflict" but not the "relational histories embedded in the epicentre of the conflict" (Lederach 2005). Such a platform would have the dynamic capacity to "generate processes and solutions in an ongoing way". In its submission to the OFMdFM Committee consultation on the TBUC strategy, Peter Osborne, Chair of the CRC, said:

> "Peacemaking and reconciliation must be major priorities within government, and adequate long-term and outcome based resources need to be committed if TBUC actions are to be implemented... At the moment, the infrastructure supporting peacebuilding and reconciliation work is being eroded. This society will suffer in the future because of that."

When asked about his 2007 comment about the failure to erect a programme of reconstruction, Bill Rolston now says that the 1998 Belfast Agreement was an exercise in "creative ambiguity" – the only kind of agreement that would have worked at that time. It "held the peace together in a wobbly fashion, although it doesn't reward integration, it rewards separateness". It was, he says, hopeless on the needs of victims and survivors and prisoner reintegration. Post-conflict societies require a major programme of reconstruction involving substantial root and branch interventions, but there was reluctance at the highest political levels in the UK to admit that social reconstruction was required. Now, says Rolston, the question still needs to be asked: "Does Northern Ireland require a major social reconstruction programme?" In the light of the Stormont House Agreement, we can further ask, does the new agreement go some way to addressing the needs, and, if not, what remains to be addressed in order for Northern Ireland to reach its full potential? The perception persists in many quarters that Sinn Féin and the DUP have consistently dragged their feet on concrete actions to support a shared society because their political support depends on the maintenance of a divided society. Can this dynamic change? Has there been a failure to respond strategically to some of the deep seated consequences of the conflict, consequences that have become enshrined in the walls and interface areas and the Pandora's box of social and economic issues that exist around them?

What actually happened following the 1994 ceasefires and the 1998 Belfast Agreement was that billions of pounds of funding via the EU peace programmes and other major funders was poured into disconnected programmes, often hobbled by short-term funding and a lack of high level strategic political support. As noted previously, the entire community development sector is dependent on funding and as Revd Carroll notes, much it is doled out according to the strategic priorities of funders – who may be working in a number of contexts and countries, and often have their own agendas and thematic priorities. Programmes may rely on 'cocktail funding', put together from a range of different sources, each with its own demands and constrictions. The funding may be in relatively small amounts and short-term, for one to three years. Short term funding cycles make it impossible for community groups to plan strategically or ahead, and community workers need to spend a disproportionate amount of time applying for funds instead of doing the work itself. Meanwhile the funding is being severely cut partly due to austerity measures and partly because, particularly abroad, of the persistent misconception that Northern Ireland's peace process is successful and further advanced than the reality, close-up, attests. Atlantic Philanthropies, one major funder, will complete all its grant making by the end of 2016. Peace III EU funding, £333 million since 2007, ended in December 2014 but Peace IV will not start until the end of 2015 and no funds have yet been allocated. The voluntary sector is "fraught with anxiety due to the pressure caused by short term funding cycles, which has increased year on year". It would be interesting to know what proportion of community workers' time is spent worrying about and applying for funding compared with time spent actually delivering the work.

Northern Ireland is not alone in facing these pressures on its community and voluntary sectors. Commenting on his wide international experience, John Paul Lederach says that while people recognise instinctively that healing and reconciliation are not linear processes, the organisation of funding is based on linear assumptions. "Projects have short time lines. Funding must respond to activities with goals and measurable outcomes." The community sector is under greater pressure to demonstrate that it can be outcome-focussed, in other words that it can get results for the money it receives. Informed by complexity thinking, my conviction is that too much attention is paid to trying to number and measure targets and outcomes which are predicated upon change taking place, and not enough attention is paid to understanding what is involved in real change and how that change will actually come about. Measuring and counting things rarely makes change happen. If it is hard to demonstrate that funding delivers results, the reasons for this are also complex.

What communities can be given credit for, if not having been able to address the fundamental causes of poverty, as the research for this book has shown, has been the reductions in levels of violence, the cross community work, and the painstaking relationship building at all levels of the system in order to maintain the peace and create the conditions for the walls to come down. OFMdFM Junior Minister Jennifer McCann MLA said during the 8 December Assembly debate: "A lot of good work is going on at the grassroots. I think we need to develop that more and we need to make sure that the programmes and projects on the ground that work are resourced and funded in the way that they need to be." Groups that receive funding to achieve a particular target often discover that they, or they alone, are not solely responsible for or have limited power over the factors that will deliver it. Changes that do occur, either for good or ill, are often in fact unintended consequences of interventions. This is why tracking the change process around the transformation of the peacewalls, from the original TBUC commitment, offers rich potential for understanding how change actually happens.

The effectiveness of the peacewalls programme will also depend on the ability of agencies to continually learn from the community groups about what is working well, and from groups' learning from each other. Community programmes work well when cross community teams are communicating effectively amongst themselves, and when they have developed the skills and capacity to build relationships and facilitate change in the very complex environment of the interfaces. Resistance may take the form of levels of inertia and/or interference by 'gatekeepers'. It may be that some funding is wasted or misused – although I saw little sign of that in Belfast other than the occasional expensively produced consultant's report with little evidence of impact.

In 2014–2015 the University of Ulster is working with the Department of Justice to evaluate the peacewalls programme and provide evidence-based research, including rerunning the 2012 Attitudes to Peacewalls study (Byrne 2012). In January 2015, Department of Justice are working with the University of Ulster to evaluate and learn from the first phase of the IFI peacewalls programme, to redevelop and expand the programme into, for example, East Belfast and the Falls/Shankill, and set out a more detailed 3, 6 and 9 year plan to address removal of the walls. The Community Relations Council is being engaged to help build the capacity of other community groups so that they can apply for Phase II funding. All being well, a second traffic barrier will be removed from Springmartin Road, and new gates will be installed at Flax Street and Townsend Street. The Housing Executive will improve the fencing and environment on the Crumlin Road north of Flax Street. Artworks will begin to appear in a number of these locations. So, a number of quite visible changes will begin to take place. Other improvements to structures and environments in interface areas will also have been facilitated by IFI groups.

Lederach notes that the unpredictability of programme delivery suggests that "practitioners should not complain that funders and evaluators do not understand the unpredictable nature of their context and work; they should become adept at articulating their theories of change". Meanwhile, those who fund and evaluate programmes "should concentrate less on results as the primary standard of success or failure. Those results, mostly forms of counting, produce data that look impressive on paper but lend little to the deeper learning process." Rather, practitioners, funders and evaluators should participate together in the "far more complex" – and, one could add, more profitable – process of exploring, "how did change happen or not happen?" (Lederach 2005).

Specifically with regard to the peacewalls, the IFI has funded eight peacewalls programmes, six in Belfast and two in Derry, with two years of funding at £250,000 per year – a total of £4 million. This funding is to deliver targets which everyone acknowledges will take a great deal longer than two years. On the plus side, in early 2015, the Irish government has given the IFI €5 million, which will cover the cost of a Phase II peacewalls programme. The IFI funding allows projects to employ dedicated peacewalls coordinators and workers but, critically, has not paid for any actual physical works to or removal of walls and interfaces. In a few cases, IFI has stumped up some extra cash for alterations, but in general, the cost reverts to the owner of the walls – the Department of Justice, the Housing Executive or the Department for Regional Development (roads) – or the land or building where the interface is located. Belfast City Council, which has also funded processes to lead to changes in the walls, likewise has not budgeted for the alterations themselves, and its peacewalls interventions are funded by Peace III and the Arts Council. OFMdFM has generated the TBUC strategy but has no mechanism for delivery of the 2023 commitment – it has been dependent on the IFI programmes to deliver the target. Each government department has had to bid and pay for alterations out of its own budget, balancing and juggling peacewalls amongst their own other priorities and against the background of reductions in budgets. Of course, many community and government stakeholders have called for a single dedicated central pot of money for taking down or transforming the peacewalls. It has also been said that the British government paid to put up the walls, and should pay to take them down. Alderman Tom Ekin suggested a rough overall cost of £30 million is required – if, as has been estimated, the cost of the walls is more than a billion a year, the cost of adequately resourcing their removal would be peanuts in comparison to the amount that could be saved or generated by the removal of the walls in the medium to long term.

My conviction is, along with a number of complexity theorists, including John Paul Lederach and Margaret Wheatley, that change actually takes place through relationships and conversations, in particular through uncomfortable, edgy conversations among diverse agents, conversations which are often informal and cause perplexity, reflection, thinking and rethinking – conversations which help to change people's minds, or to come to some new shared understanding or consensus. John Paul Lederach says that people "language themselves" into new realities. Real change is generated when processes which involve conversation, storytelling, listening, silence and humour address the shadow or previously undiscussable issues: power, difference, gender, belief. From his experience as a therapist, Denis Bradley said at the CRC June policy conference, he knows it is necessary to "face the 'unknowable' in our society".

This involves people at every level and in every place in the system being aware of and careful, even intentional about the language they use. If you want to change the organisation, says complexity theorist Patricia Shaw, you need to change the conversation (Shaw 2002). If change is to take place, says Arthur Battram, the stranglehold of memes, which imply that language and cultural assumptions cannot be questioned or challenged, needs to be broken (Battram 1998). Community workers, says Emily Ravenscroft, have a key role to play and should "examine what possibilities exist for the reinvention of already present narratives" (Ravenscroft 2006).

There is a difference between talk which is just talk and conversations which lead to change. For Lederach, for people to have a "voice" in constructive change implies "meaningful conversation and power – conversation that makes a difference". Such conversation features mutuality, proximity, access and contact. "Authenticity finds its birth in this sense of proximity." However, the centrality of meaningful conversation to effective peacebuilding presents a number of challenges including the reality that it is not easily measurable and therefore does not fit easily into an outcomes-focussed approach to funding. "How do whole societies move from violent social division to respectful engagement when the fundamental building block for social change is measured in the distance of an accessible conversation?" (Lederach 2005).

It is these conversations and the relationships which feed into them and emerge out of them at which the community groups excel; it is this web of connections which makes up the peace process in Belfast and like a spider's web it is both hardly visible and surprisingly robust.

The idea of conversation is strongly linked to that of 'space' and, indeed, time. Many interviewees referred to the 'space' in which they work. The walls create a dysfunctional and distorted place, because they inhibit natural flow and interaction between people. People are incarcerated among people like themselves, and come to see this as normal, and

Mayo Park,
Shankill

to reject, even violently, the presence of those they define as different to themselves. Space is required, says Lederach, for the creative act to emerge; the moral imagination calls for "a capacity to live in a personal and social space that gives birth to the unexpected". It is necessary to "study the space that people feel is necessary to perceive and experience a change process as genuine" (Lederach 2005).

Space to breathe, to think, to converse, to imagine a different future. The moral imagination is the:

"capacity to imagine ourselves in relationship, the willingness to embrace complexity without reliance on dualistic polarity, the belief in the creative act, and acceptance of the inherent risk required to break violence and venture on unknown paths that build constructive change" (Lederach 2005).

Pay attention to how spiders work, says Lederach: "Spiders must think strategically about space, how to cover it and how to create cross linkages that stitch locations together with a net. And they must do this time and time again, always at considerable risk and vulnerability to themselves." Consequently, constructive change is "the art of strategically and imaginatively weaving relational webs across social spaces within settings of protracted conflict." Relationships are key, particularly unusual relationships. Peacebuilding requires a "vision of relationship". "Stated bluntly, if there is no capacity to imagine the canvas of mutual relationships and situate oneself as part of that historic and ever evolving web, peacebuilding collapses."

Many of the people I interviewed for this book are precisely this type of person, building unusual relationships with and among others, crossing boundaries at risk to themselves. And while these are skills that can usefully be deployed by leaders, the best of whom already have them, it is a challenge not just for leadership; there is a need to "encourage a wide public sphere of genuine human engagement" (Lederach 2005). An interesting initiative which, consciously or unconsciously, embodies that concept is the Make It Work campaign, a loose coalition of civil society leaders – business people, education, church, and voluntary sector leaders and activists – which came together to accompany the pre-Christmas talks very informally – to encourage, support, perhaps at times to cajole the politicians during the process and to "give a voice to people who are not at the extremes" (http://www.makeitwork.today/). This is support from civil society for the talks process: "There are very difficult post-conflict issues which shouldn't be left to the politicians alone to sort out."

Lederach writes about the "critical yeast" for peace processes – getting a small set of the right people involved in the right places. Not "critical mass" but "critical yeast". Section 67 of the Stormont House Agreement suggests a "compact advisory panel", with an independent chair appointed by OFMdFM, could be established by June 2015. This is believed to be a nod to the value of the Make It Work coalition. Its key leverage is the quality of relationships the group has established with one another and with political leaders in all four interested governments. It was welcomed by politicians as a constructive and encouraging intervention. The Make It Work campaign also convened a larger group in January, attended by almost 50 people keen to keep the momentum going.

If the system is seen as a web, then a critical issue is the level of connection or disconnection between various elements or hubs in that web, which is another way of saying a critical issue is understanding where the conversations are taking place, and amongst whom – or, conversely, where there are gaps. "To bring health to a system," says Margaret Wheatley, "connect it to more of itself." And in a similar vein to Lederach, she writes:

"We can now see the web of interconnections that weave the world together; we are more aware that we live in relationship, connected to everything else; we are learning that profoundly different processes explain how living systems emerge and change."

This implies that any temporary or permanent structure or process that brings diverse groups into conversation with each other at any and across all levels of the system or web will be constructive for the ongoing peace process. I am suggesting through the pages of this book just how many people are involved in that web of interconnections around the walls: communities, civil servants, police, politicians – yes – and also architects, artists, church people, immigrant groups, business people and tourists.

There is a vicious circle and a virtuous circle. It is possible for both to be operating at the same time; or for one to be dominant over the other. It is possible for the tides to change direction. Lederach says:

"When the water flows towards fear, the relationship is defined by recrimination. Blame, self-justification and protection, violence and the desire for victory over the other. When the water flows towards love, it is defined by openness and accountability, self-reflection and vulnerability, mutual respect, dignity and the pro-active engagement of the other" (Lederach 2005).

It is, he says, possible to define constructive change as the pursuit of moving relationships from one direction to the other. The vicious circle is based on assumptions of victimhood and blame; the virtuous circle on assumptions of choice and responsibility.

The point was made during the December 2014 CRC conference that the generation that has a memory of the city without walls is being lost. It is all the more important, therefore, that progress towards the future vision of a city without walls is made soon. I began the research for this book with a genuinely open question in my own mind – whether, when and how the peacewalls and barriers should and could be removed. I gradually became convinced that overall, while appearing to offer security, this is to some degree a delusion and the walls do more harm than good. I now believe – as I have implied throughout this book – that the walls will and can come down – and that this could easily happen within the 2023 timeframe. If, as and when this happens, it will as has been said earlier, be to the credit of the communities and the community workers – and it will also be because the conditions for their removal have been emerging since at least 2007 or earlier. Communities may very quickly see that violence does not break out when a gate or fence is removed or transformed; indeed, that it abates. Communities will start to feel better about themselves as their neighbourhoods are opened up and normalised. This is my optimistic and non-cynical hope for Belfast – and I also understand both the gift of pessimism and the menace that persists from its more insidious sibling cynicism. Cynicism is the acceptable face of anger and is rife amongst people throughout Northern Ireland. Beneath the friendliness and behind closed doors, more than one person said to me, Belfast is an angry and aggressive place.

Anger, cynicism and apathy have the power to constrain peacebuilding efforts if allowed. To counterbalance the cynicism and as glowing examples of what Northern Ireland's

Townsend Street

people are capable of, I would see the 4 Corners Festival, the Make It Work campaign, the Anti-Sectarian Charter and the Compassionate City initiatives as non-cynical and profoundly well intentioned proposals to reframe the language and moral climate in Belfast, initiatives which deserve much more attention.

The catastrophe of terrorism is, since 9/11, a greater threat than it ever was in the 20th century. All violent terrorism – and at time of writing the Charlie Hebdo attack in Paris is the most recent example – confronts us with the unanswered global question of how to respond to the extreme fundamentalist mindset – of left or right – which is prepared to go to lethal lengths to impose its point or view, and is implacably opposed to a common good based on tolerance, diversity and consensus. I am happy to give the last word to John Paul Lederach, who says:

> "Human security is not tied primarily to the quantity or size of weapons, the height or thickness of the wall that separates them, not to the power of imposition and control. The mystery of peace is located in the nature and quality of relationships developed with those most feared."

APPENDIX 1

COMPASSIONATE CITY OF BELFAST CHARTER

The City of Belfast Compassionate City Campaign intends to:

Raise awareness of the impact of unresolved trauma in the population and the need for compassion and understanding.

Raise awareness of the skills for transforming suffering towards compassion for self and others.

Make Belfast a leading light of compassion as a country transforming itself from over 40+ years of violent conflict.

"Committing ourselves to the common good and through the relationships of the government and its peoples and the citizens to each other, being mindful of our divided, painful and troubled past, I will contribute to the creation of a compassionate, inclusive, tolerant and peaceful future, without recourse to violence – a society where human rights are respected and safeguarded – where every person, regardless of age, race, religion or ethnicity, gender or sexuality – will have a place and be enabled to flourish."

APPENDIX 2

ANTI-SECTARIAN CHARTER

Our vision is of a society where all people are reconciled to accept diversity and can live, work & socialise free from exploitation or sectarian discrimination in conditions of equality, freedom, security & equity.

What we do: We support any body, group or individual willing to tackle & reconcile the different narratives to our shared past which will bring about an end to inherent sectarianism. Our aim is to bust myths, rise above propaganda & embrace the mindset of peace as we create a-new cooperating as architects for the future.

We also:

> identify good practice through dialogue, practical research & projects of engagement.

> provide lectures & resources to help others reconcile diversity.

> lead by example destroying inherited, antiquated, sectarian moulds created by others.

> break down myth or propaganda by analysing historical or statistical facts.

Principles of the Reconciliation Collective Anti-Sectarian Base Code:

Regardless of religious faith, political ideology, nationality or ethnic origin society commits to the following principles:

1) The right to work free from sectarian discrimination, intimidation, attack or other prejudice.

2) The right to housing and to live in your home free from intimidation, attack or other prejudice.

3) The right to freely associate and socialise at places of choosing free from sectarian discrimination, intimidation, attack or other prejudice.

4) Respect for all places of worship and the right for practitioners to worship in a silent, peaceful, reflective, holistic method free from outside interference.

5) The requirement of every citizen to report or challenge sectarian speech, acts of intimidation, attacks or other discrimination when witnessed or heard to lawful authority.

6) The requirement of every citizen to support one another and ensure no one in society receives harsh or inhumane treatment or is discriminated against.

7) The right of children to grow up in areas free from sectarian imagery & idealism.

8) The right of children to be educated free from sectarian discrimination, intimidation, attack or other prejudice.

Defining Sectarianism: 'Sectarianism' is the belief or mindset that religion, political opinion, language, nationality or national and/or ethnic origin justifies contempt or a notion of superiority or other prejudice against a person or a group of persons within society.

BIBLIOGRAPHY

Anderson, J (2013). Imperial Ethnocracy and Demography: foundations of Ethno-national conflict in Belfast & Jerusalem. In Pullan, W & Baillie, B, *Locating Urban Conflicts: Ethnicity, Nationalism and the Everyday*. Palgrave MacMillan.

Ashe, F & Harland (2014). *Troubling Masculinities: Changing Patterns of Violent Masculinities in a Society Emerging from Political Conflict*. Retrieved from University of Ulster: http://eprints.ulster.ac.uk/29937/

Ashe, F (n.d.). *The Gender Politics of De-militarising Northern Ireland: Theorising Gender Power in the Context of Conflict Transformation*. Retrieved from http://www.hannashouse.ie/PDFs/Ashe.pdf

Battram, A (1998). *Navigating Complexity*. London: The Industrial Society.

Bell, J (2013). *Young People and the Interfaces*. Belfast: Institute for Conflict Research.

Berger, J (2008). *Ways of Seeing*. London: Penguin.

Belfast Interface Project (2012). *Belfast Interfaces: Security Barriers and Defensive Use of Space*. Belfast: BIP.

Boal, F (1995). *Shaping a City: Belfast in the late 20th Century*. Belfast: Institute of Irish Studies.

Bollens, S (2013). Bounding Cities as a Means of Managing Conflict: Sarajevo, Beirut and Jerusalem. *Peacebuilding* Vol 1: 2, pp 186–206.

Brewer, JD (2013). *Ex-combatants, Religion and Peace in Northern Ireland: the role of religion*. Basingstoke: Palgrave MacMillan.

Brewer, JD (2014). *Annual David Stevens Memorial Lecture: Religion and Politics in a Changing Northern Ireland*.

Byrne, J (2005). *Interface Violence in East Belfast during 2002*. Belfast: Institute for Conflict Research.

Byrne, J (2011). *The Belfast Peace Walls: The Problems, Politics and Policies of the Troubles Architecture* (University of Ulster: PhD Thesis).

Byrne, J, et al (2012). *Attitudes to Peace Walls*. Belfast: OFMdFM.

Carroll, L (2014). *Consultation to UN Rapporteur on Truth, Justice, Reparations and Non-Recurrence*. Unpublished paper.

Carvill, L (2013). *Women: Dealing with the Past Workshop*. Belfast: WRDA.

Commission for Victims and Survivors (2012). *Comprehensive Needs Assessment*. Belfast.

Commission for Victims and Survivors (2013). *Peace IV 2014–2020 Preparing an EU Programme for Peace and Reconciliation*. Belfast: OFMDFM.

Community Relations Council (2009). *Challenge of Change Conference*, Interface Working Group, 30 March 2009.

Community Relations Council (2011). *Report on the Joint Conference of the Interface Working Group (IWG) and the Interface Community Parties (ICP) on City Interfaces*.

Community Relations Council (2008). *Towards Sustainable Security: Interface barriers and the legacy of segregation in Belfast*. Belfast: CRC.

Conway, M & Byrne, J (2005). *Interface issues: an annotated bibliography*. Belfast: Institute for Conflict Research.

Craig, C (2010). *The Tears that made the Clyde: Well-being in Glasgow*. Argyll: Argyll Publishing.

Deloitte (2007). *Research into the financial cost of the Northern Ireland divide*.

di Cintio, M (2013). The Mutilated City. In di Cintio, M, *Walls: Travels Along the Barricades* (pp 208–257). Berkeley: Soft Skull Press.

Duffy, R & Doherty, R (2010). *Our View.* Belfast: Rita Duffy Studio.

Eames, R & Bradley, D (2009). *Report of the Consultative Group on the Past.* Retrieved 12 September 2014, from http://tinyurl.com/nvsfeqr

Edwards, A & McGratton, C (2010). *The Northern Irish Conflict: A Beginner's Guide.* Oxford: One World Publications.

InterAction (2005). *Ex-combatants and Conflict Transformation.* Belfast: InterAction

Fay, M, et al (1999). *Northern Ireland's Troubles: The human costs.* London: Pluto Press.

Forthspring 5 Decades Project (2014). *Talking about the Troubles.* Belfast: Forthspring Intercommunity Group.

Goldie, R & Ruddy, B (2010). *Crossing the Line: Key features of effective practice in the development of shared space in areas close to an interface.* Lisburn: Roz Goldie Partnership.

Graham, C (2013). *Northern Ireland: 30 Years of Photography.* Belfast: Belfast Exposed/MAC.

Greenslade, R (18 October 2013). Northern Ireland stories are not covered by British national newspapers. Retrieved from *The Guardian*: http://www.theguardian.com/media/greenslade/2013/oct/18/northernireland-derry

Haass, R (31 December 2013). *An Agreement among the Parties of the Northern Ireland Executive on Parades, Flags and Emblems, and Contending with the Past.* Belfast.

Hall, M (2007). *Building Bridges at the Grassroots: the experience of Suffolk-Lenadoon Interface Group.* Newtownabbey, Co Antrim: Island Publications.

Hammond, SA (2013). *The Thin Book of Appreciative Enquiry, 3rd Edition.* USA: Thin Book Publishing Company.

Hansard (9 October 2013). *Official Report: Victims and Survivors Service.* Northern Ireland Assembly.

Hatch, J (2013). *Transformational theology in a context of division: Examining Belfast's separation barriers through a theological lens of idolatry.* University College Dublin: PhD Thesis.

Healy, T (28 November 2014). Blog: Things you always wanted to know about Northern Ireland public finances. Retrieved from Nevin Economic Research Institute: http://www.nerinstitute.net/blog/2014/11/15/things-you-always-wanted-to-know-about-public-fina/

Heatley, C (2004). *Interface: Flashpoints in Northern Ireland.* Belfast: Lagan Books.

Herbert, D (2013). *Creating Community Cohesion.* London: Palgrave MacMillan.

Herman, J (1992). *Trauma and Recovery.* New York: Basic Books.

Hocking, BT (2012). Beautiful Barriers: Art and Identity along a Belfast 'Peace' Wall. *Anthropology Matters Journal* (14) 1, www.anthropologymatters.com.

IBM (2014). *Belfast, Northern Ireland Smarter Cities Challenge Report.*

Jamieson, RS (2010). *Ageing and social exclusion among former politically motivated prisoners in Northern Ireland and the border region of Ireland.* Belfast: Changing Aging Partnership.

Jarman, N & O'Halloran, C (2001). *Recreational Rioting: young people, interface areas and violence.* Belfast: Department of Social Work, Queen's University Belfast.

Johnston, W (2014). *The Belfast Urban Motorway: Engineering, ambition and social conflict.* Newtownards: Colourpoint Books.

Kennedy, L (10 November 2014). *They Shoot Children, Don't They? Report on paramilitary attacks on children 1990–2013.* Retrieved from http://www.michaelnugent.com/2014/11/10/they-shoot-children-dont-they-part-1/

Kernaghan, P (2000). *Watching for Daybreak: a history of St Matthew's Parish.* Belfast: St Matthew's Parish.

Kintrea, K, et al (2008). *Young People and Territoriality in British Cities.* York: Joseph Rowntree Foundation.

Kirk, R (2012). City of Walls. In Vollman, WT, *The Best American Travel Writing.*

Komarova, M & O'Dowd, L (2013). Territorialities of Capital and Place in Post-Conflict Belfast. In Pullan, W & Baillie, B, *Locating Urban Conflicts: Ethnicity, Nationalism and the Everyday.* Palgrave MacMillan.

Lederach, JP (1997). *Building Peace: Sustainable Reconciliation.* United States Institute of Peace Press.

Lederach, JP (2005). *The Moral Imagination: The Art and Soul of Building Peace.* Oxford: OUP.

Lederach, JP & Lederach AJ (2010). *When Blood and Bones Cry out: Journeys through the soundscape of healing and reconciliation.* New York: Oxford University Press.

Lennon, J & Foley, M (2000). *Dark Tourism.* London: Thomson.

Leonard, M & McKnight, M (2011). Bringing Down the Walls: Young people's perspectives. *International Journal of Sociology and Social Policy,* Vol 31 569–583.

MacGoil, S, et al (2010). *From Ashes to Aisling: Belfast Gaels and the rebuilding of Bombay Street.* Belfast: Forbairt Feirste 2010.

Mackel, C (2012). Documenting Belfast's Peace-walls. *Your Place or Mine: Joint Heritage Council/ICOMOS Ireland Conference.*

MacLennan, H (1945). *Two Solitudes.* Toronto: MacMillan.

McDowell, S (2008). Selling conflict heritage through tourism in peacetime Northern Ireland. *International Journal of Heritage Studies,* Vol 14:5 pp 405–421.

McGonagle, D (2008). *A Shout in the Street: Collective Histories of Northern Irish Art.* Belfast: Golden Thread Gallery.

Monaghan, R (2013). The Legacy of Fear in Northern Ireland. In Sinclair, S & Antonio, DJ, *The Political Psychology of Terrorism Fears* (pp 139–155). New York: OUP.

Morrow, D, et al (1991). *The Churches and Intercommunity Relationships.* Coleraine: University of Ulster.

Murray, RC (2006). Belfast: The Killing Fields. In Boal, FW, *Enduring City: Belfast in the Twentieth Century* (pp 221–237). Belfast: Blackstaff Press.

Murtagh, B (2008). *New Spaces and Old in 'Post-Conflict' Belfast: Working Paper No 5.* Retrieved 5 December 2014, from Conflict in Cities and the Contested State: www.conflictincities.org

Neill, WJ (2006). Past and Future: Imagining and Visioning the City. In Boal, FW, *Enduring City: Belfast in the Twentieth Century* (pp 195–206). Belfast: Blackstaff Press.

Nolan, P (2014). *Northern Ireland Peace Monitoring Report.* Belfast: Community Relations Council.

Northern Ireland Housing Executive (2014). *Northern Ireland Housing Market Review.*

Northern Ireland Life and Times Survey (2014). http://tinyurl.com/lasrn8t

Northern Ireland Office (2013). *Building a Prosperous and United Community.* Belfast: NIO.

Ó Dochartaigh, N (2007). Conflict, territory and new technologies: online interaction at a Belfast Interface. *Political Geography,* 26 (4), 474–91.

Ó hAdhmaill, F & Watt, P (1990). *Political Vetting of Community Work in Northern Ireland.* Belfast: Northern Ireland Council for Voluntary Action.

Ó hAdhmaill, F (2012). Community Develoment, Conflict and Power in the North of Ireland. In Jackson, A & O'Doherty, *Community Development.* Dublin: Gill & Macmillan.

OFMDFM (2013). *Together: Building a United Community.* Belfast: OFMDFM.

Patton, MQ (2011). *Developmental Evaluation: Applying Complexity Concepts to Enhance Innovation and Use.* New York: Guildford Press.

Persic, C (2004). *The State of Play*. Belfast: InterAction.

Phillips, A (2013). Looking at Obstacles. In Phillips, A, *One Way and Another: New and selected essays* (pp 29–44). London: Hamish Hamilton.

Processions, JW (1971). *Future Policy on Areas of Confrontation*. Belfast: Government of Northern Ireland.

Quinn, F (2008). *Streets Apart: Photographs of the Belfast Peacelines*. Belfast: Frankie Quinn.

Quinn, F (2010). *Murana i Belfast*. Uppsala: Global.

Ravenscroft, E (2006). *Producing Inventive Transgressions in Belfast: A rhetorical analysis of the peacelines*. (Masters Thesis) Chapel Hill.

Rolston, B (1995). Selling Tourism in a Country at War. *Race & Class* Vol 37, pp 23–40.

Rolston, B (2007). Demobilization and Reintegration of Ex-Combatants: the Irish Case in International Perspective. *Social Legal Studies*.

Shaw, P (2002). *Changing Conversations in Organizations: a complexity approach to change*. London: Routledge.

Shirlow, P et al (2006). *Segregation, Violence and the City*. London: Pluto.

Shirlow, P et al (2005). *Politically motivated former prisoner groups: community activism and conflict transformation*. Belfast: CRC.

Smith, W (2014). *Inside Man: Loyalists of Long Kesh – The Untold Story*. Newtownards: Colourpoint Books.

Soriano, K (2014). Building, Dwelling, Thinking. In *Anselm Kiefer* (pp 20–30). London: Royal Academy of Arts.

St Matthews & Avoniel Primary Schools (2007). *Your Place or Mine*. Short Strand.

Templer, S (2013). *Personal and Public Problems: Victims and Political Transition in Zimbabwe and Northern Ireland*. Queen's University Belfast: PhD thesis.

The Official Report (Hansard) (8 December 2014). Retrieved from Northern Ireland Assembly: http://data.niassembly.gov.uk/HansardXml/plenary-08-12-2014.pdf

Tomlinson, M (n.d.). *Legacies of Conflict: Evidence from the Poverty and Social Exclusion Survey 2012*. Retrieved 12 September 2014, from http://tinyurl.com/jwebsoa

Topping, M (2014). *From Dark Tourism to Phoenix Tourism: The Ethics of Cultural Translation in Urban Festivals*. Retrieved from Queen's University Belfast: http://www.qub.ac.uk/schools/SchoolofModernLanguages/FileStore/Filetoupload,479227,en.pdf

Weikop, C (2014). Forests of Myth, Forests of Memory. In *Anselm Kiefer* (pp 30–47). London: Royal Academy of Arts.

Weiner, R (1975). *The Rape and Plunder of the Shankill in Belfast: Community Action – the Belfast Experience*.

Wheatley, MJ (1999). *Leadership and the New Science: Discovering order in a chaotic world*. San Francisco: Berrett Koehler.

Williams, R (2014). *Keywords: A vocabulary of culture and society*. London: Fourth Estate.

Working Party on Areas of Confrontation (1971). *Future Policy on areas of confrontation: Final Report of the JWP on Processions etc*. Belfast: Government of Northern Ireland.

INDEX